D1551854

ELIZABETH SCHEU CLOSE

August 8, 2021

To Barbara & Bob,

Thanks for everything! Enjoy the book.

Love,
Jane

ELIZABETH SCHEU CLOSE
A LIFE IN MODERN ARCHITECTURE

JANE KING HESSION

UNIVERSITY OF MINNESOTA PRESS
MINNEAPOLIS / LONDON

Published by the University of
Minnesota Press
111 Third Avenue South, Suite 290
Minneapolis, MN 55401-2520
http://www.upress.umn.edu

ISBN 978-1-5179-0857-7 (hc)
A Cataloging-in-Publication record
for this book is available from the
Library of Congress.

Printed in Canada
on acid-free paper

25 24 23 22 21 20   10 9 8 7 6 5 4 3 2 1

FOR LISL

CONTENTS

FOREWORD

JOAN SORANNO

I have known of Elizabeth "Lisl" Close and her reputation as an arbiter of modern architecture for years. Lisl is widely recognized as a pioneer of modern architecture, but also for an aesthetic that was truly Minnesotan. Her skill in combining the honesty and function of modern design with a warmth and beauty derived from nature was remarkable. Until I read this book, however, I was unaware of Lisl's significant legacy in the state and beyond. She was a prolific architect who produced a body of work that included single-family homes, public housing, commercial, health care, and prefab projects, and RVs! The book's thoughtful and thorough telling of Lisl's story, including her family background, the obstacles she faced in her life, and her perseverance in overcoming them, helped me understand the motivated, determined force she was—and needed to be to build her legacy.

As one does when reading a great story, I discovered many connections with Lisl along the way and found myself reflecting on my own work and career. On a professional level, her approach to architecture resonated with me: a dedication to designing spaces through the lenses of her clients. Getting to know them, listening to and understanding their needs, hopes, and desires, were paramount to Lisl. This knowledge drove her designs. She developed great friendships with many of her clients, and through her architecture helped to shape the personal, intimate moments of their lives.

Similarly, I have long been motivated to design for specific communities—spiritual, cultural, and intellectual. I have been fortunate to develop wonderful relationships with individuals who are invested in bringing people together to create connection and build community around life's celebratory moments, both big and small. I see it as my job to enable those moments. Based on what I have learned about Lisl, that drove her as well.

So often there is a tug of war between architecture and landscape, but Lisl saw no conflict there. Instead, she perceived harmony and synergy between the two. This book details Lisl's sensitivity to context and site; how she thoughtfully maintained appropriate character and scale while working *with*—rather than against—the natural contours and challenges of a site. I sensed that a deep, almost spiritual connection with nature drove her ideas and fostered the close partnerships she created with landscape architects over the years.

In our practice at HGA, we have found tremendous value in working side by side with landscape architects to make sure the architecture doesn't overwhelm a site and instead that the two are beautifully integrated. We try our best not to fight history or Mother Nature but to work in partnership with them.

Like many architects who will read Jane King Hession's book, particularly women of my generation or older, I empathize with Lisl's determination to become an architect despite the barriers she faced as a woman in a field dominated by men. But I also feel a kinship with her childhood and her experience growing up in Vienna, Austria, in the family's iconic and somewhat controversial house designed by architect Adolf Loos. The author's portrayal of the culture Lisl's parents fostered there was almost cinematic: a salon where intellectuals and artists sat at the table together, broke bread, and exchanged ideas. I can imagine how living in the house shaped Lisl's thoughts about how the physical elements of movement and light could change one's perception and experience of space.

The formative years of my own childhood (although not as vivid as Lisl's) were spent in Milan, Italy. At the time, my father was an executive with Braun, the German consumer products company, and worked closely with Dieter Rams, the company's chief designer. Rams was a renowned German industrial designer closely aligned with the functionalist school, a successor to the Bauhaus. I remember various iterations of Braun's celebrated (now historic) products in our house. Of course, as a child, I didn't recognize them as significant objects of design. But thinking back, perhaps their presence in my home did influence me as an architect because they embodied many of the principles that now guide my work: beauty, functionality, simplicity, and honesty.

Lisl left Vienna for Boston in 1932, just as the shadow of Nazism began to fall over Europe. She continued her education at

MIT, where women were few––and women in architecture programs even fewer. Still, she received her degrees and found work during the Depression in the male-dominated field of architecture—a doubly difficult prospect. Her story is nothing short of remarkable.

I attended Notre Dame and graduated with a degree in architecture in 1984, decades after Lisl obtained her diplomas. I rarely saw the kind of outright discrimination she faced as she knocked on doors looking for work (just wait until you read about some of these attempts), but in my early career I did encounter an insidious, more discreet kind of discrimination. Lisl said she went into residential work primarily because clients weren't as threatened by a woman doing domestic architecture. When I left school, that thinking was still prevalent. There were assumptions about my capabilities—or lack thereof—to tackle more complex, larger-scale applications of architecture. That discrimination, while not necessarily malicious, was truly frustrating. But those of us who had the desire to learn and do something more pushed through; we were resolute in what we wanted and unwavering in asking for it. For many of us, including Lisl, there was someone who heard us and emboldened us to take the leap.

While studying at MIT, Lisl met Winston "Win" Close, a Minnesota-born fellow architect and her future husband. They eventually moved to Minneapolis, where they set up a practice together—becoming partners in work and life, teammates at the office, and companions at home. Of course, this part of their story interested me: I, too, work alongside my husband, John Cook. I met him at Meyer Scherer Rockcastle while working on the Weisman Art Museum. Over time, our relationship evolved: he became a mentor, a colleague, and a partner. Reading about the Closes' marriage and collaboration, I saw elements that reflect my own relationship with John.

The Closes had complementary rather than redundant talents, which reduced the friction that can sometimes arise. Win thought about how something would be built, while Lisl was more philosophical and abstract. John and I also come at projects from different angles, and see it as key to our partnership: I tend to focus on the "art" of architecture, and he the "science." As a couple, we're able to address both the aesthetic and technical, and we try to strike the right balance between the two.

Architecture can be an all-consuming, intense profession—conversations about projects are constant. If you're going to put in long hours at the office to build your practice, and then go home and build a family and raise children together as the Closes did, it's certainly more tolerable and pleasant if you have your life partner at your side. They were lucky to have each other, as we are.

Perhaps, when Jane asked me to write this foreword, she knew of the personal and professional connections I might make with Lisl. Or maybe she simply believed—rightly so—that Lisl's life and work would inspire those who are forging a career in architecture, or any woman trying to make her way. I thank Jane for asking me to contribute this essay. Her curiosity, knowledge, and passion for the history of modern architecture are evident throughout the book and are matched by her ability to tell a fascinating and important story.

Elizabeth Scheu Close: A Life in Modern Architecture paints a portrait of an important icon of modern architecture. But it also relates a story of tenacity, focus, and making the most of opportunity; of navigating complex political climates; of being a caring steward of nature and community; of being a good partner; of living a full life; of being a trailblazer.

BLAZING A TRAIL AS A MODERN ARCHITECT

INTRODUCTION

On December 6, 2002, the Minnesota architecture community came together to present its highest professional honor, the AIA (American Institute of Architects) Minnesota Gold Medal, to a petite, ninety-year-old woman. There had been twelve previous recipients, but that night Elizabeth "Lisl" Scheu Close became the first woman to receive the medal, which recognizes an individual whose work has had a "significant, positive impact on the Minnesota architecture community and culture."[1] At the award ceremony, presenters spoke of the many reasons Lisl merited the honor: an unshakable commitment to modernism; the design of scores of well-crafted, sensitively sited modern residences; her business acumen in founding and running a firm for decades; and her service to the AIA. In addition to illuminating her distinguished professional career, speakers also shed light on Lisl's remarkable personal life, one that began in pre–World War I Vienna, Austria, during the reign of Emperor Franz Joseph I and ended in Minnesota in the heyday of Prince. Although it was not known that night, Lisl would live another nine years after the presentation, dying just six months short of her one hundredth birthday.

One of the people who knew her best, her son Roy Close, once described Lisl as "a diminutive woman in a hard hat."[2] It is a wonderfully concise phrase that is both literally and figuratively accurate, but that also suggests the steel at the core of Lisl's being and a key to her success. Lisl left an indelible mark on Minnesota's built landscape. She was a pioneering modern architect and (with Winston Close) founded the first modern architecture practice in the state. The firm designed the first International Style house in Minneapolis as well as many of Minnesota's early modern houses, most of which still stand today. As a rare practicing woman architect and firm principal in the 1930s and beyond, Lisl served as a role model and blazed a trail for ensuing generations of aspiring female architects.

The story of how a determined young woman from Vienna became the esteemed Minnesota modern architect honored that December night is the subject of this book.

Figure I.1 Garden view of the Scheu House, Vienna, Austria. The Scheus commissioned architect Adolf Loos to design the house in 1912. Photograph by William B. Olexy, 2010.

Lisl was born to modern architecture, or very nearly so. In 1912, the year of her birth, her parents, Gustav Scheu and Helene Scheu-Riesz, commissioned iconoclastic architect Adolf Loos to design a home at 3 Larochegasse in the elegant Hietzing district of Vienna. In its unusual stepped shape and absence of ornamentation, the strikingly modern Scheu House was a cause célèbre and a shocking insertion into its architecturally traditional neighborhood. The seminal house, which is still studied by historians today, incited a range of responses from outrage to admiration from observers at the time. Lisl's socially and politically well-connected parents welcomed thousands of visitors from around the globe to the house, and within it fostered a salon for intellectual debate and a lively exchange of ideas.

Lisl lived at 3 Larochegasse for the first twenty years of her life, and at a very young age understood that her home was no ordinary house. As she grew older, she began to comprehend that architecture had the power to provoke discourse, stimulate ideas, and challenge opinions. When she was ready to pursue a university education and choose her life's work, the experience of living in the distinctive house helped shape her interests and goals. She decided to become an architect and vowed to focus on modern design.

Unquestionably, the Scheu House was responsible for igniting Lisl's interest in architecture, but her parents opened other worlds for her. Helene, a determined, ambitious, and enterprising woman, was an author, translator, and publisher of children's books. She was also involved in international peace and social welfare causes. In Helene, Lisl had the model of a professional workingwoman for a mother—a rare commodity in early twentieth-century Vienna. For this reason, Lisl was determined to pursue a professional career and was free do so without reservation. Gustav, an attorney, was an active Social Democrat and an adviser on housing matters to the city of Vienna after World War I, a time when the city faced critical housing shortages. His interest in the Garden City movement and commitment to providing shelter for those in need made a lasting impression on Lisl; throughout her career she was attracted to architectural projects, such as public and cooperative housing, that had a social agenda. Gustav, an accomplished

Figure I.2 Elizabeth Scheu, seated at left looking at camera, with her brother, Friedrich, at center in glasses, and a group of friends in Vienna, circa 1928. Courtesy of Roy M. Close Family Papers.

pianist, also instilled a deep love of music in his daughter, who studied the cello throughout her long life.

Although she considered studying at the Bauhaus, a progressive German arts school founded in 1919 by architect Walter Gropius, Lisl began her architectural education at the Technische Hochschule, or Technical University, in Vienna, where she encountered challenging conditions. The all-male faculty "didn't like having women there," and they expressed their hostility by blocking enrollment in classes, failing to provide restroom facilities for women, and issuing low grades to women.[3] The Nazis further complicated the pursuit of an education by obstructing classes on a regular basis. As they grew in number and influence, life in Vienna became increasingly perilous for Lisl because her mother (a practicing Quaker) was Jewish by birth. When it became clear that Lisl had to leave Austria, the Scheu House—once again—played an important role in determining her future. A frequent visitor to it, philanthropist and Boston department store magnate Edward Filene, arranged for her safe journey to the United States and continued education at the Massachusetts Institute of Technology. There, she met Minnesota-born Winston "Win" Close, who would be her life and professional partner for more than sixty years.

When she arrived in America in 1932, Lisl had one resolute goal: to become an architect and to design modern buildings—a bold ambition given that she did not know of a single practicing female architect and that modern design was not widely embraced by the architecture profession or the public at the time. While these facts did not dissuade her, she understood that significant obstacles stood between her and her objective.

By 1935 Lisl had earned both her bachelor's and master's degrees from MIT. She had the misfortune of entering the job market during the Depression, and further narrowed her already finite options by limiting her search to firms doing modern design or housing. This was a tall order for anyone, much less a twenty-three-year-old living alone in an adopted country. She applied for work at three architectural firms: one rejected her as a probable disruptive presence in the drafting room; another offered her an unpaid position in return for a monthly fee; Oskar Stonorov of Philadelphia, a European émigré himself, hired her. He put her to work drafting the children's facility for Westfield Acres, a large federal housing project in Camden, New Jersey. In 1936 she moved to Minnesota to join the firm of Magney and Tusler and work on Sumner Field, a Public Works Administration initiative and the first federally funded housing project in Minneapolis. In 1938 she and Win founded Close and Scheu, the first architectural practice in Minnesota dedicated to modern design. They married that same year and later changed the firm's name to Elizabeth and Winston Close, Architects.

During World War II, the Closes suspended their practice for three years. While Win served in the U.S. Naval Reserve, Lisl worked for Page & Hill Defense Housing designing prefabricated home models. She continued to work for the Minnesota-based company until the late 1950s. In all, more than ten thousand houses would be produced from her plans, including one constructed by the U.S. State Department in Berlin during the Cold War. The Closes reopened their practice in 1946. That same year, Win joined the faculty at the University of Minnesota's School of Architecture. He would subsequently serve as the university's head of campus planning and advisory architect until 1971. Lisl was the firm's principal designer and ran the office alone during those years. The couple retired from architecture in 1992.

Like many Europeans who left their histories and homelands behind to immigrate to other countries, Lisl brought her beliefs and convictions with her to America. Architecturally speaking, these included intimate knowledge of the buildings of Loos, but she also came of age during the rise of other progressive, early twentieth-century architectural movements in Europe. Undoubtedly, she would have known of the work of Gropius and other leading modern architects, including German Ludwig Mies van der Rohe, Swiss French Charles-Édouard Jeanneret (known as "Le Corbusier"), Dutch J. J. P. Oud, and Austrian Richard Neutra, to name a few. In 1932, the year Lisl arrived in the United States, the Museum of Modern Art in New York mounted its groundbreaking show *Modern Architecture: International Exhibition,* which featured designs by those men and

Figure I.3 Lisl Scheu in Minneapolis, 1938. Courtesy of Roy M. Close Family Papers.

Figure I.4 International Style buildings, such as the Lovell House in Los Angeles (1929), designed by Richard Neutra, influenced Lisl's architectural aesthetic. Photograph by Elizabeth Scheu, circa 1935. Courtesy of Roy M. Close Family Papers.

others. The exhibit, which ran from February 10 to March 23, not only introduced a radical new take on architecture to Americans but also coined the movement's best-known name: the International Style. As the exhibition catalog explained, this "genuinely new style" was so labeled "because of its simultaneous development in several different countries and because of its world-wide distribution."[4]

The architects of the International Style preferred volume over mass, planar surfaces devoid of ornamentation, the use of industrial materials, honest expression of materials, and architectural forms that followed a building's function. Fundamentally, these tenets were a rejection of historical styles and traditional methods of construction in favor of an adoption of new machine age materials and technologies and their applications to contemporary life. As stated in an exhibition publication, "The aesthetic principles of the International Style are based primarily upon the nature of modern materials and structure and upon modern requirements in planning. Slender steel posts and beams, and concrete reinforced by steel have made possible structures of skeleton-like strength and lightness."[5] Unfortunately, Lisl was not able to see the MoMA show—it closed five months before she arrived in the United States. Nor is it known whether she visited the exhibition in any of the other cities to which it toured over the next three years.[6] But it is certain that the proponents of the International Style and its principles and philosophies profoundly influenced her own architectural beliefs and future work.

Her aesthetic was further refined, however, by Austrian modernism and the Viennese architects of the 1920s and 1930s. Just prior to leaving Vienna for the United States, Lisl had the opportunity to visit the Werkbundsiedlung, an experimental housing development built a little over a mile from her home. The Siedlung, or settlement, opened to the public as the "Vienna International Werkbund Exhibition" on June 5, 1932—the day after Lisl's twentieth birthday. Organized by architect and designer Josef Frank, a leading promoter of Viennese modernism (and a Scheu House guest), the exhibition featured seventy fully furnished, single-family dwellings and row houses designed by Frank, Loos, Neutra, Margarete Schütte-Lihotzky,

Oskar Strnad, Oskar Wlach, Josef Hoffmann, and other influential Austrian architects.[7]

Over the course of its two-month run, the exhibition and model estate, which today are remembered as "among the most important architectural documents of Austrian modernism," drew more than one hundred thousand visitors.[8] For Lisl, the Werkbundsiedlung was an opportunity to consider the ways in which multiple architects applied modern ideas and new technologies to residential design. It was also a built expression of the "Neues Bauen, or New Building era in Vienna." The movement, which was closely associated with Frank, was "not primarily concerned with aesthetic or theoretical principles of design and form, focusing rather on the individual needs of the occupants."[9] The principles of the Neues Bauen, particularly regarding occupants' needs, resonated with Lisl. As Austrian architect and critic Judith Eiblmayr has observed, "Lisl was influenced by the Viennese school of architecture [and the work of] Frank, Oskar Strnad, and Oskar Wlach—a Viennese kind of modernism that always had a social agenda."[10]

Figure I.5 Terraced houses by Josef Hoffmann at the Werkbundsiedlung (1932), Vienna, Austria. Lisl visited the Siedlung, a historically important display of Austrian modernism, shortly before leaving Vienna for the United States. ÖNB Vienna: 423.013D.

Collectively, these principles shaped Lisl's core beliefs as an architect, but she was not bound by a single philosophy or style. Fundamentally, she was a pragmatist interested in solving a problem through a skillful architectural response. Above all, she strove for a well-designed building—one reduced to its essential elements—that sensitively fit the site, was constructed of attractive, durable materials, and would serve its clients long and well.

Elizabeth and Winston Close, Architects, worked on a range of building types in Minnesota, including medical, educational, and commercial. Notable among them are several buildings for the Metropolitan Medical Center (1970s) in Minneapolis; the International School of Minnesota (1987) in Eden Prairie; the Donald Ferguson Hall for the University of Minnesota in Minneapolis (1986), the Freshwater Biological Institute (1974) on Lake Minnetonka in Navarre; and the Peavey Technical Center (1966) in Chaska. However, most of the firm's commissions were residential—more than 250 houses characterized by simple geometries, efficient and clever plans, warm natural materials, ample daylight, and thoughtful integration with their sites. They include the Ray Faulkner House (1938), in Minneapolis, the first International Style house in the state; fifteen houses in the University of Minnesota–owned neighborhood of University Grove in Falcon Heights, built between 1939 and 1965, including the Closes' own residence (1953); the Hendrik and Marri Oskam House (1962), the only modern house designated by the city of Edina as a Heritage Landmark; the John and Dorothy Rood House (1947) in Minneapolis; and the Philip and Helen Duff House (1955, demolished in 2012) in Wayzata, which AIA Minnesota honored with a 25-Year Award in 1989.

Lisl described houses as "probably my primary interest" and appreciated the range of creative responses residential design allowed. "Each house is different, you never have the same problem," she said.[11] However, there was another reason she gravitated toward residential work. Female architects were a rarity when she opened her firm. Her solid education and qualifications notwithstanding,

Figure I.6 The Peavey Technical Center (1966), Chaska, Minnesota. Photograph by Phillip MacMillan James and Associates. Close Associates Papers (N78), Northwest Architectural Archives, University of Minnesota Libraries, Minneapolis.

"people [had] less reserves about letting a woman design a house or a residence or an apartment because it is not so formidable as a technical problem," she said. "And so, in trying to get a job it makes it easier."[12] This prejudice-induced dilemma was one also shared by other female architects who as "newcomers" to the field were seen, by some, as being less qualified for the business of architecture than their male counterparts.

To understand the scarcity of women in the field—and Lisl's relative position within it—some context is necessary. According to Sarah Allaback's 2008 study of the topic, *The First American Women Architects,* Mary Louisa Page, who graduated from the University of Illinois in 1879, was the first woman to earn an architecture degree from an accredited American university.[13] Allaback identifies Lisl as one of seventy-two women to do so by 1934.[14] In 1948 *Architectural Record* conducted a survey to determine how many women architects there were in the country at that time. After canvassing the nation's architecture schools and the Women's Architectural Association, it identified 1,119 women who had studied architecture to date. Those women were surveyed, and of the 231 respondents, 108, or 47 percent, were practicing architecture. Of those, "many" had their own firms, and thirty-two were members of the AIA, Lisl among them. She was one of ten women surveyed who were featured in the March 1948 issue of the magazine in which these findings were announced. The article included photographs of two of her projects and quoted Lisl as saying, "People are still inclined to snort or laugh at us, but architecture is a fine field for women. We can contribute a lot, especially in residential design."[15] Because the magazine identified architecture as "traditionally, a field for men," the "ladies" were specifically asked about "difficulties they encountered because of their sex." The article stated, "Quite a few reported the occasional trouble with contractors and laborers in the field, and several admitted to having been taken more or less frequently as secretaries in their own offices." None regretted her choice of career.

Ten years later, a survey based on data collected from state architectural examining boards identified 320 registered women architects (including Lisl) in the country, or 1 percent of the total number

Figure I.7 The Ray Faulkner House (1938) in Minneapolis was the first work built by the firm of Close and Scheu. Close Associates Papers (N78), Northwest Architectural Archives, University of Minnesota Libraries, Minneapolis.

Figure I.8 In 1953 Elizabeth and Winston Close designed a home for their family in the University Grove neighborhood of Falcon Heights. Members of the Close family lived in the house for more than sixty years. Photograph by William B. Olexy, 2014.

Figure I.9 The John and Dorothy Rood House (1947) in Minneapolis is one of more than 250 houses designed by the firm of Elizabeth and Winston Close, Architects. HB-14358-H. Chicago History Museum, Hedrich-Blessing Collection.

Figure I.10 The Philip and Helen Duff House (1955) on Lake Marion in Wayzata, Minnesota. Photograph by George Miles Ryan Studios Inc. Courtesy Gar Hargens/Close Associates. Close Associates Papers (N78), Northwest Architectural Archives, University of Minnesota Libraries, Minneapolis.

of registered architects.[16] It further revealed that seven states—Kentucky, Mississippi, Nevada, North Dakota, South Dakota, Utah, and Wyoming—could not claim a single woman architect in 1958.[17]

The paucity of women architects in practice and architectural education at the time also meant that young women who wanted to become architects had few female role models, and even fewer mentors who could shepherd them through the challenging process of getting a job. "Role models boost self-esteem . . . and foster a sense of identification with a field, combating alienation. The scarcity of female role models in architecture is thus profoundly damaging," writes historian Despina Stratigakos. Likewise, "Mentors can make a critical difference: careers are advanced not just by ambition and sacrifice, but also by having a sponsor to show you the ropes, make connections, and put your name forward for career-enhancing opportunities."[18] Female architectural role models and mentors were in decidedly short supply during Lisl's training and throughout her career.

Women architects were few and far between in the country in the 1930s. When Lisl arrived in Minnesota in 1936, however, she was not the first university-trained woman architect in the state. By then, forty-eight women had graduated from the University of Minnesota's School of Architecture, the first in 1921, and a handful practiced.[19] One was Dorothy Brink, who graduated from the university in 1924 and became a draftsperson in the office of architect William Ingemann, whom she later married. Nor was Lisl the first woman to open an architecture office in the state. Marion Parker set up a solo practice in 1919, which she closed sometime in the 1920s, and Emma Brunson opened a one-person office in 1920, which she retained until her retirement in 1968.[20]

Still, as a professional woman in a traditionally male-dominated field, Lisl was a rare bird and an object of curiosity for the press and public alike. Her European roots and unique educational and professional experience to date further set her apart from Minnesota's other early women architects, and gave her a platform from which to express her singularity. Shortly, after arriving in Minnesota, "Miss Elizabeth Scheu" shared her knowledge in a lecture titled "Modern European Housing" at a meeting of the League of Women Voters in the Curtis Hotel in Minneapolis.[21] She was likely the only architect in the upper Midwest, and beyond, qualified to do so.

In the 1940s and 1950s, local publications made Lisl the subject of several human-interest stories. While the articles did raise awareness of her accomplishments and professional stature, they often bore dismaying (and dismissive) headlines. A 1949 piece in the *Minneapolis Star* titled "Doctor, Lawyer, Dentist, Architect Agree: Women Are Own Worst Enemy" considered the question "Why don't more college-trained women reach the top of their profession?" and posited "the biggest problem a professional woman faces is the prejudice of other women."[22] In 1952 the *Star*'s "Town Toppers" column featured "Here's a Quick Look at: Mrs. Elizabeth Close." The article pointed out that despite her status as an equal partner in the "man-and-wife team of Elizabeth and Winston Close, Architects," too often she had been greeted with some variation of "Toots, I want to see the architect" by a less-than-illuminated visitor to her office.[23] Four years later, as part of a series on "the wives of prominent men in the community," the *Star* published "Woman behind the Man: Her Blueprint for Living Calls for Architectural Teamwork." The article did not provide her first name, but noted of Mrs. Winston Close, "She's an architect, too."[24] When she had the opportunity, Lisl spoke out on the challenges professional women with children faced, and was clear in her belief that "everybody with a full-time job who wants to do it justice should hire somebody to do the rest of the work. You can't do everything. There isn't enough time or energy."[25]

Lisl, who had little interest in self-promotion and did not view herself as a standard bearer for feminism, shook off the genuine—and left-handed—compliments with aplomb and just kept working. Throughout her life, however, she disliked being labeled a "woman architect," preferring "an architect who happens to be a woman." She believed her skills and accomplishments needed neither embellishment nor qualification because of her sex.

Lisl was not one for small talk. Nor did she expound on her personal or professional philosophies to any great extent. She wrote little about her own work and when questioned on it wasted few

Figure I.11 Elizabeth Scheu Close in her Minneapolis office, circa 1940. Courtesy of Roy M. Close Family Papers.

words in its description. "It was a long time ago," she would often say. She didn't seek awards, never advertised her services, and was modest about her achievements. What mattered was the quality of the work.

Today she is best remembered for the modern houses she designed, which architect Ralph Rapson, the first AIA Minnesota Gold Medalist and longtime head of the School of Architecture at the University of Minnesota, described as "carefully thought-out designs . . . in the more organic, natural tradition."[26] Not coincidentally, those houses are very like Lisl herself. They embody the essentials only. They are handsome, well designed, and durable. They are practical, efficient, and useful. They are made of strong materials that age well. They don't demand attention but they command respect. They have European roots, yet they are well suited to life in America.

The trajectory of Lisl's architectural career was indelibly shaped by the artistic, political, and economic upheavals of the twentieth century, including two world wars, the Great Depression, the rise of new technologies, and a revolution in modern art and architecture. Through it all, she proved herself eager to learn, adaptable to change, and skillful at negotiating roadblocks as she pursued a singular and successful career as a modern architect. She made her professional mark in America, but the seeds of her architectural aspirations were planted an ocean away in Austria in the early 1900s.

Figure I.12 Lisl Close, circa 1956. Courtesy of Roy M. Close Family Papers.

1

VIENNA 1912 TO 1932

A photographer captured the moment on June 2, 1919, when six-year-old Elizabeth "Lisl" Scheu was thrust onto the international stage. The occasion was a celebration in the Augarten, a large public park in Vienna, Austria, to mark the arrival of representatives of the American Relief Administration's European Children's Fund in the city. American humanitarian efforts were warmly welcomed and desperately needed in post–World War I Vienna, where food and housing shortages had led to malnutrition, squalid living conditions, and other deprivations among much of the population; children were particularly hard hit. To officially acknowledge America's lifesaving aid, members of Austria's newly elected Social Democratic Party, President Karl Seitz, Vienna's vice-mayor Max Winter, and invited guests, convened near the baroque splendor of the Augarten Palais.[1] The photograph, which appeared in a local newspaper under the title "Amerika Hilft" (America Helps), centers on a small, curly-haired girl nervously tugging at her white dress. She stands alone in front of a somber-looking assemblage of officials clad in dark suits. Her considerable responsibility was to recite a welcome poem, in English, for the American and Austrian dignitaries. Eight decades later, Lisl remembered that the poem began, "American women, American men . . ."[2]

Figure 1.1 Six-year-old Lisl Scheu welcomes members of the American Relief Administration's European Children's Fund in the Augarten, Vienna, Austria, on June 2, 1919. Courtesy of Roy M. Close Family Papers.

Lisl Scheu was well suited for the task and was chosen to perform it for two reasons. First, she was a member of an Austrian family with deep Social Democratic roots and close political ties to the ruling administration. One month prior to the event, Lisl's father, Gustav Scheu, a lawyer and a prominent Social Democrat, had been appointed city councilor for housing matters for Vienna, or "Red Vienna," as the era of Social Democratic leadership between 1919 and 1934 was known. As such, he was aware of the housing crisis that gripped the city and was actively involved in relief efforts.[3] Of equal importance was the fact that Lisl spoke English, in addition to her native German, having learned the language from her British nanny, Daisy O'Neal.[4] For these reasons, Scheu enlisted his daughter to welcome the American contingent on behalf of the children of Vienna.

Surprisingly, for one so young, the Augarten gathering was not the first occasion on which Lisl found herself in the company of Vienna's political and cultural elite. Previously, several of the officials in attendance that day, along with many other noted national and international visitors, had been guests in her family's residence—the Scheu House at 3 Larochegasse in Vienna. The remarkable house was commissioned by her father, Gustav, and mother, Helene Scheu-Riesz, and designed by early modern architect Adolf Loos in 1912, the year of Lisl's birth. It was built in Hietzing, a neighborhood in the city's thirteenth district that was steeped in tradition, rich in baroque architecture, and flush with imperial associations. Schönbrunn Palace and Gardens, now a UNESCO World Heritage site but once a hunting lodge and summer home for the Habsburgs, stands less than two miles from the Scheu House.[5] Many of Vienna's affluent citizens gravitated to the elegant neighborhood, where they built opulently ornamented villas of their own. The Scheus, too, were drawn to Hietzing, but they would build a villa of a very different sort—an unabashedly modern one that was, controversially, the first of its kind in Central Europe. As Loos later wrote, "Years ago I built the house of Dr. Gustav Scheu in Hietzing, Vienna. It aroused general disapproval. . . . One person went to the Municipal Council to ask if this type of building was permitted by the law."[6]

Not everyone disliked the house. In fact, it was an object of admiration—and curiosity—for hundreds of visitors from around the world who flocked to 3 Larochegasse. Many were luminaries in the spheres of politics, art, architecture, music, theater, literature, education, social justice, women's rights, and international peace. The house functioned as an intellectual salon of sorts, a gathering place for some of the era's most progressive thinkers and iconoclasts, each of whom signed a guest book when he or she visited. Loos had given this now historic volume to the Scheus the day they moved into the house. The architect was the first person to sign the guest book; hundreds of others would follow suit over the ensuing decades.[7]

Lisl spent the first twenty years of her life at 3 Larochegasse. The architecture of the strikingly modern house, the people who

Figure 1.2 Elizabeth Scheu, Vienna, 1919. Photograph by Franz Löwy. Courtesy of Roy M. Close Family Papers.

were drawn to it, and the spirited conversations that occurred within its walls, all profoundly affected her young life. Of the importance of the Scheu House she said, "We talked about it all the time. Everybody who came was interested in the house. That's why they came . . . and I was indoctrinated."[8] The design of the house inspired her to pursue a career in modern architecture. International interest in it broadened her worldview. And one of the people who frequented it changed the trajectory of her life by making possible her safe passage to America and education there.

3 LAROCHEGASSE

The house at 3 Larochegasse was no ordinary residence, and the people responsible for it would not have had it any other way. Both radical in design and boldly out of character with the neighborhood in which it stood, it made an audacious architectural statement.

The Scheus were ideal clients for Loos, and Loos was the best possible architect for the Scheus. All three were nonconformists and intrepid personalities who were uninterested in current architectural styles. Loos was particularly clear on this point. In his 1908 manifesto *Ornament and Crime*, he railed against—and personally attacked—the artists and architects of the prevailing Viennese Secessionist style, which, in his view, was characterized by florid surface decoration. Not only did Loos believe ornamentation was a waste of time, labor, and material, he argued it also was a deterrent to a civilization's advancement: "The evolution of culture is synonymous with the removal of ornament from utilitarian objects," he stated.[9] He applied a similar school of thought to architectural design, as the Scheus well knew.

The Scheus first became acquainted with Loos through Gustav's brother, Robert, a journalist and onetime secretary of the Austrian Chamber of Commerce, who was a longtime friend and admirer of the architect.[10] Prior to commissioning him to design their home, the Scheus would have been familiar with Loos's public works in Vienna, including the Café Museum (1899) and the Kärtner Bar (1908). They had likely seen the 1910 Steiner House, Loos's first modern villa in Hietzing, which stood less than a half mile from 3

Figure 1.3 Address plaque on the Scheu House in Hietzing, Vienna. For several decades, the Scheus welcomed visitors from around the world to 3 Larochegasse. Photograph by William B. Olexy, 2010.

Larochegasse. The unusual conformation of the Steiner House—flat on one side, curved on another, and entirely devoid of decoration—would have grabbed the Scheus' attention and suggested the kind of unorthodox villa Loos might design for them. Additionally, they would have experienced Loos's domestic interiors through friends Eugenie Schwarzwald, a progressive educator, and her husband, Hermann, a lawyer, for whom the architect designed an apartment in Vienna in 1905, or during visits to Loos's own 1903 apartment.[11] What is certain is that by 1912 Loos and the Scheus traveled in the same avant-garde circles and would remain close friends for the rest of their lives.[12] Yet despite that common ground, the three came from vastly dissimilar families and backgrounds.

Gustav Scheu was born in 1875 in Vienna to a family of fervent Social Democratic activists. His father, Josef Scheu (1841–1904), was a founding member of the Austrian Social Democratic Party. A conservatory-trained musician, he composed the party's "work song," or "Lied der Arbeit," and founded and directed the Workers' Choral Society.[13] An active unionist, in 1872 Josef founded the

Viennese Musicians' Association, the first union to represent the interests of musicians in that city. From 1895 until his death, he served as music critic for the *Arbeiter-Zeitung* (Worker's newspaper). Josef was arrested several times for his political views.

Josef's two brothers were involved in socialist circles as well. Andreas (1844–1927), a gilder by trade, was arrested in 1874 for high treason. He subsequently emigrated from Austria to England. In addition to his involvement with Social Democratic parties in England and Scotland, he was an associate of English artist and textile designer William Morris and Irish playwright George Bernard Shaw, both dedicated Socialists. The third brother, Heinrich (1845–1926), was an illustrator and skilled woodcarver. He produced engravings of such notables as Karl Marx, Friedrich Engels, and Charles Darwin. He eventually settled in Switzerland, where he became president of the Swiss Workers' Association and an arbiter for peace.[14]

Gustav Scheu, who maintained an active law practice from his office opposite the Opera House on the Ringstrasse, was well prepared for his role as housing adviser to the city of Vienna. He had a long-standing interest in housing reform and was a student of the philosophies of British town planning visionaries Ebenezer Howard and Raymond Unwin, among others. Prior to World War I, he and Helene traveled to England to meet Howard and further study his Garden City principles.[15] The Garden City emphasis on decentralized communities, cooperative ownership, single-family housing, and ample garden space influenced Scheu's own position on housing reform, which he codified in the 1919 essay "Zur Wohnungsreform" (On housing reform) and promoted during his tenure. Additionally, he was involved in founding a branch of the Garden City Association in Austria.[16] In 1920 Scheu used his political influence to have his friend Loos appointed chief architect to the city's housing department, a position Loos held for two years.[17]

Figure 1.4 Gustav Scheu and Helene Scheu-Riesz in portraits from the early 1930s. Scheu, who was born in Vienna, was a lawyer and a prominent Social Democrat. Moravian-born Scheu-Riesz was a translator and publisher of children's books. Photographs courtesy of Roy M. Close Family Papers.

Helene Riesz, an only child, was born in 1880 in Olmütz (Olomouc), Moravia (now part of the Czech Republic), to a Jewish family of wine merchants with Hungarian and Moravian roots. The family moved to Klosterneuburg, Austria, just north of Vienna, when Helene was a child. One distinguished member of the maternal Beer/Hess side of the family was Dr. Karl Landsteiner, a physician and biologist who was awarded the 1930 Nobel Prize in Medicine for his discovery of human blood groups. Prior to Austria's introduction of the euro in 2002, Landsteiner's image appeared on the thousand-schilling note. Another family member, Sophie Hess, was the longtime mistress of Alfred Nobel, the Swedish inventor of dynamite and the man who established the Nobel Prize. By marriage, Helene was related to the Hungarian-born painter Philip de László, known for his portraits of English aristocrats and royalty, including those of Princess Elizabeth of York (later Queen Elizabeth II) and Kings George VI and Edward VII.

Helene studied English and philosophy at the University of Vienna and became associated with the Social Democratic movement through which she met Gustav Scheu.[18] They married in Vienna in 1904, and their son, Friedrich "Friedl" Josef, was born in 1905. By all accounts, Helene was a dynamic, strong-willed, domineering woman with myriad talents and interests. She was an ardent pacifist who became a Quaker and was active in the international Quaker community, the International Congress of Women, and child education and welfare efforts. A writer, translator, and educator, she published her first novel, *Becoming*, in 1904 at the age of twenty-four. She also wrote for the *Neue Freie Presse* (New free press). Her primary literary interest, however, was children's literature; she provided German translations for scores of children's books.

Like her husband, Helene was committed to the welfare of children and the improvement of social conditions in post–World War I Vienna. Working with international Quaker organizations, she conceived an after-school program that utilized classrooms to provide hot cocoa and a warm haven for cold, hungry children. These "cocoa rooms" soon evolved into reading rooms, where Helene strove to provide quality literature, especially international folktales, to nourish the minds of the children. Her friend George Cadbury, a fellow Quaker and son of the founder of the British Cadbury confectionary company, contributed to the effort in two ways: he supplied three tons of chocolate for the program and provided funds for Helene to start her own publishing house.[19] Helene named the house *Sesam-Verlag* (Sesame Books) after English writer and social critic John Ruskin's *Sesame and Lilies*, a favorite text she had translated. She also believed books were the "Open Sesame" keys to the world of reading and knowledge. Books in the Sesame series were diminutively scaled to fit comfortably in children's hands.[20] One of her most notable achievements at Sesame Books was the 1923 German translation of *Alice in Wonderland*, for which she commissioned Vienna-born artist Uriel Birnbaum to create richly colored, evocative illustrations.[21]

Loos, the son of a stonecutter, was born in 1870 in Brno, Moravia (in the Czech Republic), not far from Helene's birthplace. Although he was determined to become an architect, he had little formal training in the field. In 1893 he traveled to the United States, visiting New York, Philadelphia, and Chicago. While in America, he attended the World's Columbian Exposition and elsewhere admired a range of building types from soaring skyscrapers to utilitarian grain silos. Once back in Vienna, he wrote essays for the *Neue Freie Presse* on the topics of design, fashion, and culture. Through Vienna's salon and café society, he cultivated friendships with such progressive thinkers as composer Arnold Schoenberg, poet Peter Altenberg, artist Oskar Kokoschka, and essayist Karl Kraus. He also met numerous well-to-do retailers, intellectuals, and industrialists for whom he designed shops, apartments, and residences.

His earliest known commission in Vienna was the interior design of the Ebenstein Fashion House (1897), a fine tailoring company that the sartorially elegant Loos frequented.[22] In 1910 he designed the facade and interiors for the Kniže Tailor Salon, a men's clothing concern. Typically, in his commercial and residential interiors, Loos rejected ornate or applied ornamentation and relied on handsome materials, often highly honed or polished stone and wood, and finely crafted construction to create an aura of luxury, sophistication, and warmth. At Kniže, these materials included black granite and high-gloss cherry. In 1911 Loos designed the Michaelerhaus, a multistory retail/apartment building in Vienna that stood across a plaza from the Hofburg, the imperial palace of the Habsburgs. Although its interiors were sumptuous and finely detailed, the building's facade lacked adornment. This ignited outrage among the public and city officials alike. An injunction to block construction of the Michaelerhaus was lifted on the condition that flower boxes be placed on the building's upper windows. It was during this firestorm of controversy that the Scheus commissioned Loos to design their new home.

Loos began designing villas in the early 1900s, as his well-to-do clients moved from the heart of the city to leafy districts on the outskirts of town. The Scheu House was one of a handful of villas Loos designed in Hietzing between 1910 and 1913.[23] The Scheus' lot was located at what was then the dead end of Larochegasse, directly across the street from a school that Lisl would later attend. The house abutted a wall that terminated the short, residential street; on the other side of the wall stood a factory that manufactured children's blocks. For the Scheus, he designed a four-story (including basement), flat-roofed house comprising roughly 3,300 square feet of space. The two levels that rose above the ground floor were successively smaller in area, thereby creating space for outdoor roof terraces. Due to its unusual stepped conformation, the villa was derogatorily nicknamed "the giant's staircase."

The house's entry was via an asymmetrically placed exterior stairway, which rose from street level to an elevated ground floor. The ground floor comprised an entry hall, kitchen, dining room, glass-walled terrace, library, and salon—labeled "the music and work room" on the original plan. The plan allowed easy flow among main living areas, as well as a view between them. The first floor consisted of three bedrooms, a maid's (or Daisy's) quarters, a bathroom, and one of two roof terraces.[24] The top floor, which was used as a rental unit, was accessible via a spiral staircase that rose from street level. It contained a vestibule, bedroom, bathroom, and access to the second roof terrace. Although the exterior of the house,

Figure 1.5 Architect Adolf Loos designed a starkly modern house for the Scheu family in Vienna in 1912. Photograph by Otto Mayer, circa 1904. Wikimedia Commons.

which was finished in smooth, white stucco, was devoid of decoration, Loos provided visual interest and a sense of scale through fenestration patterns. The house was nearly flush with the sidewalk on the street side. Behind it was a large garden planted with raspberry and gooseberry bushes, and apricot and sour cherry trees.[25]

City officials objected to Loos's plan for several reasons. One concern was that should the wall and the factory abutting the Scheu House be demolished (as they eventually were), what kind of structure could be constructed to adjoin the unusual villa at 3 Larochegasse? To allay their apprehensions, officials required Loos to suggest a design solution. Of greater concern was the fact that the house included roof terraces, which could be directly accessed from bedrooms and other private rooms of the house. This was nothing less than an architectural and cultural affront—one lacking precedent in Vienna, or anywhere in Central Europe. As Loos wrote, "It was thought that this type of building would have been fine in Algiers, but not in Vienna. I had not even thought of the East when I built this house. I just thought that it would be pleasant to be able to step out onto a large common terrace from the bedrooms . . . in Vienna just as much as Algiers."[26] As architectural historian Benedetto Gravagnuolo has observed, it was Loos's insistence on building a terraced house in Vienna and his "deliberate refusal to make any concessions to current taste and to the conventional image of the Austrian house" that led directly to the "pure, radical and extremely modern shape of this stepped white shell" of a house.[27]

Figure 1.6 According to Lisl, the city granted her mother a permit to build the controversial Scheu House on the condition that she grow ivy up its walls. Photograph circa 1920s. Courtesy of Roy M. Close Family Papers.

Lisl's bedroom opened onto one of the terraces and, as a child, she used it as a play area and sleeping porch in fair weather. Her use of the space was precisely what Loos had foreseen. As he explained of the terraces, or "raised streets," he later included in his design for a large municipal housing unit in Vienna, "Children can play on the terrace without the danger of being run over by a car, etc. . . . This safe and quiet street of terraces gives them the chance to pass the whole day in the open."[28] Although the family enjoyed the terraces, neighbors objected to their presence and damned the house as an eyesore and an unwelcome intrusion in their (or any other) Viennese neighborhood.

The Scheus did not debate the uniqueness of the house. "It was very untypical of a Vienna villa," Lisl later said. "My mother had a very hard time getting a building permit. She finally hit on the brilliant idea of taking my brother down to the offices whenever she was asking for this permit. He was such a darned nuisance that they finally gave it to her."[29] According to Lisl, the city granted the permit on the condition that the Scheus grow ivy on the bare exterior walls. As amusing as the story is, it may be apocryphal. Loos scholar Ralf Bock has observed that the facades of Loos-designed villas were often wrapped in a tangle of vines. Loos believed greenery provided a kind of protective "skin" on the house, akin to fur on an animal or clothing on a human. It offered a measure of privacy and security from "neighbors' gazes and from the public eye."[30]

Loos also made a clear distinction between the exterior or city facade of a house, which he believed should reveal little of a personal nature about its occupants, and the interior or private realm, where individuality could be expressed: "The house should be discreet on the outside and show its great wealth within," he said.[31] Gravagnuolo has called this the "otherness" between the "silent coolness of the shell and the warm welcome of the space it encloses. The exterior does not say, on the contrary it conceals, contradicts what it contains inside."[32] This counterpoint is evident in the Scheu House, where the stark geometry and plain white "shell" of the villa's exterior is deliberately at odds with the warm, textured interiors.

Loos used honey-colored, matte-finished oak for parquet floors, wood-beamed ceilings in the dining room and hall, paneling (which extended to door height in some areas), built-ins, and bookcases. Persian rugs covered floors and defined seating areas, and vertically striped English wallpaper adorned some walls. According to Lisl, Loos chose the furnishings and finishes for the house, including a Chippendale dining room set made of oak.[33] Intimately scaled spaces included a wood-paneled inglenook with a redbrick fireplace and upholstered banquettes (Plate 1). Loos made the compact space even more welcoming by dropping the ceiling in the nook. Helene was so fond of the inglenook, she used a drawing of it on the cover of her 1947 book *Open Sesame: Books Are Keys*. Large windows and terrace doors allowed light to infuse interior rooms. One window, consisting of a grid of blue, yellow, and clear panes, fascinated Lisl as a child. She remembered trying to capture its color and light in drawings.[34]

Figure 1.7 The Scheus used the flexible hall space in many ways. Here, Helene Scheu-Riesz (right) and a friend utilize it for conversation. Undated photograph. Courtesy of Roy M. Close Family Papers.

Although interior finishes were handsome and finely crafted, Loos's choice of oak and brick intentionally lacked the gloss and shine of the more opulent materials, such as the lacquered mahogany and polished stone he specified for other projects. He was sensitive to a homeowner's character and aware of "how the client wanted to leave an impression on his guests," as Bock has explained. In the case of Scheu, the simple, "puritan" finishes in his house "stressed the vital meaning of family in Gustav Scheu's life. He descended from a family of labor leaders and founders of the Social Democratic

Figure 1.8 "Frau Marie," a family employee, in the dining room of the Scheu House. Loos specified oak for the room's Chippendale furniture. Undated photograph. Courtesy of Roy M. Close Family Papers.

Figure 1.9 The blue, yellow, and clear panes of this window in the Scheu House fascinated Lisl. She often tried to capture its colors in her drawings. Undated photograph. Courtesy of Roy M. Close Family Papers.

Movement in Vienna. . . . Loos designed and furnished the house according to his character."[35] Appropriately, the unassuming finishes suited the Social Democratic values the Scheus professed, and the bookcase-lined rooms and multiple intimate seating areas fostered conversation and gathering at the couple's frequent salons (Plate 2).

Remarkably, Lisl spent extended time during her youth in another Loos-designed residence. Rosemarie "Madi" Rosenfeld, Lisl's closest childhood friend, and her parents, Valentin Rosenfeld, a lawyer, and Eva Rosenfeld, an educator, lived in a two-story Biedermeier villa in Vienna with interiors redesigned by Loos in 1917. Although the plan of the Rosenfeld House differed significantly from that of the Scheu House, the interiors shared matte-finished oak paneling, beams, parquet floors, and extensive bookshelves.[36]

Not surprisingly, growing up in the Scheu House profoundly influenced Lisl's life and career. First and foremost, it "indoctrinated" her in the power of architecture to shape one's perception of space, movement, and light. It raised her awareness of how the size and relationship of rooms, a drop or rise in ceiling height, and the color and texture of materials can affect habitation. She understood that architecture had the ability to incite emotions, invite social interaction, and promote gathering. On some level, she knew the house, which was specifically designed to suit her family's needs, was the result of a close collaboration between her parents and Loos. She would carry these lessons forward in her own professional career.

What she did not and could not understand at the time was the important role Loos and the Scheu House would play in the history and evolution of modern architecture in Europe. Loos would prove to be a "major figure of Vienna's avant-garde" whose buildings and writings left a lasting mark on that city. His impact spread far beyond Austria and his work directly influenced the philosophies of such seminal modern architects as Marcel Breuer, Rudolf Schindler, and Le Corbusier.[37] In addition to being the first terraced house built in Central Europe, the radical design of the Scheu House is seen as a premier example of Loos's aspirations toward "extreme, geometric purism."[38] Architectural historian Kathleen James-Chakraborty has observed that Loos's "renunciation of applied ornamentation"

Figure 1.10 Historic view of the Scheu House salon. A bust of architect Adolf Loos stands in a niche in the bookcase. Undated photograph. Courtesy of Roy M. Close Family Papers.

Figure 1.11 A compact spiral service staircase connects the ground floor of the Scheu House to the basement. Photograph by William B. Olexy, 2010.

and "the cubic starkness of the facade of the Scheu House of 1912 can, like the subtly detailed facade of the Willow Tea Rooms [a 1903 building in Glasgow by Scottish architect Charles Rennie Mackintosh], be seen as a precursor of the modern movement's obsession with the white box."[39]

THE GUEST BOOK

In addition to providing shelter for the family and a framework for their daily lives, the villa served as a gathering place for the Scheus' many friends, colleagues, and associates, and as a guest house for visitors who, in some instances, stayed with the family for months. The house was also an architectural magnet for those in the vanguard of modern design. "People came from all over the world to look at [the house]. We had a constant influx of visitors . . . from all over—America, England, France, Egypt. They came to stay and study," Lisl stated.[40]

In *The Architecture of Red Vienna, 1919–1934*, scholar Eve Blau places the importance of the house in the broader context of early twentieth-century public housing reform movements, with which Gustav Scheu was connected. "The Scheu residence in the Vienna suburb of Hietzing (XIII), which was a gathering place for left-leaning intellectuals and artists (including among others Eugenie Schwarzwald, philanthropist and feminist educator, and the writer Robert Musil, author of *The Man without Qualities*), also functioned as the intellectual and spiritual center of the Austrian garden city movement, whose adherents assembled there," Blau writes.[41] The significance of these get-togethers made a lasting impression on Lisl, who would later ascribe her own interest in public housing to her father's collaborative efforts to improve conditions in post–World War I Vienna.

Visitors to the house between October 1913 and March 1967 signed, wrote, drew, composed, and painted in the guest book Loos gave the Scheus when they moved into the house.[42] As such, the book provides documentation of the astonishing array of individuals, many of whom were world renowned, whose conversations enlivened the Scheu House salon for more than half a century. It also offers an indelible impression, from the perspective of one extraordinary family and house, of the richly creative, politically volatile city that was Vienna before, between, and after two world wars.

As Lisl described—and the guest book attests—the Scheu House was a popular gathering place for "a very large and interesting group of people." Many were friends or colleagues of the Scheus, while others were members of international groups and organizations with which they were associated, such as town planners and advocates of the Garden City movement, Quakers, suffragists, and pacifists. One of the most distinguished proponents of peace and social welfare to visit the house was Jane Addams, the founder of Chicago's Hull House and a future Nobel Peace Prize laureate.[43] "My mother always enjoyed bringing [together] people who would argue with each other, politely, and have different points of view." Other individuals were drawn to the Scheu House for purely architectural reasons—it was designed "by a famous modernist," she said. "I heard many discussions about architecture from people who came to see the house, so it was an important subject for me."[44]

In addition to Loos, the first person to inscribe the book, among the earliest signers were several acclaimed Austrian artists and architects, including expressionist artist Oskar Kokoschka; Mela Koehler, a painter, illustrator, and printmaker associated with the Wiener Werkstätte; and Josef Frank, an architect and graphic and textile designer. Other visitors included noted British architect and town planner Henry Vaughan Lanchester; Dutch architect Aldo van Eyck; and Austrian American architect Richard Neutra, whose future wife, Dione Niedermann, as a young woman, lived with the Scheus for several months while she studied cello in Vienna.[45] In 1962 architects Colin Rowe and Peter Eisenman traveled to the house from Cambridge, England, where both were living at the time. One or two artistically inclined individuals sketched impromptu portraits of a young curly-haired Lisl in the book.

Many journalists and war correspondents also gravitated to the Scheu House. Among them were Frederick Kuh of the Chicago *Sun-Times*, Marcel Ray of the *New York Times*, syndicated columnist Drew Pearson, and CBS radio announcer Frazier Hunt.

Austrian composers Alban Berg and Anton Webern were guests, as was Hungarian-born conductor George Szell.[46] Film and theater personalities included German American actress (and two-time Academy Award winner) Luise Rainer; French cabaret singer Yvette Guilbert, who was immortalized in several sketches and posters by artist Henri de Toulouse-Lautrec; English set and costume designer Tanya Moiseiwitsch; and English filmmaker (and reputed spy) Ivor Montagu.

Among the many American writers who visited the house were poet Ezra Pound, who signed the book and added a whimsical self-portrait in 1928; screenwriter Anita Loos (no relation to Adolf Loos), author of *Gentlemen Prefer Blondes*; poet and anthologist Louis Untermeyer; poet Theodore Roethke; Pulitzer Prize–winning playwright and novelist Thornton Wilder; and journalist and author John Gunther, who was a close friend of the Scheus. European writers included Austrian satirist and playwright Karl Kraus; Hugh Lofting, the British author of the Doctor Dolittle series of children's books; Irish playwright C. K. Munro; French writer and critic Léon

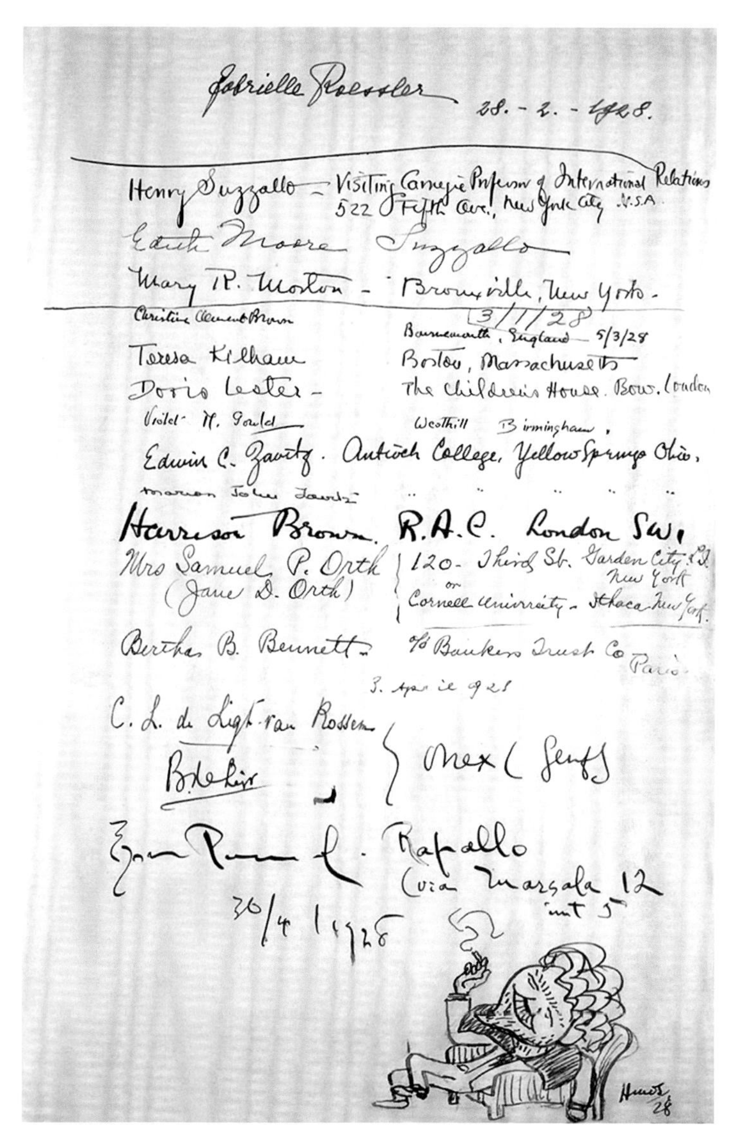
Gabrielle Roessler 28.-2.-1928.
Henry Suzzallo – Visiting Carnegie Professor of International Relations 522 Fifth Ave., New York City U.S.A.
Edith Moore Suzzallo
Mary R. Morton – Brownville, New York.
Christine Clement Brown 3/1/28
Bournemouth, England 5/3/28
Teresa Kilham Boston, Massachusetts
Doris Lester – The Children's House. Bow. London
Violet M. Gould Westhill Birmingham.
Edwin C. Zavitz. Antioch College, Yellow Springs Ohio.
Harrison Brown. R.A.C. London SW.
Mrs Samuel P. Orth (Jane D. Orth) 120 - Third St. Garden City N.Y. New York or Cornell University - Ithaca New York.
Bertha B. Bennett % Bankers Trust Co Paris
Rapallo Via Marsala 12 int 5
30/4/1928

Figure 1.12 Beginning in 1912, visitors to the Scheu House signed a guest book given to the family by Loos. Many of the signees were, or would become, world famous. In 1928 writer Ezra Pound added his autograph and a playful self-portrait. Courtesy of Roy M. Close Family Papers.

Werth; and German Jewish children's book author Josefa Metz. At the time of her visit in 1916, few in Vienna could have foreseen the rising tide of anti-Semitism and Nazi aggression that would lead to the deaths of millions of Jews—and others—during World War II, including that of Metz in the Theresienstadt concentration camp in 1943.

The guest book documents multiple visits to 3 Larochegasse by Boston department store magnate and philanthropist Edward Filene, and Cambridge, Massachusetts, city planner John Nolen. In addition to being close family friends, the two men helped to facilitate Lisl's immigration to the United States, her admission to the School of Architecture at the Massachusetts Institute of Technology, and provided financial support, a place to live, and friendship during her years there.

ARCHITECTURAL STUDIES IN VIENNA

While there was never any question in Lisl's mind that she would earn a university degree and pursue a professional career, these achievements were not a given for most young Austrian women of the era. In fact, it was "'almost unthinkable' for a woman to work in any technical profession in Austria during the final years of the monarchy" and beyond.[47] Those who successfully aspired to a career, including "bourgeois young ladies of some professional ambition," were limited to the pursuit of "a school teaching career . . . one of the few avenues open," to women in the early twentieth century.[48] However, because Lisl had grown up with the advantage of a university-educated, working mother as a role model, and had met many professionally accomplished women from around the world at 3 Larochegasse, she believed her goal was an achievable one. She briefly considered a career in law or chemistry but by high school had decided to become an architect primarily because of her experience growing up in the Scheu House. "The house was such a bone of contention in Vienna, people used to argue about it and it was clear to me that architecture was an important field to be in because there was so much talk about it," she said.[49] To put the boldness of her decision in perspective, she was not aware of a single practicing woman architect in Vienna or Europe when she committed to architectural studies.[50]

At the time, only a handful of female European architects were at work, but there were trailblazers among them. Irish designer Eileen Gray (1878–1976) was noted for her tubular steel furniture and modern residences, notably E-1027, her own villa in Roquebrune-Cap-Martin, France, completed in 1929. German-born Lilly Reich (1885–1947) was an architect and exhibition designer known for her independent work as well as for her collaborations with architect Ludwig Mies van der Rohe.[51] Swiss architect Flora Steiger-Crawford (1899–1991), the first woman to graduate from the Federal Institute of Technology in Switzerland, designed modern furniture and houses. Her firm, established in 1924 with her husband, is credited with designing the first modern house in Switzerland.[52] The French architect and furniture designer Charlotte Perriand (1903–1999) worked from her own studio as well as in collaboration with architects Le Corbusier (Charles-Édouard Jeanneret) and Pierre Jeanneret. She made significant contributions to the furniture designs of the Jeannerets, and created interiors for Unité d'habitation (1952), Le Corbusier's Brutalist housing block in Marseilles. As accomplished as these women were, their designs were not widely published at the time, if they were published at all. For this reason, it is doubtful that Lisl knew of any of these pioneering female architects or viewed them as role models.

This lack of visibility would have been the case for early women architects in Austria, as well. The 2016 exhibition titled *Calliope Austria: Women in Society, Culture and the Sciences* identifies six "women pioneers of the early 20th century" who were born, trained, or worked as architects in Austria.[53] Ella Baumfeld Briggs (1880–1977) was born in Vienna and worked as an architect there from 1924 to 1927. By necessity, she earned her architecture degree in Munich around 1920, as women were not permitted to study architecture in Vienna at that time. Moravian Liane Zimbler (1892–1987) studied and worked in Vienna—primarily as an illustrator and fashion designer—until she became "the first female civic architect in Austria" in 1938. Viennese Friederike Dicker (1898–1944) studied at the School of

Applied Arts and worked in Vienna as a stage and interior designer until she went to Prague in the mid-1930s. She died in Auschwitz concentration camp in 1944. Anna-Lülja Praun (1906–2004), born in St. Petersburg, studied architecture in Graz, Austria, during the 1920s. Her "creative period as an independent architect" began in 1952 in Vienna. Austrian Adelheid Gnaiger (1916–1991) graduated from the Technische Hochschule in Vienna in 1937, five years after Lisl left for MIT. After working for a firm in Zurich, she established her own architectural practice in Vorarlberg, Austria, in 1950. As an eighteen-year old university- bound student, Lisl was unaware of these pioneering women.

Nor was she familiar with the work of Margarete Schütte-Lihotzky (1897–2000), who was born in Vienna and became the first woman to attend the city's School of Applied Arts, where she studied architecture under Oskar Strnad. Her interest in functional design led to collaborations in the 1920s with Loos, Josef Frank, and others at the Friedensstadt settlement, a Social Democratic housing initiative in Vienna. She later designed two houses for the 1932 Werkbundsiedlung in Hietzing, a showcase of Austrian modern design that Lisl visited shortly before leaving Vienna for MIT. She is best known for her design of the "Frankfurt Kitchen," a well-planned, efficient model kitchen engineered to lessen the burden of housework on women, thereby increasing their freedom. Beginning in the mid-1920s, more than ten thousand kitchens were mass-produced and installed in public housing units in Frankfurt and other German cities. In 1926, when Lisl was fourteen, Schütte-Lihotzky left Austria for Frankfurt. In 1930 she moved to the Soviet Union, where she remained until 1937. During World War II, her political activism and work in the resistance resulted in her four-year imprisonment in Germany. Schütte-Lihotzky eventually returned to Vienna, but not until long after Lisl had immigrated to the United States.[54] Lisl was not aware of Schütte-Lihotzky or her work until late in her own life, and it is doubtful that Schütte-Lihotzky ever knew of Lisl.[55] Architecturally and politically the two women had much in common. When viewed through the lens of the documented histories of Austrian women architects of the early twentieth century, Lisl and Margarete Schütte-Lihotzky had the longest and most prolific professional careers.[56]

Lisl began her architectural education at the Technical University in Vienna, where she studied for two years under less than ideal conditions. Although she was disappointed that the university's curriculum did not embrace modern design, she encountered far more serious problems there. "It was obvious from the beginning that the school was unsympathetic to women, and there were no women professors," she said.[57] Even more troubling, "Studying in Vienna was very difficult and very awkward because there were too many political hassles and fights. If you went to the university, you had a good chance that you might not get into a class that you wanted because . . . there were Nazis and they obstructed the classes deliberately. It was politically a very unpleasant place to be," she said.[58] "I remember walking out of class one day because the Nazis had decided to close it . . . but I knew they would not touch me because I had blonde hair."[59] For Lisl's brother, Friedl, who was

Figure 1.13 Lisl began her architectural studies at the Technische Hochschule in Vienna but found conditions there hostile to women. Photograph by Jane King Hession, 2010.

studying law at the University of Vienna, the situation was becoming unsafe. "The Nazis were being aggressive . . . attacking people they thought were evil, socialist, or Jewish and tossing them out from the university and beating them up. . . . I remember my brother coming home with a torn jacket once."[60]

In addition to being at risk for their socialist views, the Scheus were also in peril because of Helene's Jewish parentage. Although Helene did not consider herself to be Jewish—and did not raise her children as such—it was a dangerous point to debate in Austria in the 1930s. Of her upbringing, Lisl asserted, "I wasn't Jewish. My mother's parents were, though. So, from Hitler's point of view we were contaminated. In Hitler's view, we were Jews."[61]

Looming threats to her safety aside, Lisl had another compelling reason to leave Vienna: her mother. Ironically, although Helene was deeply involved in international child welfare efforts and published children's books, "she was more theoretically interested in children than in her own children," observed Anne Ulmer, Lisl's daughter. "She didn't do well nurturing them."[62] Lisl stated it more succinctly: "My mother did nothing with me."[63] Yet, Helene was also an opinionated and controlling person. "My mother was a manipulator. . . . That's why I left Vienna. . . . I had to get out of the house," she said. Roy Close, Lisl's son, concurs. "She really didn't get along with her mother, as everybody in the family knows, and I think she took advantage of the opportunity to go to the United States, in part, so she could put an ocean between her and her mother."[64] As contentious as the relationship was, Roy believes his mother and Helene shared at least one personality trait. "[Helene] was a very enterprising person. . . . Lisl very definitely got that quality from her. Lisl was not afraid to do things."[65]

LEAVING VIENNA

Lisl was the first member of her family to leave Austria and come to the United States; she did so with the encouragement and support of Edward Filene. Filene, who knew Lisl wanted to become an architect, suggested MIT would be an excellent place to continue her studies. She applied, was accepted, and received a partial scholarship for the academic year 1932–33. It is not clear how much influence Filene wielded over Lisl's acceptance, but it is likely that the wealthy and prominent businessman smoothed the road for her in some way. What is evident is that the childless philanthropist served as a surrogate parent, legal protector, and guardian angel for the twenty-year-old when she arrived, alone, in the United States. "He was my mentor because he kept me alive. My parents couldn't pay tuition at MIT. I am sure Filene helped," Lisl later said.[66] He even went so far as to sign a U.S. government "Affidavit of Support" for Lisl, stating that he was "willing and able to receive, maintain, support, and be responsible for [Elizabeth Scheu] while she remains in the United States."[67] The affidavit was a critical document for Lisl to secure the necessary visas that would allow her to remain in the country and embark on the road to citizenship. She left Vienna in early August 1932, traveling to London via Belgium. From there, she sailed on the *American Merchant*, arriving in New York on August 29.

Figure 1.14 Philanthropist and Boston department store mogul Edward Filene was a family friend and frequent visitor to the Scheu House. Aided by his benevolent support, Lisl traveled to America and continued her education at MIT. Photograph by Blank & Stoller. Courtesy of Roy M. Close Family Papers.

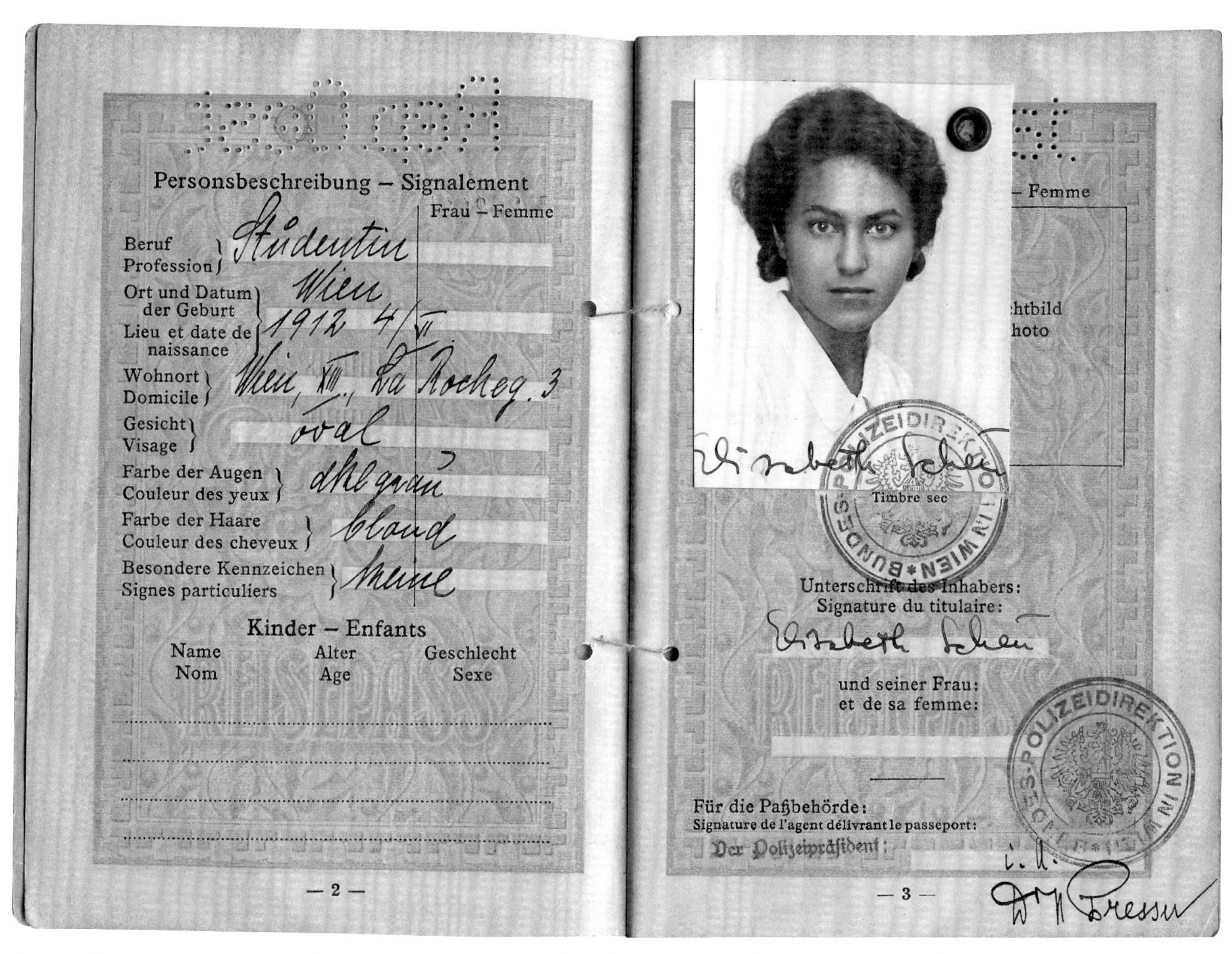
Personsbeschreibung – Signalement

Frau – Femme

Beruf / Profession: Studentin

Ort und Datum der Geburt / Lieu et date de naissance: Wien 1912 4/VII

Wohnort / Domicile: Wien, XIII, La Rocheg. 3

Gesicht / Visage: oval

Farbe der Augen / Couleur des yeux: dklgrau

Farbe der Haare / Couleur des cheveux: blond

Besondere Kennzeichen / Signes particuliers: keine

Kinder – Enfants

Name / Nom	Alter / Age	Geschlecht / Sexe

— 2 —

Elizabeth Scheu

Timbre sec

BUNDES-POLIZEIDIREKTION WIEN

Unterschrift des Inhabers:
Signature du titulaire:

Elizabeth Scheu

und seiner Frau:
et de sa femme:

Für die Paßbehörde:
Signature de l'agent délivrant le passeport:
Der Polizeipräsident:

— 3 —

Figure 1.15 Elizabeth Scheu's passport. Lisl left Vienna in early August 1932 and arrived in New York Harbor on August 29. Courtesy of Roy M. Close Family Papers.

Filene was not her only friend in the Boston area. John Nolen, then a prominent city planner in Cambridge, and his family opened their home to Lisl and gave her a place to live during her first year at MIT. The Nolens welcomed Lisl as warmly as the Scheus had welcomed the Nolens' daughter Barbara five years earlier when she was married in the garden of their home in Vienna.[68] Although she would not return to Austria to live, Lisl did travel to Vienna twice prior to the war; once in the summer of 1934 and later that winter, when her father was seriously ill.

Gustav Scheu died in Vienna on March 9, 1935. Helene moved to the United States in 1937. Family members and her biographer, Susanne Blumesberger, stress that she did so because of an affinity for the United States, not because she felt threatened by rising anti-Semitism or the deteriorating political situation. "She made no connection to her Jewish heritage or her political ideology," said Blumesberger.[69] Nor was proximity to Lisl, who lived in Minnesota at the time, a determining factor. "I don't think she was welcome in Minneapolis, frankly," stated Roy Close, but she did visit on occasion.[70] Instead, Helene settled in New York City, where she lived in London Terrace, a block-long apartment complex in Manhattan's Chelsea neighborhood. She also spent time in North Carolina, both in Chapel Hill and on coastal Ocracoke Island, where she helped organize an artists' workshop. While living in America she founded the Island Press Workshop, a publishing company. She remained in the United States until 1954.[71]

Figure 1.16 The Scheu family in the garden of 3 Larochegasse, 1928. From left to right: Gustav Scheu, Helene Scheu-Riesz, Lisl Scheu, family friend Denise Olivier, and Friedrich Scheu. Courtesy of Roy M. Close Family Papers.

Friedl Scheu, a Vienna-based correspondent for the London *Daily Herald*, left Austria in 1938. "When the Nazis came in, Friedl went out that night. He was very high on the list of people they wanted to get. He was a socialist, he was a foreign editor of the workers' party paper there, and a lawyer. They wanted him for various reasons," said Ulmer.[72] Friedl described his narrow escape in his book, *The Way into the Unknown: Austria's Changing Destiny, 1929–1938*. On March 12, the day Hitler's troops marched into Austria, Scheu attempted to cross the border from Austria into Czechoslovakia, where he planned to continue his reportage from Prague, but he was turned back by Czech authorities. Through the intervention of friend and fellow *Daily Herald* and *New York Times* correspondent Eric Gedye, Scheu was quickly and officially reassigned to Prague. He was also provided with the necessary papers to cross the Czech border, which he successfully did on his second attempt. His wife, Herta, joined him soon after, but their two-year-old daughter, Helga, remained behind in Vienna. As the Germans advanced on Czechoslovakia, Friedl and Herta fled to London, where they remained for the next sixteen years.[73] In addition to his work as a foreign correspondent and foreign editor of the British magazine *News Review*, Scheu was the author of several books, including *British Labor and the Beveridge Plan* (1943) and *Humor as a Weapon: Political Cabaret in the First Republic* (1977). He died in 1985, at the age of eighty, in Vienna.

3 LAROCHEGASSE, REVISITED

Miraculously, the Scheu House survived the war intact and in the possession of members of the extended Scheu family, one of whom was "close to the Nazis."[74] In 1954 Friedl, Herta, and their now three daughters — Helga, Veronica, and Caroline — returned to Vienna and took up residence at 3 Larochegasse. At the invitation of her son, Helene also returned to the house that same year. In 1960 Helene sold the villa, but she lived there until shortly before her death in 1970. The house, which is no longer owned by the Scheu family, remains little changed today.

Lisl returned to Vienna — and the Scheu House — for the last time in April 2001. Accompanied by family members, she traveled to the city to donate the leather-bound guest book to the Wien Museum. Of the gift Lisl explained, "I thought I should take it back to Vienna, where it was born."[75]

It is impossible to overstate the importance of the Loos-designed Scheu House to Lisl's identity, life, and career. In her later years, she mentioned it frequently and always with pride. She spoke of its architecture, her childhood there, friends and family, of the hundreds of people who were drawn to the house, of the conversation and music that resonated within its walls, of how the house shaped the person and the architect she would become. One of her reminiscences was of the last time she saw Adolf Loos in the house. It occurred roughly a year before his death in 1933, not long before her departure for America. Lisl and a few fellow students from the university had gathered in the living room to study for an exam. Loos, who was "old and feeble," entered the room with his nurse. "He went around the house, touching the wood, looking at it all, saying good-bye to the house," she said. "I have never forgotten it."[76]

2

BECOMING AN ARCHITECT IN AMERICA

Figure 2.1 Lisl *(front left)* and shipmates on transatlantic crossing from London to New York, 1932. Courtesy of Roy M. Close Family Papers.

When Edward Filene suggested that Lisl continue her architectural education at the Massachusetts Institute of Technology, he gave her sound advice. In 1868, seven years after it was founded, MIT became the first university in the United States to offer a four-year course in architecture. It began accepting women in 1885, and in 1890 Sophia Hayden became the first woman to graduate from MIT with a degree in architecture.[1]

In 1932, the year Lisl arrived at MIT, the School of Architecture was established and William Emerson became its first dean. At that time, the school was housed in the Rogers Building in Boston and was the only university department that had not moved across the Charles River to MIT's new campus in Cambridge in 1916; it would not do so until 1938.[2] The physical separation of the School of Architecture from other disciplines at MIT was not entirely accidental. "The School had throughout its early history far more affinity with architects practicing in Boston than with its parent academic institution," stated Lawrence B. Anderson, who earned a master's degree in architecture at MIT in 1930, began teaching there in 1933, and became dean of the School of Architecture and Planning in 1965.[3] This relative autonomy, as well as the predominance of part-time students and faculty, "led to the development of a degree curriculum in which the School furnished its own instruction in science, mathematics, history, and structures."[4] For Lisl, it was an ideal situation. "We were in a little old building on Boylston Street. I thought it was a wonderful school because they were very welcoming," Lisl said. "I jumped into being at MIT totally."[5]

ARCHITECTURAL EDUCATION AT MIT

Lisl was given credit for two years of study at the Technische Hochschule and placed in the third year of a four-year degree program at MIT. Because she was fluent in English, she did not face a language barrier. She did encounter other challenges, including a lack of familiarity with the U.S. system of measurements, which was both new to her and fundamental to her architectural studies. "I hadn't become familiar with feet and inches—I was thinking meters, a different vocabulary," she said.[6] Nor had her schooling in Vienna prepared her for the kind of studio design problems she encountered at MIT. "Of course, the first sketch problem we had . . . I couldn't do it and I flunked." But she gratefully acknowledged that "Dean Emerson was a very thoughtful man. He called me and said, 'Don't be discouraged. It will be OK and you will catch up.'"[7] She did and soon found the program's framework to be the "same idea" as her course of study in Vienna, in that "we took the history of architecture, structural design . . . all sorts of technical things."[8] Another significant, but stimulating, way in which the MIT program differed from that of the Technische Hochschule was that students from three Boston-area schools often tackled the same design problem: "[We] had projects that would be done simultaneously by Harvard, MIT, and the Boston Architectural [Club], competing each against the other," she said.[9] Lisl earned a first honor in one of those competitions for her design of a museum.

Figure 2.2 The Rogers Building on Boylston Street in Boston, seen here in a photograph from 1905, was home to MIT's School of Architecture until 1938. Photograph by Thomas E. Marr. Boston Pictorial Archive, Boston Public Library.

Early on, she learned that the work of European modernists was little known at MIT, let alone included in the curriculum there or anywhere else. It would be another five years before Walter Gropius and Marcel Breuer left Europe for the United States to teach at the Harvard Graduate School of Design and, in the process, introduced American architectural education to the International Style.[10] Nor did anyone know that she had grown up in a radically modern house designed by a progressive architect that had incited an architectural uproar in Vienna. "They didn't know the name Loos," she later recalled, adding wryly, "they do now."[11] Instead, she described the curriculum at MIT as "still domes and pendentives," referring to the structures that topped ancient and classical buildings and their underlying system of triangular supports. By this she meant the program was still deeply rooted in the rigorous, soon-to-be-outdated traditions of the École des Beaux-Arts, the influential school in Paris at which many nineteenth- and early twentieth-century American architects had trained. The Beaux-Arts emphasized a reverence for the classical orders, symmetry, and exquisitely rendered drawings, among other firmly held conventions, all of which was of little interest to Lisl. As Lawrence Anderson later confirmed, the design staffs of both Harvard and MIT were "headed by genuine Beaux-Arts gurus" in the 1930s.[12] He further noted that the country's leading architecture schools, including MIT, "were all part of the Beaux-Arts system for quite a long time."[13]

However, new ideas were beginning to infiltrate the curriculum at MIT. In the early to mid-1930s, Anderson and other young faculty members had been exposed to and "influenced by modernism, so we were finding ourselves the Young Turks in the school."[14] Although senior faculty and local practicing architects did not initially embrace these new trends in pedagogy and design, they eventually "saw the handwriting on the wall."[15] At around the same time, the school evaluated its program regarding the "profession of architecture and future requirements of its practitioners."[16] It concluded that "design was to remain the central theme of all good architecture," but acknowledged that "the techniques of its application must continually adapt themselves to the evolution of the technical and social environment."[17] This manifested itself in "steps to adjust design courses to conditions encountered in actual practice by means of specialized seminars and projects" and included studio projects related to "lighting, building materials, and other elements basic to a new theory of architectural design."[18] Lisl's time at MIT coincided with this sea change, elevating the quality of her architectural education and level of preparedness for professional employment.

She also enhanced her knowledge base by traveling to other regions of the United States. While at MIT, Lisl was invited by a fellow student to accompany her on a cross-country driving trip.[19] After leaving behind the traditional architecture of New England and passing through the Dust Bowl–parched southern plains, the women arrived in New Mexico, where Lisl had her first powerful encounter with American architecture. "It was fascinating. I got to see the Taos pueblo and that church, that famous church in Taos. . . . It was the most wonderful building I had seen in America." Surprisingly, Lisl saw modernity in the eighteenth-century structure. "It was the first building that really made me excited about architecture from what I had seen in this country. I was not interested in classic or Roman, or you know, those styles. And nobody else was doing modern. . . . It was simple and it was strong, a lot of things that I admired," she explained.[20]

Figure 2.3 In the mid-1930s, Lisl accompanied an MIT classmate on a cross-country drive to the Southwest. Here she takes the wheel. Courtesy of Roy M. Close Family Papers.

Lisl documented the distinctive landforms and striking buildings she discovered on the journey in a series of black and white photographs. They include images of San Francisco de Asis Mission Church in Ranchos de Taos (the church she admired), Native American cliff dwellings, buttes and other rock formations, Yellowstone National Park's Mammoth Springs in Wyoming, the Grand Canyon in Arizona, and the soon-to-be completed Hoover Dam on the Arizona/Nevada border. The women also traveled to Los Angeles, where Lisl photographed the Lovell House and other recent works designed by architect Richard Neutra, a fellow Austrian. The built and natural wonders she saw on the trip made an immediate and lasting impression on her: "They became part of my architectural education," she stated.[21]

One of the requirements for an undergraduate degree in architecture at MIT was a thesis. Lisl's chosen topic was "A Production Plant for Pre-Fabricated Houses." The choice was significant for two reasons. First, her argument for producing factory-made "efficient, clean, simple, and pleasant homes" to alleviate the problem of people "living crowded together in noisy, dusty, unhealthy and unpleasant cities where slums breed sickness and crime" likely sprang from her Social Democratic roots and her father's commitment to solving societal problems through housing reform. "We are conscious of the vital influence of physical surroundings on the healthy, mental development of the individual and the race," she wrote.[22] Second, the thesis uniquely qualified her for future employment. Seven years later, when the Page & Hill Company of Shakopee, Minnesota, was looking for a qualified architect to design a series of factory-made houses for their firm, they hired Lisl partly on the strength of her undergraduate thesis work in prefabricated housing. She would design twenty-five prototypes for the firm.

Figure 2.4A Lisl photographed many natural and built wonders on her trip, including New Mexico's San Francisco de Asis Mission Church in Ranchos de Taos. Photograph by Elizabeth Scheu. Courtesy of Roy M. Close Family Papers.

Figure 2.4B Lisl admired the simplicity and strength of the Hoover Dam. Photograph by Elizabeth Scheu. Courtesy of Roy M. Close Family Papers.

Lisl received a bachelor of science in architecture from MIT in 1934 and went straight into the school's graduate program, where she was the only woman in a class of twelve students. One classmate was Winston "Win" Arthur Close, the man who would become her personal and professional partner for the next six decades.

WINSTON CLOSE

Win was born in 1906 in Appleton, Minnesota, the third child and only son of Arthur and Clara Close. His father, who once worked for the railroad and co-owned Close & Lathrop Groceries in Appleton, died in the flu pandemic of 1918, leaving twelve-year-old Win the sole male in the family. He took an early interest in drafting and furniture design. He had "a terrific sense of perspective and that translated pretty easily for him into design work," said son Roy.[23] In contrast to Lisl's early "indoctrination" with modern architecture, Win did not grow up in or around it. "I was born in a small town in western Minnesota and I had never seen an architect" prior to college, he said.[24]

In 1923 Win entered the University of Minnesota to study architecture, and he proved to be a talented artist and designer. He won student prizes and was a member of the Scarab Fraternity, a national architectural society. His undergraduate student projects, as well as those of his contemporaries at the university in the late 1920s, demonstrate the rigor and precision of a classically influenced architectural education. After earning his bachelor of science in architecture in 1927, he worked as a draftsman for a series of Minnesota firms, including Toltz, King, and Day; Long and Thorshov; Ellerbe & Company; and Erickson & Company.[25]

Figure 2.5 Winston Close (foreground) at the University of Minnesota. Roy Childs Jones, head of the School of Architecture from 1937 to 1954, is at left. Undated photograph. Courtesy of Roy M. Close Family Papers.

In 1930 he took a hiatus from work to expand his knowledge of architecture—and the world—through travel. Just as European-born Lisl had discovered American architecture on her cross-country journey in the mid-1930s, Minnesota-bred Win was introduced to an array of ancient and classical architecture during a five-month bicycle tour of Europe. Unlike Lisl, who used photography—and a strong sense of light and shadow—to record her observations, Win employed his considerable gifts as a renderer and watercolorist to create a collection of evocative portraits of sites that captured his attention.

Santa Maria della
Salute - Venice
WOE
5-22-30

Figures 2.6 A and B In 1930 Winston Close embarked on a five-month bicycle trip in Europe. He used his artistic talents to create a series of sketches and watercolors, including these drawings of Chartres, France, and Santa Maria della Salute in Venice. Courtesy of Anne Ulmer and Roy M. Close Family Papers.

These included views of cathedrals, basilicas, palaces, bridges, canals, villages, squares, gardens, ruins, and coastlines in Italy, France, and England. Although neither knew it at the time, Lisl's and Win's youthful peregrinations would provide valuable insight into the cultural roots of their respective life partners.

With scholarship assistance, Win entered graduate school at MIT in 1934. While at MIT, he gained additional work experience in the Cambridge office of city planner John Nolen, the longtime friend of the Scheus. He met Lisl in a studio led by Minnesota-born assistant professor Lawrence B. Anderson, who was a former classmate of Win at the University of Minnesota and a good friend.[26] "[Anderson] was a marvelous teacher," Lisl recalled. Apparently, Lisl (and Win) made a lasting impression on Anderson as well. When asked in 1992 to name students who stood out during his tenure at MIT, Anderson put them on a short list that included architects Harry Weese, Walter Netsch, and Gordon Bunshaft, who was a member of Lisl and Win's graduate school class.[27]

Of first meeting Win, Lisl recalled, "He just looked interesting and I, being the only woman, probably was interesting to him. So, we spent a year competing against each other, in a way, but also talking a lot about architecture."[28] Win's graduate thesis was titled "A Transportation Terminal for Duluth, Minnesota," and Lisl's "A Municipal Bathhouse." Her topic was inspired by the architecturally impressive public baths and indoor swimming pools constructed in Vienna during the Social Democratic era to provide the city's underprivileged citizens access to basic hygiene and healthful exercise.[29] As Roy Close observed, the subjects of his mother's MIT theses "were characteristic of the kinds of things she would be interested in. Very much the social impact of architecture or the social potential, in terms of a swimming pool and [a factory] that would create modular housing that would be inexpensive."[30]

Lisl and Win earned their master's degrees in 1935, and soon after turned to the task of finding jobs. They did so, however, during the Great Depression—the worst economic downturn in U.S. history.

FINDING WORK

Win, who had seven years of professional employment in Minnesota behind him, returned to Minneapolis to join the firm of Magney and Tusler as chief draftsman. He immediately went to work on Sumner Field, a project of the Public Works Administration (PWA)—an initiative of President Franklin D. Roosevelt's New Deal. It was the first federally funded housing project in Minneapolis.[31]

Lisl encountered more daunting obstacles on the road to employment. "That was a time when it was very difficult to get a job in architecture, in the Depression," she said.[32] Admittedly, she intensified the challenge by limiting her search to only those firms that were doing modern architecture and/or housing. "I wanted to be in housing because of my father's involvement with it."[33] As Lisl embarked on her job quest, she discovered that being a woman, in an era when female architects were a rarity, further complicated her mission. In the end, she applied for work at three architectural firms: William Lescaze of New York, Richard Neutra of Los Angeles, and Kastner & Stonorov of Philadelphia.

She admired the work of Swiss-born William Lescaze, who in 1932, with his former partner George Howe, designed the PSFS (Philadelphia Saving Fund Society) Building, an elegant, streamlined, modern skyscraper. "I went to see him but he said he couldn't hire a woman because it would disrupt his drafting room," Lisl explained.[34]

Next, she wrote to Neutra, whose Lovell House in Los Angeles she had photographed on her cross-county trip. She hoped she might "have an in there" for two reasons. The Viennese-born Neutra, who had trained at the Technische Hochschule, had been a guest in the Scheu House, and his future wife, Dione, had lived with the Scheus for "quite a while" when she studied cello in Vienna as a young girl. Neutra replied that of course she would be welcome to come, "but it would cost me $20.00 a month, rather than the other way around, and I couldn't afford that," Lisl said.[35]

Finally, she applied for a job with Kastner & Stonorov. Oskar Stonorov, who was born in Germany and educated in Italy and Switzerland, interviewed Lisl over lunch. There they discovered their common European roots and shared socialist leanings, as well as an interest in modern design. "He was an émigré, like I was," she said. She never met Kastner, but Stonorov hired her as a "draftsman."

In the types of buildings they designed and the modern aesthetic they brought to those structures, the firm was an ideal fit for Lisl. Kastner & Stonorov had recently completed the Carl Mackley Houses (1934) in Philadelphia, a project sponsored by the American Federation of Hosiery Workers. It was one of the earliest examples of International Style workers' housing in the United States and the first low-rent housing project built by the PWA. Stonorov was responsible for the "essential ideas" of this "most European and modernist of the early PWA projects." His determination to create housing that "included communal features, such as rooftop laundries and community buildings, while catering to worker aspirations for a middle-class lifestyle with garages and a swimming pool," echoed many of the fundamental Social Democratic ideals that Gustav Scheu promoted in his housing initiatives in post–World War I Vienna.[36]

Figure 2.7 Designed by Oskar Stonorov and built by the Public Works Administration in 1934, Philadelphia's Carl Mackley Houses were one of the earliest examples of International Style workers' housing in the United States. Lisl briefly lived in the complex. Dallin Aerial Surveys, Special Collections Research Center, Temple University Libraries, Philadelphia, Pennsylvania.

Through a bit of good fortune, Lisl became a resident of the Carl Mackley Houses when Stonorov's fiancée, Elizabeth Foster, lent her an apartment in the architecturally inspiring complex.

For Stonorov, Lisl worked on Westfield Acres in Camden, New Jersey, a Federal Housing Development project for more than five hundred families, sponsored by the Camden Labor Housing Committee.[37] The 1939 Federal Writers' Project guide to New Jersey describes Westfield Acres, which was built with $3 million of PWA funds, as a "model housing project [that] covers 25 acres and includes 18 units with a total of 514 structures of simple design," further noting, "Spacious inner courts provide adequate sunlight and ventilation. Kitchens are equipped with electric ranges and mechanical refrigerators."[38] Marion Greenwood, a Brooklyn-born muralist whose work was influenced by the Mexican muralists Diego Rivera and José Clemente Orozco, painted a large mural on the wall of the social room at Westfield Acres. According to Greenwood, her design was inspired by local factory and shipyard laborers, some of whom worked on the construction of the housing complex.[39]

Specifically, Lisl was assigned to draft the children's facility. She admired Stonorov's "humanistic attitude" when it came to housing design. "He thought about the people who were going to live there instead of the bureaucrats who were running the place," she said.[40] During the design phase of Westfield Acres, Stonorov would "run afoul" of federal authorities when the individualized elements he proposed, such as recessed porches, windows of differing sizes, and garden spaces, conflicted with the more economical standardized unit plans that the housing officials preferred. Stonorov disagreed and argued that rigid standardization served to "stigmatize apartment life and failed to provide for the development of a potential community life."[41] Similarly, Lisl would rail against regimentation in a project for her next employer. Photographs, drawings, and models of both the Carl Mackley Houses and Westfield Acres were featured in *Architecture in Government Housing,* a 1936 exhibition at the MoMA in New York City. The show featured six projects of the Housing Division of the Public Works Administration that "exemplify or show the influence of modern architecture principles."[42]

Figure 2.8 While employed by Stonorov, Lisl worked on the design of Westfield Acres (1938) in Camden, New Jersey, a low-income housing project sponsored by the PWA. In this photograph of the project's social room in the 1940s, a model of Westfield Acres can be seen in foreground at right. American muralist Marion Greenwood painted the labor-inspired scene on the back wall. Westfield Acres Housing Project Social Room Murals, Camden, New Jersey, 1935–43; Treasury Relief Art Project: Missouri, New Mexico, New Jersey, New York; Records of the Public Buildings Service, Record Group 121; National Archives at College Park, College Park, Maryland.

Lisl respected Stonorov both personally and professionally. "He was wonderful. He hired me. . . . I was a female [but] he didn't say I was going to be disruptive. He gave me a starting salary, which was modest, but then two weeks later he raised me. He was terrific to work for."[43] Stonorov was also a multi-talented man. In addition to his architectural work, he was a sculptor and an exhibition designer; most significantly he was the chief organizer of *Sixty Years of Living Architecture,* the renowned exhibition on the work of Frank Lloyd Wright that opened in 1951 at Gimbel's Department Store in Philadelphia and traveled internationally for several years.[44]

Although her employment with Stonorov was "a plum hire" for Lisl, it would be brief.[45] In 1936 Win called Lisl from Minnesota and advised her of an opening with Magney and Tusler, one of a consortium of firms working on the Sumner Field project. She took the job. As Roy Close observed, "It says something about her interest in my father that after a year [with Stonorov] he persuaded her to move to Minneapolis because there was an opening at the Magney firm for a designer. She started at the rate of seventy-five cents an hour."[46]

Figure 2.9 View of Minneapolis in 1935, the year before Lisl moved to Minnesota. Norton & Peel, Minneapolis Skyline, 1935. Minnesota Historical Society, St. Paul, Minnesota.

MINNESOTA

Lisl moved to Minnesota in February 1936, during a year of temperature extremes. That winter the wind chill in the Twin Cities plunged to minus 67 degrees Fahrenheit. A few months later, the Upper Midwest endured a heat wave that produced one of the hottest summers on record.[47] Soon after she arrived in Minneapolis, Win departed for Europe where he participated in a study tour of European housing led by Helen Alfred, a social worker and the executive secretary of the National Public Housing Conference, an organization that lobbied for housing reform.[48] The trip was planned to coincide with meetings of the International Federation for Housing and Town Planning that was founded in 1913 by Ebenezer Howard, whose theories on Garden City planning had shaped Gustav Scheu's own housing work in Vienna after World War I. On the trip, the group visited England, France, the Netherlands, Germany, Russia, and Finland.[49] During Win's absence, Lisl took up residence in his

Figure 2.10 One of several housing blocks at Sumner Field (1938), the first federally funded housing project in Minneapolis. Lisl Scheu and Winston Close worked on the project for the firm of Magney and Tusler. The project was demolished in 1998. Library of Congress, Prints and Photographs Division, HABS MN 27-MINAO, 34B-3.

vacated rooms at the Ogden Hotel in downtown Minneapolis and went to work for Magney and Tusler.

Sumner Field Homes, in North Minneapolis, was built on land formerly characterized as "slums" by city officials.[50] To clear the land, the city razed predominantly African American and Jewish neighborhoods. Like Westfield Acres, Sumner Field Homes was a federally funded, low-income housing project comprising multiple flat-roofed, residential blocks. On the project's thirty-acre site, four dozen two- and three-story buildings housed roughly 450 two- and three-bedroom residential units and community spaces. Within the project, there was racial segregation.[51]

Figure 2.11 Elizabeth Scheu in Minnesota, circa 1938. Courtesy of Roy M. Close Family Papers.

Lisl was assigned to work on the buildings' elevations. Although she had been instructed "what to do and what not to do," she did not follow instructions to the letter. Instead, as Stonorov had done at Westfield Acres, Lisl ignored directives and added certain features she believed would provide a more pleasurable living experience for residents—notably balconies—because, she felt, "it was important living in an apartment [to be] able to go outside or air your baby."[52] She knew "this was a no-no," and predictably her superiors were not pleased by her architectural insubordination.

Lisl and Win continued to work for Magney and Tusler for two more years, during which time they took on a few independent projects under the banner of "Close & Scheu Architects, of the Office of Magney and Tusler," none of which were realized.[53] Eventually, they both felt the firm was "not happy with what we were doing," she said.[54] Even more to the point, "we were interested in modern architecture and they weren't."[55] In 1938 Lisl and Win left Magney and Tusler and founded Close and Scheu—the first architectural practice in Minnesota dedicated to modern design.

3

MINNESOTA'S FIRST
MODERN ARCHITECTS
INTERSTATE CLINIC

On April 1, 1938, Winston Close and Elizabeth Scheu opened Close and Scheu, their new architectural firm in Minneapolis. Although they chose one of the oldest neoclassical buildings in the city—the 1898 Long & Long–designed Andrus Building (now Renaissance Square)—as their base of operations, they resolved to focus their work on modern design.

They established their practice before they got married: "First things first," Lisl said.[1] The pair was motivated to tie the knot when an apartment became available in a Southeast Minneapolis building in which their friends, University of Minnesota political science professor Asher "Christy" Christensen and his wife, Allison "Hap," lived. "They got married because they could not rent this apartment as an unmarried couple," explained their son Roy Close. "On April 11, 1938, they walked to city hall over the lunch hour where they met Hap and Christy, who served as their witnesses. They got married and then they walked back to the office and continued work for the rest of the day."[2] The practicality of his parents' incentive to wed, as well as their refusal to allow the ceremony to interrupt the flow of the workday, was "totally" typical of their relationship, said Close. "They had very, very little romance in their daily lives."[3] The local press, however, did take notice of the union and ran a photograph of the recently married couple under the headline "Architect Weds Architect." The caption (incorrectly) identified "Mrs. Winston Close" as "the only woman architect in the city."[4] When Lisl was pregnant with their first child in 1940, she and Win changed the name of their firm to Elizabeth and Winston Close, Architects.

ARCHITECT WEDS ARCHITECT

MINNEAPOLIS JOURNAL PHOTO

Mr. and Mrs. Winston Close, Minneapolis architects, were feted last night by the Minnesota chapter, American Institute of Architects, in celebration of their recent marriage. Mrs. Close is the only woman architect in the city. She is a native of Vienna. In the picture members of the chapter are giving gifts to the young couple.

Figure 3.1 Although Lisl was not the only woman architect in the city, as this caption claimed, the local press considered the Closes' marriage in 1938 to be a newsworthy event. Undated clipping. Courtesy of Roy M. Close Family Papers.

To open an architecture firm during the Depression—a time when many architects were out of work and the construction industry had slowed to a crawl—was risky. To establish a practice limited to modern design—a style the general public had not yet adopted—was even riskier. For a twenty-six-year-old woman to cofound an architecture firm was almost unheard of.[5] But that's exactly what Lisl and Win did. Although success was far from guaranteed, project by project they built a solid and lasting practice.

CLOSE AND SCHEU MODERN

Lisl and Win were successful, in part, because they worked well together and respected each other's abilities. "They were perfectly paired, in many ways, the love of music, outdoors, many things. They were also well paired for the business of architecture," observed architect Gar Hargens, who joined the firm in 1968, while a student at the University of Minnesota's School of Architecture, and owns it today. Yet they also possessed complementary skills. "Win was clever, he was inventive, but he was also rather linear—here's an idea, it's my idea, it's a good idea, it's the idea we will follow," Hargens said.[6] Architect Georgia Bizios, who worked for the firm in the 1970s, noted that Win was "very disciplined as an architect" and understood the "implications of every design decision." He was "always thinking about how it would be built."[7]

In contrast, "Lisl often led with sketches and concepts," Hargens said. She would "get a more philosophical idea and a stronger design concept, then she would continue to work with that and embellish that, but she would also give more latitude to whoever was working with her."[8] In terms of planning, she was able to "wring the most out of spaces and make them very efficient." In the fluidity and ease of her process, Bizios described Lisl as a "facile" designer.[9] Architect Julia Robinson, who worked for the firm in the 1960s, observed that Lisl also had a "golden touch" when it came to working with people. "Her clients were devoted to her," and for them she created buildings that "had a high level of design and were beautifully put together."[10]

The couple ultimately worked well in partnership because "they knew what they believed and what they wanted to do. They focused on that," said Hargens.[11] As one observer noted, in Minnesota "they were pioneers in rejecting the stylistic approach of the past, in making their work completely contemporary with the times." This worked to their benefit when it came to attracting talented young architects to their office, especially those "who could not find other offices who so closely held to the cause of modern architecture."[12] Philosophically, they were in sync, observed Lawrence Anderson. "They were modernists to the end."[13]

For Lisl and Win, a building was modern if it was functional, efficiently planned, and served the needs of the client. Modernity also meant the elimination of any unnecessary elements or adornment. As Anderson stated, Win was "an extremely careful functionalist. Everything had to work in its proper place. If anything wasn't serving that purpose, why, it shouldn't be there. That was one of the rather extreme but somewhat admirable preachings of the modern movement."[14] For this reason, they were drawn to the tenets of the International Style, including an emphasis on volume over mass, a preference for planar surfaces, the elimination of ornamentation, an honest expression of materials, and the rejection of historical styles, in their design work. Unlike many architects of the International Style, however, Close and Scheu did not favor stark, white exteriors or interiors in their houses. Instead, they brought warmth to those spaces using wood, brick, and other textural materials.

Lisl's architectural preferences were also rooted in the buildings of the Neues Bauen or New Building era of Vienna in the late 1920s and early '30s. Architecturally, the movement was less concerned with aesthetics than with addressing the specific needs of inhabitants. Its proponents sought to "free themselves from the limitations of style and symbols, focusing at all times on the occupant, even at the stage of planning the layout."[15] Lisl and Win felt so strongly about this approach they developed a system through which they could identify myriad client needs and tailor plans accordingly. In the process they achieved clever, compact planning that realized the maximum potential of every space.

MODERNISM IN MINNESOTA

When Lisl and Win established themselves as modern architects in Minneapolis, they had little to no professional competition in Minnesota, and Minnesotans had minimal exposure to modern architecture and design. Upon her arrival in 1936, Lisl became the first European-born proponent of the International Style to work in the state. Until Close and Scheu opened its doors two years later, no modern architects were practicing in Minnesota. Relatively speaking, the state was slower to embrace modernism than some other regions of the country.

By the mid-1920s the International Style was beginning to flourish in California, largely due to the work of Rudolf Schindler and Richard Neutra, two Austrian-born (and Technische Hochschule–educated) progressive architects who had established residential practices in Los Angeles. Individually, each man designed several iconic, early modern houses on the West Coast, one of the most influential being Neutra's 1929 Lovell House—the International Style masterpiece that Lisl photographed on her cross-country journey in the 1930s.

On the East Coast, as previously mentioned, MoMA's 1932 exhibition on the International Style raised both public and professional interest in modern architecture. Five years later, the arrival of Walter Gropius and Marcel Breuer at Harvard's Graduate School of Design would begin to transform American architectural education

—and future generations of architects—by mainstreaming European modernism into curricula. By 1938 Chicago's New Bauhaus and Armour Institute of Technology were also led by noted European modernists. As it did at many other architecture schools, modernism would begin to infiltrate the course of study at the University of Minnesota in the mid-1930s. But the program would not be headed by a devout modern architect until Ralph Rapson arrived in 1954. Today the state's landscape is dotted with significant buildings by such international masters of the modern movement as Edward Larrabee Barnes, Pietro Belluschi, Breuer, Philip Johnson, Erich Mendelsohn, Rapson, and Eliel and Eero Saarinen. However, not one of these men had built a single building—or had the promise of a commission—in Minnesota when Close and Scheu realized its first project: an unabashedly International Style residence in Minneapolis completed in 1938.

Even though modern design had not yet taken root in Minnesota, the state was moving into the modern age in significant ways. The birth of new industries, technologies, and lifestyles created a demand for building types that had previously not existed. Architectural responses to those demands, and the materials used in their construction, were "modern" in their very functionality and innovation. One remarkable building, completed in 1900 in the Minneapolis suburb of St. Louis Park, illustrates this point. The 125-foot-high Peavey-Haglin Experimental Grain Elevator was built to test the suitability of fireproof, reinforced concrete for grain elevator construction. In its marriage of form and functionality—and rejection of traditional materials and methods of construction—the building was nothing short of a modern marvel—one that transformed an industry.

During the 1930s some students at the School of Architecture at the University of Minnesota were leaving Beaux-Arts classicism behind to experiment with modern design in studio projects. One 1932 student project by Robert Cerny, later a partner in the firm of Thorshov and Cerny, was way ahead of its time. Cerny's streamlined design for "A School of Architecture," which featured a square plan, open court, light framing, and strip windows, was strongly influenced by the International Style. Eighteen years later, in 1960, when Cerny designed a new building for the university's School of Architecture, which is still in use today, he referenced his prize-winning student scheme for inspiration. Other striking examples of student projects embracing modern design were produced by Edward Barber, John Magney, and George Rafferty, to name a few. During their professional careers, all three would produce significant buildings in the state.

Architect Frank Lloyd Wright, who had long challenged conventional notions of architecture, brought his own American brand of modernism to Minneapolis in 1934. His free-flowing plan for the Nancy and Malcolm Willey House radically rethought how space could be experienced in the American middle-class residence. The 1935 Richard Elliott House in University Grove, a University of Minnesota–planned community of architect-designed houses in Falcon Heights, is another residence that merits mention in the context of early modernism in Minnesota. Architects Roy Childs Jones and Rhodes Robertson designed the house for Elliott, chair of the university's Department of Psychology. The small, stripped-down, cubic house, which the *New York Times* described as being "influenced by the modest scale of the worker houses designed by Bauhaus architects," is notable as the first departure from traditional home styles in the Grove.[16] Jones, who in 1937 would become the second head of the university's School of Architecture, and Robertson were both on the architecture faculty at the time. Robertson, who also worked as a draftsman and designer for the firm of Hewitt and Brown, has been described as "one of the most talented designers to work in Minnesota."[17] In 1947 Lisl would collaborate with him on the John and Dorothy Rood House in Minneapolis.[18]

Given such technological developments, architectural experimentations, and cultural shifts, it would be an oversimplification—as historian Gwendolyn Wright has made clear—to believe that "European émigrés and their loyal American disciples brought Modernism to the United States, as if in a suitcase."[19] Minnesota, like most of the country, was ripe for architectural change in the 1930s.

If modern architecture was an acquired taste for many Minnesotans, the modern house, with its flat roofs and simple volumes devoid of ornamentation, was an even tougher sell. Most Americans inextricably linked a home and its comforts with traditional architectural styles and familiar house types, such as Colonial Revival, Victorian, Tudor, California Bungalow, or other vernacular styles. Most of them, like a child's drawing of a house, featured sheltering gabled roofs that offered a sense of protection. They also offered endless opportunities to personalize (and accessorize, as budget allowed) one's private castle with shutters, window boxes, brackets, porches, railings, and countless other forms of embellishment. Such homes were relatively easy to procure, finances permitting. Ready-made houses could be ordered by style or model name from one of many companies, including the American retailer Sears, Roebuck and Company, which offered illustrated catalogs of home plans and kits for purchase. Beginning in the 1930s, the modern house offered prospective homeowners a new, if not an immediately embraced, option.

In 1938 *Life* magazine collaborated with the *Architectural Forum* to initiate a nationwide debate on the merits, or lack thereof, of modern architecture to residential design. That September, in "Eight Houses for Modern Living," *Life* reported on an experimental program in which four typical American families, who lived in different regions of the country and had varied income levels, were asked to describe their "dream homes." The magazines then assigned a pair of "famous American architects," one "traditional" and one "modern," to create affordable house plans for each family that embodied their ideals and were "beautiful and stirring designs for modern living."[20] The implied question at the heart of the discussion was "does the average American want to live in a modern house?" *Life* argued that houses were like any other commodity, but the housing industry was trailing behind other industries producing products essential to contemporary life. "Great corporations advertising nationally keep Americans tingling with the yen to own new automobiles, new radios, new refrigerators, new devices of all kinds . . . but there is no national advertising to make people want new houses."[21]

All eight house schemes were published in the magazine. "To help settle the urgent building question of how well Americans like 'modern' houses," *Life* asked its readers to choose the houses

Figure 3.2 The *New York Times* likened the Richard Elliott House (1935), designed by Roy Childs Jones and Rhodes Robertson in University Grove, to Bauhaus-style workers' residences. Photograph by William B. Olexy.

they preferred for each family. When the votes were tallied, traditional house designs were chosen for three of the four families. Frank Lloyd Wright's design for the Blackbourn family of Minneapolis was the only "modern" scheme selected, but it was the most popular of all of the eight published houses. The Blackbourns agreed and wanted to construct Wright's plan until costs became prohibitive. Left with no other option, they built the traditional house architect Royal Barry Wills had designed for them. It still stands today on a quiet cul-de-sac in the Minneapolis suburb of Edina.[22]

Although "Eight Houses for Modern Living" was not a comprehensive or scientific study, the results of the voting suggested a strong preference for traditional home design among the American public. It also revealed certain prejudices about the modern house, which readers described to as "too institutional," "too uncomfortable looking," and not unlike "a chicken coop."[23] The firm of Close and Scheu was launched during this national debate.

FIRST PROJECTS

To do the kind of work they wanted to do in 1938, and to build an architecture practice dedicated to modern design, the Closes needed to connect with like-minded clients. Fortunately, the University of Minnesota, where Win was then a lecturer in the architecture school, proved to be a fertile source of individuals who were not only in the vanguard of their respective professions but were also interested in new architectural ideas.

The Closes explored at least a dozen projects before their first built work was completed in late 1938. Among them was a possible residence for behavioral psychologist B. F. Skinner, who was on the faculty at the university from 1936 to 1945, and his wife, Yvonne. Over time, the Skinners and the Closes discussed a handful of options, including one proposed by Win that involved "looking at possible building sites with the idea that maybe you and the Feigls and ourselves might start a community."[24] Although the Skinners responded that "the idea of starting a community sounds swell," their preference was to construct a house in University Grove, in which qualified members of the faculty and administration were eligible to build houses on university-owned land. In 1941 Skinner's promotion to associate professor entitled him to do so. "As long as we are eligible for the Grove, at long last, we want to build there," wrote Yvonne.[25] Ultimately, uncertainty over rising costs and the availability of building materials in the early 1940s, coupled with an upcoming sabbatical, scuttled the Skinners' plans to build a Close-designed house. However, they would live in the Grove from 1941 to 1945 in a preexisting house.[26]

While he was in Minnesota, Skinner began work on his novel *Walden Two,* which was published in 1948. Reputedly, he based the characters of the architects, responsible for the design of the utopian community around which the story revolves, on Lisl and Win. In the text, he described them as being "a young couple interested in modern housing," adding, "one of them [was] an attractive young woman with a slight accent which I took to be Viennese."[27]

In 1938 the Closes were involved in feasibility studies and planning for at least two unrealized housing projects. At the request of University of Minnesota comptroller and vice president William Middlebrook (who set aside the land for University Grove in the 1920s), they developed preliminary plans for "low-cost group houses," consisting of sixteen four- and five-room, two-story units with garages. Lisl produced appealing watercolor perspectives for the complex, to be known as "University Terrace" (Plate 3). The project did not move forward owing to zoning restrictions and hesitation on the part of the university.[28]

Beginning in late 1937, Lisl and Win were part of a small group of idealistic individuals who attempted to launch an ambitious collaborative housing initiative. They were inspired by the principles of the Cooperative movement, which originated in the United Kingdom in the nineteenth century and promoted democratic group ownership of land, goods, and housing for the mutual economic benefit of all participants. The mission of the St. Paul–based "Cooperative Housing Study Group" was to provide "better housing at low cost" through "cooperative efforts" and group ownership.[29] It adhered to the fundamental principles of earlier cooperatives, which included "unrestricted membership, [with] no discrimination for race, religion, color, politics, etc.," something that could not be said of all Twin Cities communities at the time (Plate 4).

Professionally, Close and Scheu conducted feasibility studies and selected a prospective site, off Como Avenue in St. Paul near where Luther Seminary now stands, for the cooperative to purchase.[30] Personally, Win and Lisl actively recruited at least sixty potential members, many of whom were associated with the University of Minnesota, to join the group. Although interest was high in certain circles, others objected to the plan, fearing the "cooperative" aspect of the clustered row houses smacked of socialism or worse. Rather than fight them, Lisl and Win, humorously, joined them. "We started to call the project 'Trotsky Heights,' because the Trotskyites were

Figure 3.3 Frank Lloyd Wright designed the Malcolm and Nancy Willey House in Minneapolis in 1934. It stands across a cul-de-sac from Close and Scheu's "Opus One," the 1938 Ray Faulkner House. Photograph by Steve Sikora, 2007.

very much in the news at the time. We thought we might as well shock people thoroughly," she said.[31]

The project failed because of lack of financing. "We had a group who was interested in doing this, but the bank wouldn't lend us money—wouldn't lend them money. They said, you can't do this because it was modern and had a flat roof," she said.[32] Among the interested participants was Ray Faulkner, the man who—with colleagues Edwin Ziegfeld and Gerald Hill—would commission the first built work by Close and Scheu.[33]

OPUS ONE

"Opus One," the residence known as the Faulkner House, was built at the dead end (later a cul-de-sac) of Bedford Street Southeast in Minneapolis, on a lot Faulkner described as "without question . . . the most wonderful spot on earth. Well, anyway in southeast Minneapolis."[34] Interestingly enough, Close and Scheu were not the first modern architects to design a house for the property. "Richard Neutra had designed a house for that same site for a university professor who had since moved elsewhere," recalled Win. "We once talked to [Neutra] about the house," which was not built.[35]

The cul-de-sac, which stands in the Prospect Park neighborhood and overlooks the Mississippi River Valley, was already home to one architecturally distinctive residence: the 1934 Willey House by Frank Lloyd Wright.[36] That house was designed for Malcolm Willey, a professor of sociology at the University of Minnesota, and his wife, Nancy, who was inspired to contact the world-famous architect after reading his autobiography. While the Willey House was an important commission for Wright, it was far from being his first built work. When the house was completed, Wright was sixty-seven years old and had been practicing architecture for more than four decades. The Closes admired Wright's work and early in their careers "went on a pilgrimage . . . visiting all the Wright buildings" in and around Minnesota. Lisl described Wright as "a wonderful architect in many ways," but characterized his furniture designs as "not strong."[37]

Although the two houses were built a mere four years apart and were both contemporary insertions in the architecturally traditional neighborhood, they broke with convention in radically different ways. The design of the Willey House was rooted in the Wisconsin-born Wright's long-standing interest in an American architecture—one inspired by its unique landscapes, notably the midwestern prairie. Spatially, its flexible, open plan reflected an increasingly informal American lifestyle. Conceptually, it prefigured the affordable, modularly planned Usonian houses Wright would design in the future.[38] Characteristically, the one-story redbrick Willey House was distinguished by its low profile, deep, overhanging eaves, and horizontal trellis that extended from the roof edge over the terrace doors.

In contrast, the Closes' brand of modernism, as evidenced in the Faulkner House, had very different origins. Its rectangular geometry, flat roof, unadorned planar surfaces, strip windows, and use of unconventional materials were inspired by the International Style (Plate 5). As different as their approaches were, both Wright and the Closes understood their clients' interest in affordable houses that were suited to a changing American lifestyle and expressive of the modern era.

Ray Faulkner and Edwin Ziegfeld met in graduate school at Harvard University. By 1933 each had joined the faculty at the University of Minnesota: Faulkner in the General College and Ziegfeld in the School of Education. "Ray and Edwin had both received [an] MLA (Master of Landscape Architecture) from Harvard in the late 1920s, at a time when modern art and modern architecture were opening a new and exciting field in that venerable institution," wrote Sarah Faulkner, Ray's widow.[39] They expressed that interest through "Art Today," a course they taught at the University of Minnesota. "The field of contemporary art was the chief concern of the course. And contemporary architecture continued to be of tremendous interest to them," she added. In Minneapolis they met Gerald Hill, a Minnesota graduate and faculty member in the General College. He taught "Music Today," a course similarly inspired by modern trends.

In 1941 Faulkner, Ziegfeld, and Hill wrote *Art Today: An Introduction to the Fine and Functional Arts,* a book that was a "direct outgrowth" of the courses they taught at the university and was intended to be "an introduction to those arts of form and color with which we come

Figure 3.4 The Ray Faulkner House (1938) was the first modern house in Minneapolis inspired by the International Style. Lisl's sketch of the residence hints at its once unimpeded view to the Mississippi River Valley below. Drawing by Elizabeth Scheu. Courtesy of Close Associates Papers (N78), Northwest Architectural Archives, University of Minnesota Libraries, Minneapolis.

into contact every day."[40] Each art form—architecture, planning, and interior design among them—was considered from the perspectives of human needs, organization (design), and materials and processes. Therefore, as architectural clients, the three bachelors brought a sophisticated knowledge of design, not to mention enthusiasm, to the project. They "were only too delighted to find the Closes and excited about the possibility of actually building in the modern style," wrote Sarah Faulkner.[41] Likewise, Lisl and Win found the men to be "ideal clients."[42]

Of paramount importance to all parties was the creation of a house that took "advantage of the site and the exposure and the view," but also "fit the modern style of living." Site orientation and sun and wind exposure were also well considered. As a result, the house became "closed" on the north side as a buffer against the cold, and open to the south—where main living areas clustered—to maximize light and view. The fact that the house was designed for three bachelors, and not a family with children, uniquely affected the floor plan. Instead of needing one master and several smaller bedrooms on the second floor, the clients required three bedrooms of equal size.

Because the house consisted of simple volumes and flat roofs, Lisl and Win chose materials that fit the "very simple character" of the residence. The exterior was sheathed in a combination of horizontal redwood siding and resin-bonded plywood. Roof overhangs blocked the summer sun (but let in winter sun) and sheltered the walkway that flanked the garage. "Then we played around a little with things like color," Lisl said, which manifested itself in a blue-tinted concrete driveway and sidewalk.[43] While this was intended as a bit of whimsy on the part of the architects, after a passerby suffered a fatal heart attack in front of the house, the *Minnesota Daily* speculated that the shocking blue concrete might have been to blame.[44]

Interior finishes for the two-story, three-bedroom house included exposed brick, gumwood veneer, and Homasote, a pressed card-

Figure 3.5 To complement the simple geometric forms of the Faulkner House, the architects specified durable, unfussy construction materials, including redwood siding and resin-bonded plywood. Gar Hargens/Close Associates and Close Associates Papers (N78), Northwest Architectural Archives, University of Minnesota Libraries, Minneapolis.

board wall board more commonly used for "chicken coops" and for lining the inside of train cars than for residential purposes.[45] But Lisl and Win liked the durability and modular possibilities of the material, which was produced in large sheets.[46] The use of warm and textural materials on the interior of the Faulkner House is reminiscent of Loos's material selections for the Scheu House in Vienna.

Financing the house was a challenge, as it had been for the cooperative housing project the Closes attempted to develop earlier that same year. "Chiefly, it had a flat roof and it was a boxy kind of a house; pretty hard to get a thing like that financed by any of the lending companies," said Win.[47] The lenders' fear was that the house, which cost a little over $12,000 to build, would have no resale value—a concern that would soon prove to be unfounded.[48] The group engaged in some creative financing. Faulkner and Ziegfeld provided landscape design services for the Closes' next project in return for a reduction of their costs. The couple also accepted two watercolors by Faulkner as part of his payment—a bartering system they would continue to employ with future clients. Lisl and Win generated an interesting collection of paintings, sculptures, and other art objects produced by their talented clients.

The three men had been living in the house for a little over a year when Faulkner and Ziegfeld received job offers from Columbia University. In 1939 they sold the house to Benjamin Lippincott, an associate professor of political science at the university, and his wife, Gertrude, a modern dancer. Unlike the original owners, who were committed to modern ideals, the Lippincotts were not interested in the house because of its architectural pedigree. As Gertrude Lippincott explicitly stated, "We mainly bought a 'modern' house not because of its particular style or [for] aesthetic reasons, but merely because we wanted a house and it was available."[49] A year later they hired the Closes to design an addition for their residence (Plate 6). Hill, who remained in Minnesota, subsequently commissioned the firm to design a cabin for him on Lake Vermilion in St. Louis County, Minnesota. It was completed in 1943.

As the first dwelling in Minneapolis inspired by the International Style, the Faulkner House was an object of curiosity, dismay, dislike,

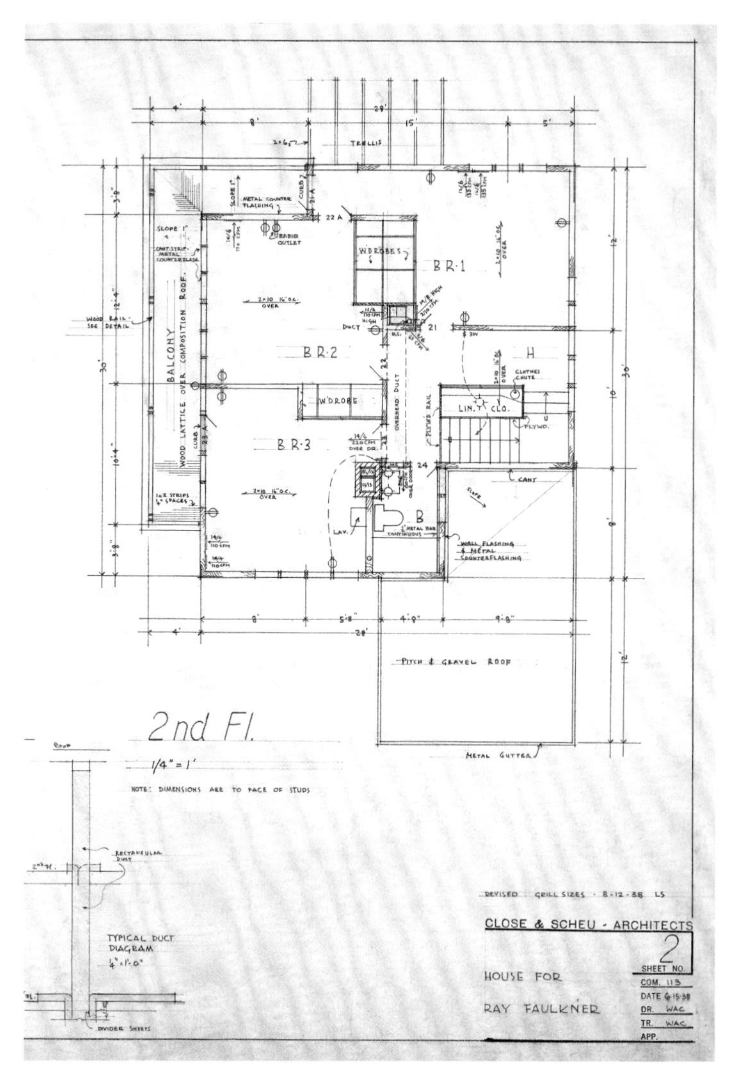

Figure 3.6 Second-floor plan of Faulkner House. Because the Closes designed the residence for three bachelors, all three bedrooms are equal in size. Close Associates Papers (N78), Northwest Architectural Archives, University of Minnesota Libraries, Minneapolis.

Figure 3.7 Living room of the Faulkner House. Interior finishes included Homasote, gumwood veneer, and brick. Close Associates Papers (N78), Northwest Architectural Archives, University of Minnesota Libraries, Minneapolis.

interest, and admiration. Its uniqueness was documented in at least two articles in the university's campus newspaper, the *Minnesota Daily*. One noted that "Ray Faulkner, who professes Art with capital A's," built a house that "is a show piece, a splendid example of modern architecture." The house also received a second mention in an article promoting a benefit for Spanish children to be held in Faulkner's home. As if the evening's program of "dance numbers . . . modern water colors, and a bust of the much-discussed 'La Pasionaria,' Loyalist Spain's famed woman leader," were not enough of a draw, the piece announced that Faulkner's new home "of Viennese architecture in the modern style," would be on display for the first time.[50]

Significantly, the house raised regional awareness of—and initiated debate about—the evolving role of modern architecture in residential design. It would not have happened without adventurous

Figure 3.8 Benjamin and Gertrude Lippincott, the second owners of the Faulkner House, hired the Closes in 1940 to expand living areas, including the dining room. Close Associates Papers (N78), Northwest Architectural Archives, University of Minnesota Libraries, Minneapolis.

clients who shared the Closes' progressive views. As art historian Lauren Soth insightfully observed, "All five individuals were committed to modernism in the arts. The house they collaborated on was a physical manifesto of their beliefs."[51]

The Faulkner House was an important commission for Lisl and Win. Not only was it their first built work, it made a clear statement about their architectural philosophies. For the couple, who never advertised their services, the house was a full scale, three-dimensional declaration of the type and quality of work they resolved to do.

The striking architecture of the Faulkner House—and the positive word of mouth it generated—initiated a wave of new clients for the Closes. In addition to residential commissions, new opportunities included the design of a state-of-the-art medical clinic in Red Wing, Minnesota, that doubled as a gallery for abstract art, and a low-budget, off-the-grid rustic cabin sequestered in the Wisconsin woods. Their next in-town commission was a Minneapolis residence for a couple who, like Faulkner, Ziegfeld, and Hill, had more than a passing interest in modern architecture, and little inclination to live in anything other than a modern house.

A FUNCTIONAL HOUSE FOR AN ASTRONOMER

Willem Luyten, who headed the Department of Astronomy at the University of Minnesota for three decades, was an astronomer of international repute now credited with determining the stellar motions of more than 544,000 stars.[52] He and his wife, Willemina, were both raised and educated in the Netherlands. Fortunately, in 1939, when they were ready to build a house of their own on East River Terrace in Minneapolis, they met the Closes through a mutual friend.

In terms of home design, Lisl later described the Luytens as "not particularly wedded to the American idiom. They knew a lot about modern architecture because [the Netherlands] was a very active center of modern design."[53] In the 1910s, the Netherlands became "a laboratory for an unusual variety of architectural experiments," among them de Stijl (the style), originally an art movement that explored harmony and order through the purity of rigid geometries and primary colors.[54] Its proponents included architect Theo van Doesburg and artist Piet Mondrian. Architecturally, de Stijl was most fully realized in the 1924 Rietveld Schröder House in Utrecht, designed by architect Gerrit Rietveld with considerable input from Truus Schröder, the young widowed mother who commissioned its design. Although the exterior of the house—an asymmetrical composition of layered white and gray concrete planes and colorfully painted slim steel supports—was striking, the interior was revolutionary. Schröder wanted a house in which she could "break free of what she experienced as the smothering conventions of middle-class domesticity."[55] Minimal interior walls, replaced where possible by sliding panels and folding doors, fostered an "exceptionally multifunctional and adaptable space," devoid of "useless frills." Schröder described the house as a "stripped home, there is only that which is necessary for its residents, it's what you call functional."[56]

Because the Luytens also were interested in functional design and wanted a residence that was in sync with their lifestyle, they approached the Closes with very definite ideas on the subject. In fact, Willem Luyten went so far as to build a cardboard model of the number and arrangement of rooms the family required, and later conducted sun exposure and solar gain calculations to project how window area could positively affect winter heating costs.[57] Yet as forthcoming as the Luytens were, the Closes believed the planning process would benefit from more information.

In their quest to design efficiently planned and livable houses, the Closes took functional design to a new level by adopting a system by which they could gather information and develop an architectural program for a residence. They quantified the wants, needs, and possessions of each prospective homeowner and ascertained how they lived their daily lives. Such in-depth research was not generally undertaken for residential projects at the time. "Nobody would think of building a skyscraper without a program, but in those days, everybody just bought their house off a shelf or [from] a catalog," Lisl said. In her opinion, that was a mistake and "not a very good way to get what you really needed."[58] Fundamentally, the Closes believed a house could and should be as efficiently planned for use as was a laboratory, hospital, or other commercial building. The key to efficient planning was for both architect and client to honestly assess what was needed—and not needed—in the house they would create together.

Serendipitously, in 1938 the Closes discovered the book *Plan Your House to Suit Yourself,* by Tyler Stewart Rogers, which proposed a useful strategy for identifying a client's residential requirements. On the book's first page, Rogers explained that the key to planning a house that "suits you in every particular" is to "organize your desires so concretely that they can be expressed clearly to the artisans who will erect it for you. . . . The important thing is to know precisely what you want!"[59] The first step in achieving "rational planning" of a house was to create an "Inventory of Family and Possessions." Helpfully, the book provided said inventory form, which Lisl and Win used for the first time on the Luyten House.

The eight-page form was an exhaustive accounting of all family members' lifestyle preferences from sleeping and bathing to hobbies and entertaining, as well as a complete inventory of family possessions—furniture, pots, pans, plates, cutlery, garments, hats, shoes, books, sporting equipment, toys, and pets, to name a few. With this knowledge in hand, design and planning of a well-organized, clutter-free, individualized residence could proceed. In addition to the inventory, a survey of the Luytens' penchants and peculiarities revealed a preference for morning sun and a sensitivity to noise. Also requested were "a door on the upstairs landing for shaking mops," a "drawer for current bills," a cabinet for motion picture equipment and three hundred reels of film, as well as storage for a platter used for serving a twelve-pound bird.[60]

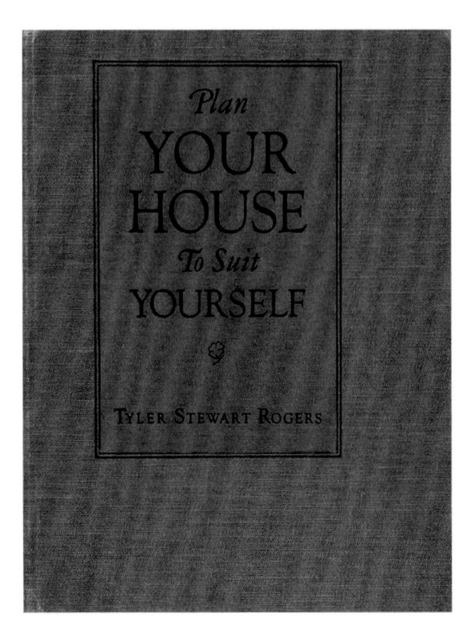

Figure 3.9 The Closes used an inventory form that they discovered in the book *Plan Your House to Suit Yourself* (1938), by Tyler Stewart Rogers, to assess a client's needs and wants in a house. Courtesy of Roy M. Close Family Papers.

The Closes found the inventory approach to be constructive for several reasons. First, it was an excellent way to make sure everyone agreed on the fundamentals, especially the clients. "Sometimes [couples] butted heads. . . . They couldn't agree. So, this was a good way to get out points where there might be friction," Lisl said. It also proved to be a "useful tool" because it allowed clients to get "a general idea of how this house, in their mind, was going to work . . . and tell us in a direct way." At first, Lisl and Win gave prospective homeowners their sole copy of *Plan Your House to Suit Yourself* and asked them to pencil in their preferences in the book. "Then we erased it and gave it to the next client. Eventually we made up our own questionnaire," she said.[61] They used the form from 1939 onward, and Close Associates uses it to this day.

Because the functions and relationships of the rooms in the house helped the Closes generate the floor plan, they designed the Luyten residence from the inside out. For this reason, for the Closes the house became "an elevation problem. . . . All the windows had to be certain sizes [and placements] because of the use of the room behind," Lisl said. Finding a satisfying solution proved to be a time-consuming challenge for the couple. "We studied it in model and we studied it in drawings. Our previous employers never would have permitted this amount of study in the early phases," Win recalled.[62] Another challenge was that the Closes were determined to use casement and awning windows—more commonly utilized in Europe at the time—instead of the double-hung windows that were readily available in the United States, because casements offered views unobstructed by an additional horizontal sash. As they were

Figure 3.10 Lisl's perspective sketch of the Willem and Willemina Luyten House (1939), Minneapolis. Close Associates Papers (N78), Northwest Architectural Archives, University of Minnesota Libraries, Minneapolis.

Figure 3.11 The Willem and Willemina Luyten House (1939) in Minneapolis. The Luytens, who were raised in Holland, brought to the design process sophisticated knowledge of European modernism and strong ideas about what they wanted in a house. Photograph by Richard C. Lundin II.

Figure 3.12 Living room of the Luyten House. The wood paneling, integrated bookshelves, and ceiling beams are reminiscent of those in the Loos-designed Scheu House in Vienna. Close Associates Papers (N78), Northwest Architectural Archives, University of Minnesota Libraries, Minneapolis.

Figure 3.13 The Starke and Jinny Hathaway House (1941) is built into a hilly site in the Prospect Park neighborhood of Minneapolis. HB-10242-I, Chicago History Museum, Hedrich-Blessing Collection, and Close Associates Papers (N78), Northwest Architectural Archives, University of Minnesota Libraries, Minneapolis.

not obtainable in Minnesota, each window was individually designed and custom made.

The Closes had used some redwood on the exterior of the Faulkner House, but the two-story, flat-roofed Luyten House was sided almost entirely in it. Lisl and Win favored the material for its character, durability, and low maintenance. Flat roofs and redwood siding "sort of became our vocabulary for quite a long time," Lisl said. Their use of the wood, which is native to the Pacific Northwest but not to Europe, was a departure from the palette of more industrial materials commonly used by architects of the International Style. However, the natural material warms and texturizes the exterior of the house and resonates with the trees and other landscape features of the site, which the Closes disturbed as little as possible. The original site plan reveals that only one tree was removed to make room for the house.[63]

Interior finishes for the three-bedroom, two-bath house included Homasote, gumwood, plaster, and brick, with linoleum and hardwood used for floors. Wood beams, like those used by Loos in the hall and dining room of the Scheu House in Vienna, span the living room ceiling.

The Luytens were pleased with their new residence, but some neighbors were "alarmed" by the house, which was the only modern one on East River Terrace at the time. Win recalled one neighbor was disturbed because light reflected off the bright new redwood siding into their windows and "made their color scheme pink, which they hadn't intended."[64]

The Luyten House led to a 1941 commission for University of Minnesota professor and clinical psychologist Starke Hathaway, a cocreator of the Minnesota Multiphasic Personality Inventory (MMPI) test, and his wife, Jinny, for a residence in the Prospect Park neighborhood. That same year, the Closes also designed a house on East River Terrace for Lennox Mills, a professor of political science at the university. Each house was functionally planned to accommodate the homeowners' unique lifestyles and needs.

INTERSTATE CLINIC

The Closes' first commission for a medical facility was not initiated by a university faculty member but by two physicians from Red Wing, Minnesota, a city on the Mississippi River roughly fifty miles southeast of Minneapolis. The building, known as the Interstate Clinic, was a fusion of functional design, state-of-the-art medical technology, and world-class modern art (Plate 7). When Drs. Edward H. Juers and Raymond F. Hedin decided to build a medical clinic on Third and Dakota Streets in Red Wing, they turned to Hedin's brother-in-law, painter and photographer John Pierce Anderson, for advice. Anderson, son of Alexander Anderson, the inventor of Puffed Rice (once promoted as "The Eighth Wonder of the World") was a patron of modern artist Charles Biederman. Anderson and Biederman, who were brothers-in-law, were well connected in local and international art circles.[65] Because they knew of the Faulkner House, they suggested the Closes design the new clinic.

Lisl believed Anderson and Biederman had an ulterior motive when they steered Juers and Hedin their way. "Clearly, John and Charles Biederman had a very strong inclination for modern art, so they encouraged their relatives, I'm sure, to go with us," she said. But as artists, "they were eager to have a place to show their very new and very modern constructions . . . steel and wood shapes. Very abstract shapes and large scale." They got their wish. When the clinic was completed in 1940, three works by Biederman, including *#7, New York,* a large, colorful three-dimensional construction that became the "centerpiece of the waiting room," were hung in the clinic, Lisl recalled. The size and highly abstract nature of the work baffled some patients. "People used to wonder what those things were, whether they were an eye chart, or something," she said.[66] But the Closes appreciated Anderson's and Biederman's artistic contributions to the project and their support of modern art and architecture.

Figure 3.14 Interstate Clinic (1940), Red Wing, Minnesota. Glazed white tiles sheathed the simple, geometric volumes of the building. HB-06586-A, Chicago History Museum, Hedrich-Blessing Collection.

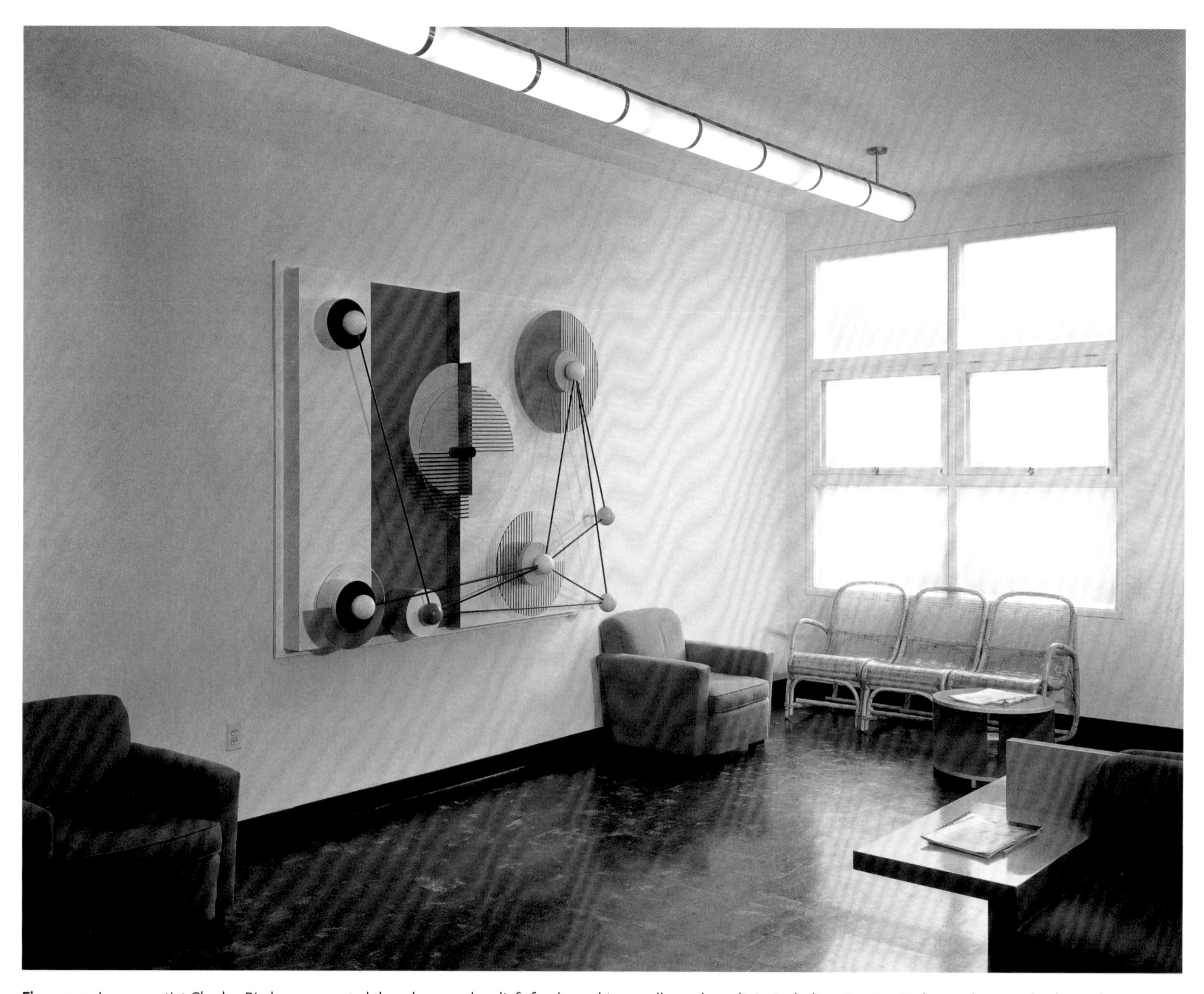

Figure 3.15 In 1940 artist Charles Biederman created three large-scale reliefs for the architecturally modern clinic, including *#7, New York,* seen here on display in the waiting room. The Hedin family later donated the wood, metal, Plexiglas, and paint construction to the Tweed Museum of Art at the University of Minnesota Duluth. HB-06586-H, Chicago History Museum, Hedrich-Blessing Collection.

Programmatically, the clinic was planned to address the "increasing specialization in the medical profession [and] the need for group practices . . . in small and medium-sized communities." Office space and examining rooms were provided for six physicians, a dentist, and an "x-ray specialist." Primary design considerations for Close and Scheu were a main control point near the entrance and flexibility of movement among the examining, diagnostic, and procedure rooms that flanked a main corridor.[67] Interior finishes included plaster, tile, and birch and pine plywood. A color scheme of light gray, blue, and yellow, suggested by Anderson and Biederman, who also designed furniture for the waiting room, concentrated the cooler colors in rooms with western exposure, and yellow in those to the east. Ample daylight entered the building through clear and diffused glass.

The simple, asymmetrical geometry of the exterior of the L-shaped, flat-roofed building was sheathed in glazed white tile and plywood. It was devoid of any ornamentation save a continuous strip of bright blue paint on the fascia. Access to the visually arresting building was via a double-tiered stairway that was partially sheltered by a cantilevered overhang.

Hedrich-Blessing, a highly regarded architectural photography firm based in Chicago, documented the building in a series of striking black and white images that were published nationally, including in the February 1942 issue of the *Architectural Forum*. The text that accompanied the photographs pointed out the building's framing system in which joists ran parallel to the long perimeter walls, noting that this "unusual framing facilitates piping and wiring." Such efficient planning and clever problem solving would become a hallmark of the firm's design approach.

An article in the *Red Wing Daily Republican* was more effusive in its analysis and praise of the clinic: "The entire building is functionally designed to provide the maximum of efficiency and at the same time the highest degree of beauty without any superfluous decoration and without an inch of wasted space." The writer added, "The architecture of the exterior of the building is so unusual that it at once commands immediate attention. Its lines are straight and

Figure 3.16 Close and Scheu used birch plywood throughout the building to handsome effect, including for the stair rail and pharmacy walls. HB-06586-P, Chicago History Museum, Hedrich-Blessing Collection.

plain, but the effect achieved is beautiful, as well as novel." For these reasons, the article predicted that the clinic "seems destined to win national recognition as one of the most modern medical buildings in the country."[68] As for the modern art installation by Anderson and Biederman, it was deemed "unlike anything seen in this vicinity, though similar decorations have been introduced to a limited extent in Europe and the East."[69]

By the late 1960s, the expanded and renamed Interstate Medical Center had outgrown its original facilities and moved to a larger building. The handsome Close-designed building was demolished on July 25, 1985.[70]

SKYWATER

In 1941 Joseph Warren Beach, a literary critic and head of the University of Minnesota's English department, and his wife, Dagmar Doneghy Beach, a writer, asked the Closes to design a small cabin for an isolated site on the St. Croix River near Osceola, Wisconsin. The Beaches, who lived on University Avenue in Minneapolis across the street from Memorial Stadium, needed a quiet weekend retreat for reading and writing as far away from the busy campus as was feasible—especially during football season.

Lisl described the steep, wooded site as "a magical place in many ways . . . quiet and beautiful." But the potential construction site was "daunting" because there was no road, no water, and no electricity. "It was pretty primitive in many ways," she said.[71] The location of the site, on a bluff high above the river, inspired the cabin's poetic name, "Skywater," as Dagmar believed it stood midway between sky and water.

The Beaches were away from Minnesota during much of the planning and construction of Skywater, so they gave the Closes free rein in its creation, including exactly where and how to build it. "The design was essentially a question. Should it be a house dug into the hill or projecting from the hillside into the trees, a treehouse?" Lisl stated. They ultimately decided to build into the hill on a ridge 150 feet above the river. The 576-square-foot cabin cost $1,200 to build (roughly $22,000 in 2019) and was constructed of local native stone and redwood. The sod roof of the two-room cabin was supported by a system of five-by-eight-foot wood planking and a built-up roof membrane, which also wraps the back wall of the cabin, topped with a layer of gravel. Two feet of earth fill, an extension of the hillside above, completes the roof and seamlessly blends the cabin into the landscape. Three of the cabin's four walls were totally or partially embedded in the earth, providing natural cooling during the summer months; the fourth, an expanse of glass, allowed natural light and solar gain in the living area. The Closes described Skywater as demonstrating "an optimal situation for earth shelter and solar heating."[72] A distinguishing feature of the cabin was a cantilevered, horizontal trellis above the glass wall, which was designed to accommodate an existing oak tree. The trellis at Skywater appears to have been inspired by a Frank Lloyd Wright design. It is a simpler, more rustic version of the one above the terrace doors of Willey House in Minneapolis, which stands across the cul-de-sac from the Faulkner House.

Today, Skywater is almost indistinguishable from its site and appears to be a natural outgrowth of it. But it was not easy to build. One major problem was getting material and equipment to the site, to which there was no road. The farmer who sold the land to the Beaches helpfully lent his horses and a cart to get materials, such as lumber, fireplace brick, floor tile, and a kerosene stove, to the site. Even the finished cabin was "very primitive. There was no running water, there was no electricity. In other words, the usual comforts were not available," said Lisl.[73] Winter access to Skywater was impossible.

To stay within the project's low, Depression-era budget required considerable creativity on the part of the Closes. Local stone, "picked up along the site," was used for the fireplace and exposed walls; inexpensive hollow tile was employed for the floors. A trash can, horizontally recessed in the earthen wall of the kitchen, became the "refrigerator." The Beaches allotted an additional $50 for furniture and other necessities. Win and Lisl came up with an ingenious and low-cost design in which one chair and one table could be produced from a single sheet of fir plywood; once pieces were assembled,

Figure 3.17 Skywater, the Joseph and Dagmar Beach Cabin (1941), in Osceola, Wisconsin. The horizontal trellis was designed to accommodate an existing tree. HB-10242-E, Chicago History Museum, Hedrich-Blessing Collection, and Close Associates Papers (N78), Northwest Architectural Archives, University of Minnesota Libraries, Minneapolis.

Figure 3.18 Skywater, living room. Local stone, gathered on-site, was used for the fireplace and interior walls. HB-10242-B, Chicago History Museum, Hedrich-Blessing Collection, and Close Associates Papers (N78), Northwest Architectural Archives, University of Minnesota Libraries, Minneapolis.

clothesline was strung across the chair frame to create its back.[74] Other items, including kitchen equipment, were sourced at Goodwill. A prize find was an iron cooking kettle, purchased for $1.75. Suspended from a kettle crane in the fireplace, it became Dagmar's "stew pot." A local blacksmith made the crane and a set of andirons from a piece of salvaged trolley tracks. An article on the "peaceful retreat," with photographs by Hedrich-Blessing, was published in *Progressive Architecture* in December 1948.

As modest and rustic as the cabin was, the Beaches often entertained their worldly friends and colleagues there. Guests included writers Sinclair Lewis and Robert Penn Warren, and architect and structural innovator R. Buckminster Fuller. Following Joseph Beach's death in 1957, Dagmar asked Lisl to design a guest cabin on-site, as she did not want to visit Skywater alone.[75] She built the second cabin out from the hillside, like a tree house, an option originally considered for the first cabin (Plates 8 and 9). The light frame structure, completed in 1961, included the amenities of electricity, running water, a screened porch, and a bathroom. In October 1983, the Closes purchased Skywater from the Beaches' son Northrop. Members of the Close family still own it today.[76]

The Closes had no lack of clients in the late 1930s and early '40s, but after the United States entered World War II in December 1941, things changed. Materials became more difficult to secure and many people, increasingly unsure of what the future would bring, shied away from embarking on new projects. Life changed for the Closes personally, as well. Win enlisted in the U.S. Navy and remained on active duty until the end of the conflict. His military assignments meant multiple moves for the couple and their toddler daughter, Anne (born in 1940). For all these reasons, the Closes suspended their architectural practice in 1942. Three years would pass before they permanently returned to Minnesota.

Figure 3.19 Lisl and Win created an efficient and economical design for Skywater's furniture. All components for one chair and one table were cut from a single sheet of plywood. Courtesy of Roy M. Close Family Papers.

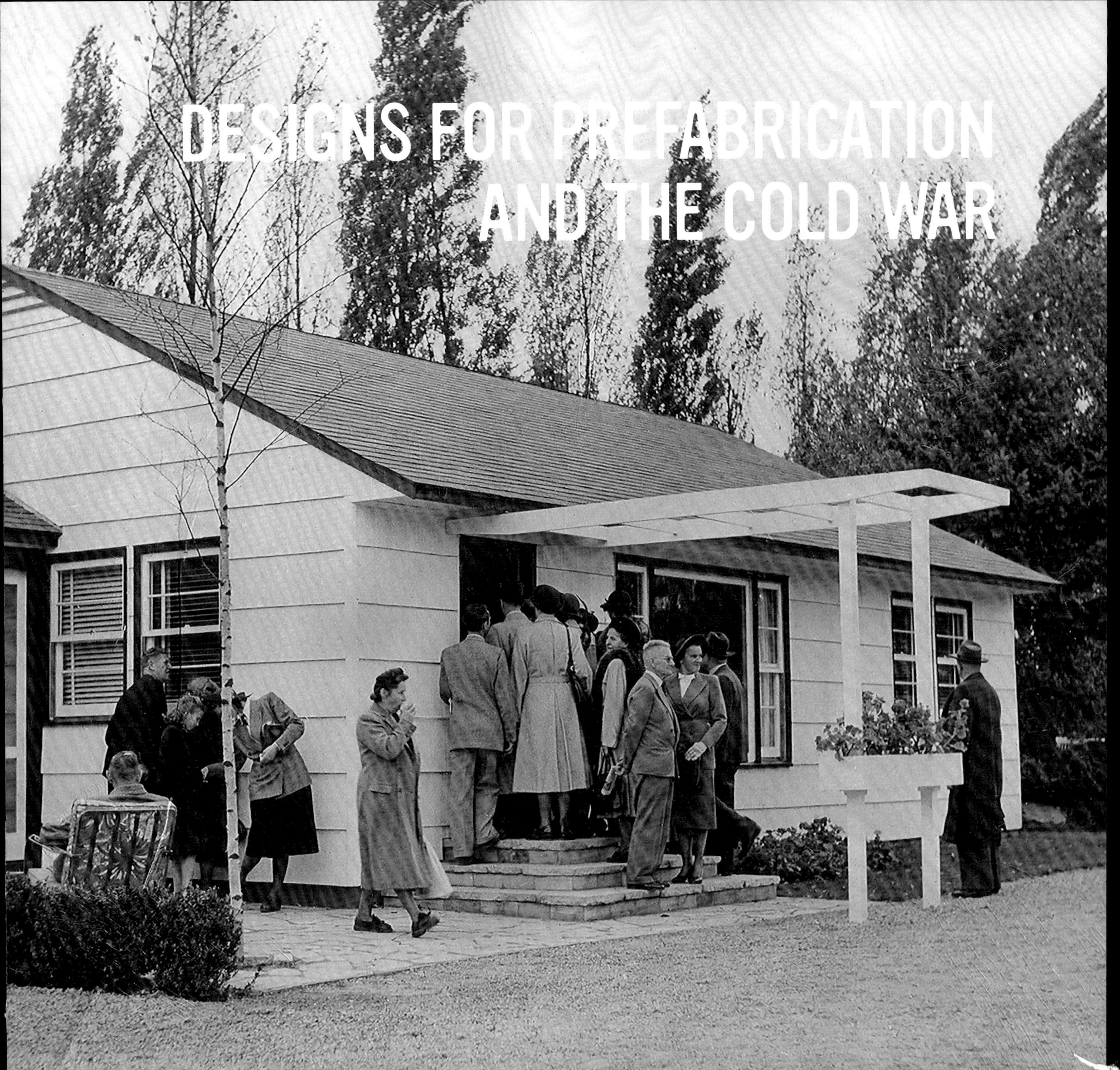

DESIGNS FOR PREFABRICATION AND THE COLD WAR

As was true for many Americans, World War II upended the lives and livelihood of Lisl and Win Close. In January 1942, the War Production Board was established to coordinate the manufacture of defense machinery and commodities. To accomplish its work, the WPB instituted wartime rationing of gas, heating oil, metals, and other materials, including those used in the building trades.[1] For architects and prospective homeowners, this made it nearly impossible to build during the war. "Our work here was stopped by the priority orders," Win explained to a client in 1942. "The office is dormant."[2]

The building and repurposing of peacetime factories for wartime production, however, were big business for the government—and welcome work for architects who were fortunate enough to secure contracts. Win was hired to design machine layouts for ordnance facilities in Des Moines, Iowa, and Eau Claire, Wisconsin. In the latter city, he worked on the "conversion of a tire factory to manufacture 30 [caliber] cartridges."[3] The job resulted in a move to Eau Claire for Win, Lisl, and their young daughter, Anne, in the summer of 1942.

Although the Closes dutifully continued to correspond with their clients, ultimately most projects were halted or postponed. "The war does take on concrete shape at times, even in Wisconsin," Lisl wrote to Dagmar Beach, who was hoping to build a second cabin at Skywater in Osceola that summer. "Although we may be still able to get lumber, you might find it quite difficult to get hardware and nails and so on. Especially hardware," she cautioned.[4] Even automobile travel was becoming a challenge. Of the Closes' desire to visit a project that was under construction, Win wrote, "If we can conserve enough gas we'd like to come out . . . so that we can see how the place is developing."[5]

In February 1943, Win enlisted in the Naval Reserve of the United States as a lieutenant (junior grade).[6] Following indoctrination at the U.S. Naval Air Station at Quonset Point, Rhode Island, he reported for active duty at the Bunker Hill Naval Air Station near Kokomo, Indiana.[7]

Lisl's life changed in many ways, too. Not only was she now a mother, she no longer had an office in which to work or a partner with whom to work. This became a challenge when the Page & Hill Company approached her about a project that would keep her gainfully employed during the war and for many years to follow. Not one to let obstacles get in her way, Lisl set up a drafting board in her new residence, found someone to care for Anne a few days a week, and went to work.[8]

PAGE & HILL

The Page & Hill Company was founded in Minnesota in 1903 as a manufacturer of Western red cedar utility poles. By the early 1930s, it had diversified its output and found an additional use for cedar logs through the production of a series of log homes. The houses had all the "rustic charm and pioneer ruggedness" of the traditional American log house but with "modern conveniences." Marketed under the name "Real Log Houses," each model consisted of precut components that were fitted and numbered at the factory for easy assembly on-site. Promotional materials promised that "P&H exclusive log construction is readily adaptable to a wide range of uses and needs—from small cabin to pretentious lodge."[9] The successful enterprise produced and shipped log homes to twenty-eight states.[10]

The outbreak of World War II and government restrictions on any residential construction other than defense program housing ended Page & Hill's line of log houses. While it was true that the government urgently needed affordable and easy-to-assemble housing to shelter the tens of thousands of workers who were flocking to new war-industry production plants across the country, log cabins were not the answer.[11] Cleverly, Page & Hill shifted focus to a contemporary line of prefabricated houses more suited for defense program housing. The company already possessed expertise in manufacturing precut, factory-made components, but it lacked the architectural skill to design the attractive, well-engineered, contemporary residences the WPB was willing to fund.

While at a WPB meeting in Washington, D.C., Hart Anderson, Page & Hill's vice president in charge of sales, learned of Lisl's credentials as an architect as well as her 1934 undergraduate thesis work at MIT on a production plant for prefabricated houses. In December 1941, Page & Hill Defense Housing, as it was then known, hired the Close firm to design prefabricated house models at the rate of two dollars per hour. Given Win's existing contract work and subsequent active duty in the Naval Reserve, Lisl assumed responsibility for the Page & Hill commission.

It is not known if Anderson hired Lisl based on the topic of her thesis alone, or on the strength of its content. If the latter, he would have discovered much of interest in her outside-the-box thinking. The stated goal of her thesis was to propose a way to meet the "urgent social and economic need to provide a type of house that is better planned, better built and better equipped than the house that is available at the present time." The factory production of prefabricated houses, she argued, was the solution. To that end, she proposed a production plant that would utilize "carefully applied industrial principles, coupled with the greatest possible compliance with the wishes of their clientele" to mass-produce quality housing within the financial reach of a large audience.[12]

Prefabrication, defined as "the mass production of interchangeable building parts," was not a new idea. Architects in America and Europe had been experimenting for many years with some measure of the technology, which had the potential to lower costs and control quality.[13] Beginning in 1908, the Sears, Roebuck and Company sold precut kit homes through its *Sears Modern Homes* catalogs. In the 1910s, Frank Lloyd Wright and Arthur Richards created a line of American System-Built Homes that utilized standardized, precut elements designed to be shipped to sites for assembly. In the 1920s, to address housing shortages in Europe, architects including Walter Gropius, Ernst May, and Marcel Breuer experimented with prefabricated building systems using concrete and steel.[14] Other experiments with prefabrication used lightweight materials and inventive structural systems, including R. Buckminster Fuller's "Dymaxion House" of 1927, Richard Neutra's "Diatom" houses of the 1920s, and similar experiments by Monroe and Irving Bowman of Bowman Brothers, Architects. As Irving Bowman wrote in "An Industrial Approach to Housing" in 1932, the firm's interest was

Figure 4.1 From 1941 until the late 1950s, Lisl designed prefabricated houses for Page & Hill of Shakopee, Minnesota. As this advertisement from 1956 states, Page & Hill Homes were marketed in fifteen states. Courtesy of Roy M. Close Family Papers.

not limited to the design of prefabricated houses but encompassed issues of "structure, manufacture, erection, finance, and sales."[15] In her thesis, Lisl likewise argued a holistic approach to prefabrication and cited the Bowmans, Fuller, Neutra, and thirty other published sources in her bibliography. Although her Depression-era treatise predated the post–World War II prefabricated housing boom by more than a decade, it did coincide with a "renewed interest in the potential of prefabrication to create affordable housing" following the stock market crash of 1929.[16] Lisl was also inspired by the 1933–34 Century of Progress International Exposition in Chicago. Not only was that World's Fair a platform for contemporary design and cutting-edge technologies, it also showcased futuristic methods of home construction, new materials, and unconventional uses for them. Fair organizers erected thirteen modern houses along Lake Michigan, the most famous of which was "The House of Tomorrow," by George Fred Keck. The house featured materials and products not always associated with home construction by General Electric, the Libbey-Owens-Ford Glass Company, Reynolds Metals, and the Goodyear Tire and Rubber Company.

Lisl's thesis argued that one of the most critical factors in the affordable machine production of prefabricated houses was "the use of as few materials as possible. . . . The problem therefore consists of finding a material that combines as many of the necessary qualities [of] strength, insulation value, hardness" as possible. To this end she focused on relatively new "plastic" materials, specifically Bakelite, as the ideal choice. This "completely synthetic product" was invented in 1907 by Belgian chemist Leo Baekeland as "a liquid resin that would not burn, boil, melt, or dissolve in any commonly available acid or solvent."[17] Additionally, the "resinoid product" could be "machined to great exactness . . . can be finished to any shape or color, has a high insulating value, and requires practically no maintenance." Therefore, she proposed manufacturing the "structure and shell of the house, the pipes and plumbing fixtures, doors, built-in closets, and possibly even some of the furniture" from the material. In doing so, Lisl may have been the first to propose a mass-produced Bakelite house. She clearly understood she was suggesting an untried application of the material, which had to date been used for smaller items, including "pipe joints, I-beams, gear wheels, bath tubs, soap dispensers, trays, and bracelets." Yet she believed she was making "no rash assumption." In fact, she argued her seemingly radical concept made more sense in the modern age than "the attempt to squeeze old construction methods into new ways of construction."[18] In her proposed use of Bakelite alone, her thesis was prescient, as subsequent twentieth-century experimentation with unimagined applications of thermoplastic materials would prove.[19] Although she would not be designing Bakelite houses for Page & Hill, innovative thinking would serve her well in her work for the company.

While Lisl had theoretically explored prefabrication for her thesis, she had not, to date, designed a prefab house that had been built. To understand what was necessary on the manufacturing end, Page & Hill arranged for her to commute from Kokomo to Chicago to learn

Figure 4.2 View of the Page & Hill factory in Shakopee, Minnesota. Norton & Peel, *Interior, Shakopee Workshop*, 1942. Minnesota Historical Society, St. Paul, Minnesota.

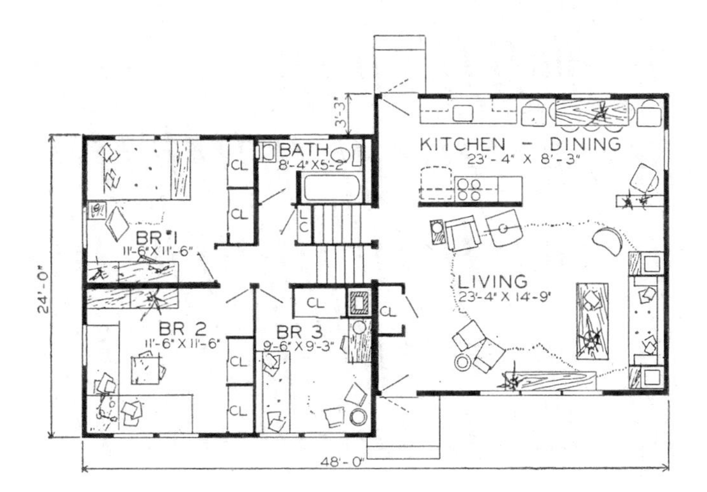

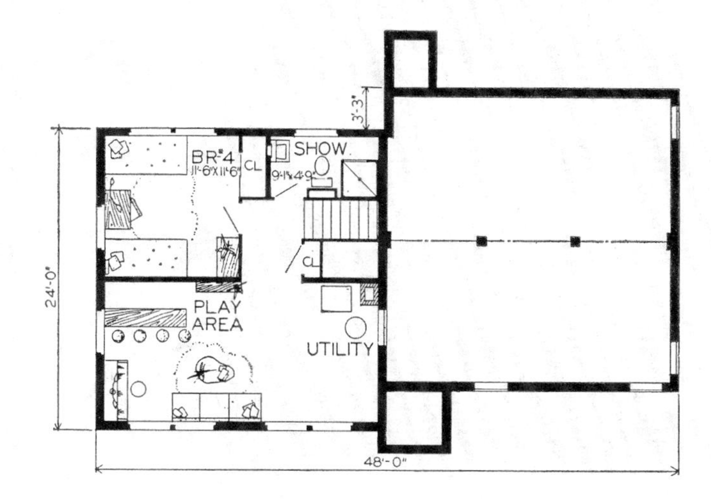

Figure 4.3 Floor plans for the split-level, four-bedroom, Close-designed "Andover" model Page & Hill Home. Courtesy of Roy M. Close Family Papers.

how it was done.[20] The company prided itself on its architecture and engineering and spent "$50,000 over a three-year period" on architectural services.[21] In addition, the design and production of a Page & Hill prefab house involved many complexities that differed from those related to conventional construction. First among them was the requirement that each house be designed to pack and ship in a single truckload. Although the technology of the mass production of entire houses was a modern concept, stylistically the houses Lisl designed for Page & Hill "weren't very modern," she said. "They were just ordinary houses. Very inexpensive."[22] They addressed a very pressing contemporary need: the rapid mass production of affordable housing for those in need of shelter.

After the war, Page & Hill segued from defense housing to the production of prefabs for a new generation of American homeowners. For the company, Lisl designed several series of plans—each with multiple models—sold by Page & Hill Homes and its subsidiary Pagemaster Homes. The one-, two-, and split-level houses, which were marketed under such vaguely evocative but nondescriptive names as "Andover," "Devonshire," "Hiawatha," and "Jubilaire," were available with two to four bedrooms. The "typical house [was] 40 × 24 feet, with three bedrooms, a fireplace and a deluxe kitchen," according to a company spokesperson.[23] Houses were delivered by truck to completed foundations on the owners' lots, where contractors would supervise assembly of the factory-made elements. The company strove to make the process as seamless and rapid as possible; its best time from model sale to owner move-in was twenty-seven days.[24]

Like their defense program housing predecessors, Page & Hill's postwar houses were not architecturally modern in style but pushed the envelope in the degree of shop fabrication involved for each model; the company focused on achieving the maximum amount possible. For example, Lisl was charged with designing exterior wall systems in which windows, doors, and screens were inserted, and hardware, siding, and finishes were applied, at the company's

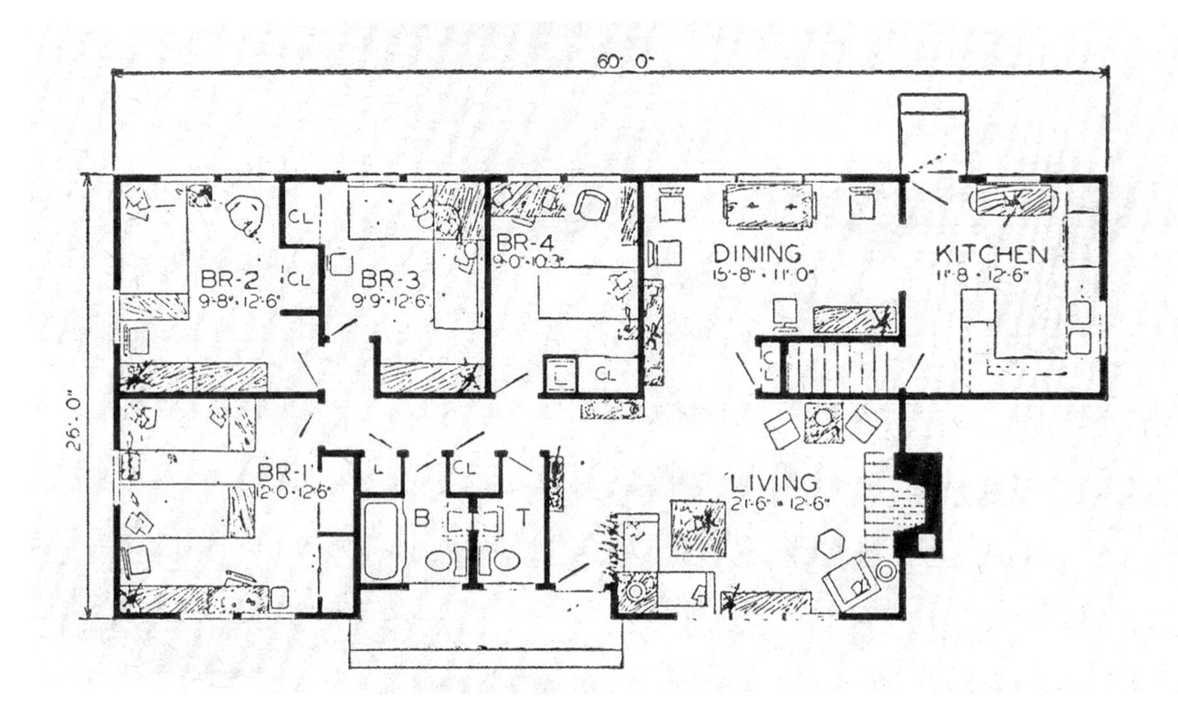

Figure 4.4 Floor plan for the four-bedroom, one-level, Close-designed "Devonshire" model Page & Hill Home. Courtesy of Roy M. Close Family Papers.

Figure 4.5 Lisl created this painting of a Page & Hill model house for promotional materials. Close Associates Papers (N78), Northwest Architectural Archives, University of Minnesota Libraries, Minneapolis.

main plant in Shakopee.[25] This efficiency would translate to faster, easier, and less expensive assembly on-site. Additionally, all designs and construction methods were required to conform to Federal Housing Authority engineering standards. Office records show Lisl devoted many billable hours to preparing narrative descriptions and specifications for FHA's engineering bulletins.

According to Lisl, more than ten thousand Page & Hill houses of her design were shipped to and assembled in fifteen states in the Midwest and Northwest. Developers purchased units to quickly and affordably populate entire neighborhoods in America's burgeoning suburbs. Local Twin Cities examples include the Vista View neighborhood in Burnsville and Acorn Ridge, a community of Page & Hill homes in Minnetonka.[26]

Prefabricated houses were also an ideal way to shelter an influx of workers in a new company town. In 1956 Page & Hill shipped more than one thousand dwellings—at the rate of twenty houses per week—to taconite mining concerns, including the Erie Mining Company, on the Iron Range in northern Minnesota. The company provided prefab homes for laborers and administrative staff in the newly incorporated town of Hoyt Lakes where "crushers, grinders, magnetic separators, and heat-hardening furnaces are rising on land that was wilderness only a few months ago."[27]

Lisl continued to work with Page & Hill into the late 1950s, developing plans for prefabricated housing for married students and designing models for new company lines. To retain an edge in the highly competitive, booming prefab market, later series included such "special feature" options as cathedral ceilings, decorative garage doors, and built-ins. In 1957 a catastrophic fire destroyed the company's Shakopee factory. Although Page & Hill remained in business, production of prefabricated houses at the plant ended, and with it most of Lisl's work for the company.

In addition to her designs for Page & Hill, Lisl developed prefabricated plans for at least three other companies during the 1950s and '60s, including "Precision-bilt System" houses for the Fullerton Lumber Company of Minneapolis; prototype factory-built mobile homes for the Iseman Corporation of Sioux Falls, South Dakota; and

Figure 4.6 The cover of the August 1956 issue of *PF—The Magazine of Prefabrication* featured a row of Page & Hill homes in an unidentified Minneapolis subdivision. Courtesy of Roy M. Close Family Papers.

Figure 4.7 A Page & Hill model home built in Acorn Ridge, a development in the Minneapolis suburb of Minnetonka. Norton & Peel, *House on Acorn Ridge*, 1956. Minnesota Historical Society, St. Paul, Minnesota.

Plate 1 The Scheu House (1912) in Vienna, Austria. Adolf Loos dropped the ceiling in the inglenook to create an even more intimate and inviting space. Photograph by William B. Olexy, 2010.

Plate 2 A south-facing, recessed window, with built-in seating, provides a view to the garden from the Scheu House salon. Photograph by William B. Olexy, 2010.

Plate 3 One of Close and Scheu's first projects was University Terrace (1938), a low-cost group housing complex. It was not built. Watercolor perspective by Elizabeth Scheu. Close Associates Papers (N78), Northwest Architectural Archives, University of Minnesota Libraries, Minneapolis.

Plate 4 The principles of the Cooperative movement inspired this unbuilt row house project (1938), which was intended for a site in St. Paul near the current location of Luther Seminary. Watercolor perspective by Elizabeth Scheu. Courtesy of Gar Hargens/Close Associates.

Plate 5 With its flat roof, stark exterior, and blue-tinted concrete driveway, the Ray Faulkner House was a controversial addition to the Prospect Park neighborhood of Minneapolis in 1938. Photograph by Jane King Hession.

Plate 6 Benjamin and Gertrude Lippincott purchased the Faulkner House in 1939. The following year they hired the Closes to expand the house (addition at left), nearly doubling its size. Saari and Forrai Architectural Photography.

Plate 7 The Interstate Clinic (1940), Red Wing, Minnesota, was the first of several clinics and medical office buildings the firm would design. It was demolished in 1985. Watercolor perspective by Elizabeth Close. Courtesy of Gar Hargens/Close Associates.

Plate 8 Skywater, cabin for Joseph and Dagmar Beach (1941) in Osceola, Wisconsin. The first cabin at Skywater was built into a hillside and sheltered by the earth. Photograph by Jane King Hession.

Plate 9 The second Skywater cabin (1961), built as a guesthouse, projects out from the hillside. Photograph by Jane King Hession.

Plate 10 The brochure *America at Home* for the 1950 Berlin International Industrial Exhibition featured a prefabricated house, designed by Lisl, on its cover. The small house played a big role in a high-profile exercise in American propaganda during the Cold War. European Recovery Agency, *Amerika zu Hause: Zur Erinnerung an die Deutsche Industrie Ausstellung* (Berlin, 1950).

Plate 11 In 1940 the Closes designed the Tracy F. Tyler House, their first completed project in University Grove in Falcon Heights, Minnesota. Photograph by William B. Olexy.

Plate 12 Living room of the Tyler House in 2017. Streamlined cabinetry includes a sixteen-foot sideboard and a birch storage cabinet flush with the fireplace wall. Courtesy of Spacecrafting.

Plate 13 The Elizabeth and Winston Close House (1953) in University Grove. The original galley kitchen of the Close House was renovated in 2006. Photograph by William B. Olexy.

Plate 14 Living room of the Close House. *Maya*, a statue by sculptor John Rood (for whom the Closes designed a house in 1947), can be seen in the garden. The Bechstein piano originally stood in the Scheu House in Vienna. Photograph by William B. Olexy.

Plate 15 In 1964 Lisl designed the "Atrium Contemporary" for the Weyerhaeuser Company's Registered Homes program. This plan for the nationally distributed prefabricated house shows how living areas surround an outdoor courtyard or atrium. Close Associates Papers (N78), Northwest Architectural Archives, University of Minnesota Libraries, Minneapolis.

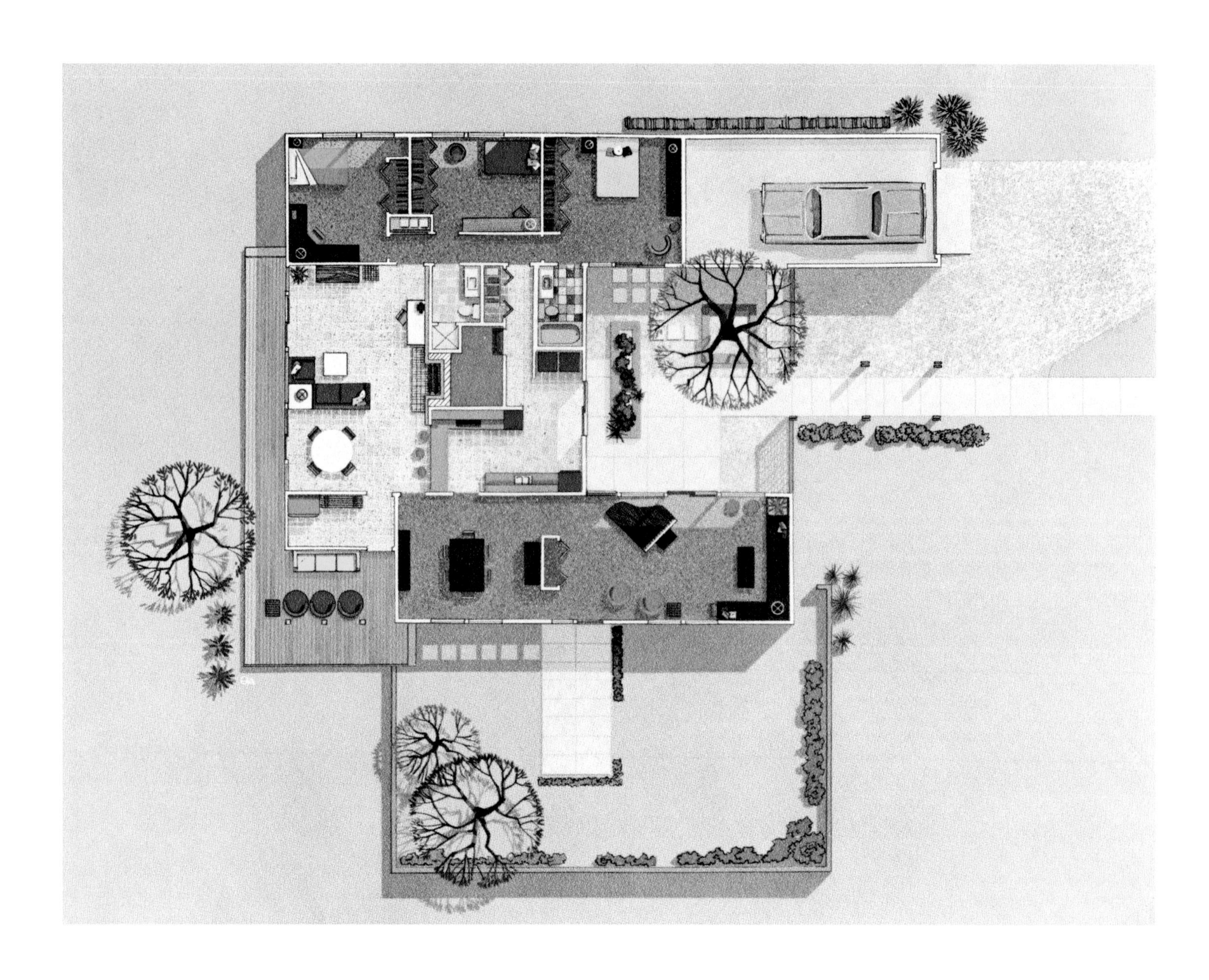

Plate 16 Interior perspectives of the "Atrium Contemporary" illustrate the airy spaciousness of the plan and the relationship between interior rooms and the outdoor atrium. Close Associates Papers (N78), Northwest Architectural Archives, University of Minnesota Libraries, Minneapolis.

FAMILY ROOM. In the family room, a spectacular window wall overlooks a spacious wooden deck and second private garden area, providing a feeling of spaciousness. The fireplace will encourage relaxation with your family and generous counter space makes for convenience and livability.

LIVING ROOM. An all season view of the atrium adds a feeling of pleasant openness to this beautifully appointed room. And the high, exposed-beam ceiling and specially designed built-in lighting combine to create an atmosphere of friendly warmth and hospitality.

Plate 17 The Hendrik and Marri Oskam House (1962) on Indianhead Lake in Edina, Minnesota. Glazed Dutch brick, built-in seating, and a wood beamed ceiling bring warmth to the modern interior. Period furniture and decorative items were purchased from Barret Pohl, a modern furniture store that operated in Dinkytown, near the University of Minnesota. Photograph by William B. Olexy.

Plate 18 View of the Oskam House from Indianhead Lake. Photograph by William B. Olexy.

Plate 19 The Jason and Lorentina Quist House (1947), Edina, Minnesota, is one of many houses designed by the Closes that have been purchased and renovated by a new generation of homeowners. Photograph by William B. Olexy.

Plate 20 The Fry House (1956), designed for landscape architect Marion and Robert Fry, was built into a steep, wooded hillside in St. Paul. This entry hall staircase, photographed in 2015, leads to main living areas on the second floor. Courtesy of Spacecrafting.

Plate 21 Glass walls wrap second-floor living spaces of the Fry House and allow expansive views. Courtesy of Spacecrafting.

Plate 22 The Gove and Elsie Hambidge House (1958) in Roseville, Minnesota. Six bedrooms, a kitchen, dining and living rooms, a study, and a dark room encircle the central courtyard of the house. A towering copper fireplace hood visually anchors the courtyard. Photograph by William B. Olexy.

Plate 23 Lobby of the Freshwater Biological Institute (1974) in Navarre, Minnesota. The building received an AIA Minnesota Honor Award in 1975. Photograph by William B. Olexy, 2014.

GRAY FRESHWATER CENTER
LOWER LEVEL

Plate 24 In addition to laboratories, the Freshwater building included multidisciplinary spaces such as this lounge, which faces a marsh and Lake Minnetonka's Lafayette Bay. Photograph by William B. Olexy, 2014.

a prefabricated contemporary atrium home for Weyerhaeuser's nationally distributed "Registered Home" series. She also conducted research and development on the architectural uses and machine production of plastic structural elements for Polystructures, a Minnesota-based company.

A PREFAB PAWN IN COLD WAR BERLIN

Lisl may have characterized her prefab designs for Page & Hill as "just ordinary houses," but during the Cold War one played an extraordinary role in a highly publicized, propagandistic display of the comforts and prosperity of life under the American system of democracy, a potent statement at a time when Europe was recovering from the ravages of World War II and the Iron Curtain ideologically separated East from West.

Figure 4.8 Watercolor rendering of the George C. Marshall House, the showpiece of America's contributions to the German International Industrial Exhibition in Berlin, 1950. European Recovery Agency, *Amerika zu Hause: Zur Erinnerung an die Deutsche Industrie Ausstellung* (Berlin, 1950).

By the summer of 1950, the U.S. Department of State already had well-formed plans for the American contribution to the first German International Industrial Exhibition in Berlin, then a politically divided city. The undisputed showcase was to be the George C. Marshall House, which "symbolized" the European Recovery Program and America's role in it.[28] Designed by architect Bruno Grimmick and built as a trade pavilion by the U.S. State Department, the Marshall House was the city's first postwar International Style building.[29] The glass-walled, colonnaded structure housed a 250-seat cinema, a library of American books, scale models of typical American communities, and an "electrically animated diorama of an [American] industrial community."[30] More than 750,000 people visited the Marshall House during the fair's two-week run.

In late July 1950, a little more than two months before the exhibition's opening on October 1, that plan was augmented when an idea was hatched to include a "model U.S. constructed house as a symbol to visitors . . . of the U.S. standard of living." It was further suggested that the model be a "house of modern prefabricated construction complete with the latest furnishings and utilities."[31]

It is not documented why a Close-designed Page & Hill "Jubilaire" house was chosen over hundreds of other models marketed by dozens of American companies engaged in prefabrication at the time. By August 18, however, the choice had been made by Bernard Wagner, a German-speaking American architect from the United States Housing and Home Finance Agency, who also selected furnishings for the house and served as its "curator" during the exhibition.[32] The stated purpose of the "Model American Home" was to "graphically represent the high living standard of the American wage-earner," and by extension "the fruits of American democracy and free enterprise."[33] More plainly stated, it was intended to demonstrate that life was better in the free world and to make that point behind the Iron Curtain.

A sum of $25,000 was allotted for the purchase of the house, its furnishings, and shipment from Minneapolis to Berlin.[34] It arrived in ninety-four crates shortly before the opening of the fair and was assembled on-site in ten days. The floor plan of the six-room

Figure 4.9 In 1950, the U.S. State Department shipped a "Jubilaire" Page & Hill house from Minnesota to Cold War Berlin to serve as the "Model American Home" at the German International Industrial Exhibition. Here, workers in Berlin unload boxes containing prefabricated sections of the house. National Archives, Text Division, RG59, 862A.191, box 5225.

Figure 4.10 During the exhibition's two-week run, 43,000 people visited the "Model American Home." National Archives, Text Division, RG59, 862A.191, box 5225.

"ranch house" measured twenty-four by sixty-one feet, including a breezeway and garage. It was fully equipped with the most current conveniences and comforts of American domestic life, including a thermostat-controlled furnace, electric range, washing machine, vacuum cleaner, Mixmaster, and television. Roughly 43,000 "enthralled" visitors—many from the Soviet sector of the city—were guided through the house, in groups of ten, by specially trained young German women from the Berlin Free University.[35] State department memos reported the "average German" was left "gasping" or "too dazed to comprehend" the marvels of the house.[36] To quantify the advantages of life in America, visitors were provided with a pamphlet detailing such things as the number of automobiles, televisions, and radio sets in the country; how many people were covered by Social Security and life insurance; and the average yearly earnings of a cross-section of workers, including policemen, bus drivers, auto mechanics, and miners.[37] In addition to accommodating a flood of daily visitors, the house also hosted special-interest tours, including one Wagner led for a group of thirty German architects.[38]

The State Department declared the "achievement" of the American Model House and the Marshall House to be the "gratifying demonstration of what can be accomplished in selling the American democratic way of life."[39] In pairing the grand, International Style Marshall House and the small, prefabricated Page & Hill house, the State Department inextricably linked the two, in what one newspaper described as a "striking joint display of American economic strength on the international front and social achievement on the home front."[40] In the politically charged atmosphere of Cold War Berlin, Lisl's prefab design packed a powerful punch (Plate 10).

The house retained a measure of potency even as the fair closed. As the State Department had anticipated, a decision had to be made about the fate of the house. Unlike the Marshall House, which was

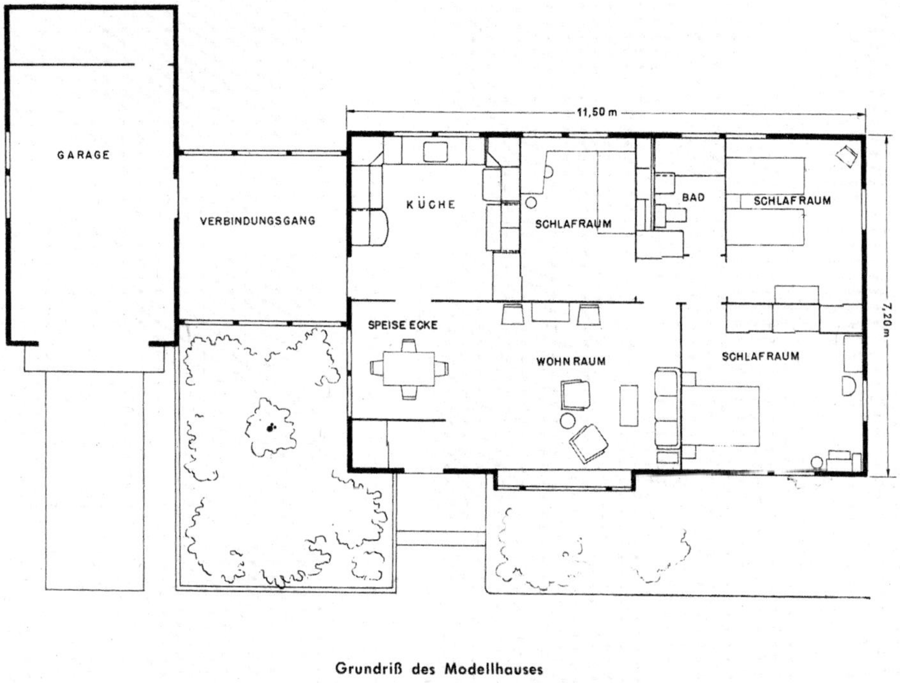

Grundriß des Modellhauses

Figure 4.11 The floor plan of the "Jubilaire" as published in 1950 in *America at Home*, a promotional brochure. European Recovery Agency, *Amerika zu Hause: Zur Erinnerung an die Deutsche Industrie Ausstellung* (Berlin, 1950).

Figure 4.12 Living room of the "Model American Home" at the German International Industrial Exhibition. National Archives, Text Division, RG59, 862A.191, box 5225.

erected as a permanent structure (and still stands) in what is now the Berlin Exhibition Grounds, for unclear reasons the model house could not remain on-site. Initially, the State Department planned to raffle it off, and broadcast the raffle, on the final day of the exhibition. They reasoned: "Should an east sector resident win, we would very much welcome it because publicity of a favorable or unfavorable action by east authorities would be extremely valuable propaganda for U.S."[41] They scuttled the idea because of the "questionable legal propriety" of a raffle. Another plan was floated to dismantle the house and relocate it for an alternate use. However, a Page & Hill representative stated, ironically, that although the house was assembled from prefabricated parts, it could not be disassembled and "must either be moved as a unit or wrecked."[42] If it could be moved, one thought was to "select some needy person

Figure 4.13 A woman from the Berlin Free University demonstrates a television set for visitors. National Archives, Text Division, RG59, 862A.191, box 5225.

or needy family for receipt of house. . . . Disposal in this fashion could be favorably exploited with certainty."[43] Although no paper trail exists to document the final disposition of the house, historian Greg Castillo writes, "Given the dearth of building materials in Berlin at the time, I doubt that it was simply demolished and hauled away as construction debris. Certainly, the furniture and appliances must have found new uses."[44]

Lisl did not see, nor was she invited to visit, the house in Berlin. She is not mentioned in now unclassified State Department documents, and she was not credited for the design of the small house that played a big role in a high-profile exercise in American propaganda during the Cold War. Remarkably, no one involved in the process was aware that the house, shipped from Minnesota to Germany to epitomize the freedoms of American democracy, was designed by a young architect who had left Austria for the United States to escape Nazi aggression. Had they known, the compelling human interest story would have made a useful addition to the "125 tons of propaganda material" that was disseminated during the run of the fair.[45] Lisl's role in creating the house went unrecognized, except in Minnesota, where a *Minneapolis Star* article titled "Shakopee House Goes to Berlin" ascribed the design to the firm of Elizabeth and Winston Close, Architects.[46] The American Model Home was the only structure designed by Lisl that was built in Europe.

Figure 4.14 Visitors were enthralled by the ultramodern kitchen of the "Jubilaire," which was equipped with such marvels as an electric range and a Mixmaster. National Archives, Text Division, RG59, 862A.191, box 5225.

5

HOUSES AND HOUSING

Figure 5.1 Elizabeth and Winston Close, circa 1952, with a model of the Robert and Lois Pflueger House, Ortonville, Minnesota. Courtesy of Roy M. Close Family Papers.

In the postwar years—with the baby boom in full swing and prosperity on the rise—the widely held aspiration of homeownership was becoming an achievable goal for many Americans. Numerous Minnesotans, hopeful to transform those dreams into realities, turned to the firm of Elizabeth and Winston Close, Architects. As a result, the office was busier than ever.

The Close family returned to Minneapolis in 1946 with their, now, two children; son Roy was born in Kokomo in 1944. They moved into a large house on Dell Place near Loring Park, which doubled as an office and workshop. That same year, Win embarked on a teaching career at the School of Architecture at the University of Minnesota. In 1950 he became the university's head of campus planning and in 1959 its advisory architect, the latter a position he held until 1971. In that capacity, he led several major campus expansion efforts, including the master planning of the university's new West Bank campus and Washington Avenue Bridge in Minneapolis and its campuses in Duluth and Morris, among many other initiatives.[1] Lisl ran the firm, was its principal designer, and interacted with clients. Although they did not work together on a daily basis, each valued and respected the other's opinion and, when possible, conferred on concepts and designs. "We always talked about [projects] with our kids over dinner. And he would come and look over my shoulder on weekends," she explained.[2] Because Win had a full-time job at the university, "follow-through was usually by me," she said.[3]

An associate described their office partnership during those years as "not always an equal division of effort," as Win's "major efforts were directed to his assignment as advisory architect to the University of Minnesota. The force that was necessary to maintain and expand the architectural practice was largely supplied by Elizabeth Close."[4] Gar Hargens, AIA, concurs. "We weren't aware of Win" prior to his retirement from the university. "A lot of us have always felt Lisl ran the office alone for so many years, she ran the office really when Win came back," he said. "They would make major decisions together . . . but day-to-day she was the one who was watching the checkbook, staffing, all of that."[5] After Win left the university, where he had managed other architects' projects rather than his own, and

Figure 5.2 The Walter and Johnnie Heller House (1954), University Grove, St. Paul, Minnesota. The sensitive siting of the house, its low-slope roof, strip windows, and textural vertical siding are all characteristic of the designs of the Closes' firm. Photograph by William B. Olexy.

returned to Close Associates, as the firm was then known, "he was like a kid in a candy store," said Hargens. In retirement he could participate more actively in the firm and take the lead on a project.[6]

Over the years, Lisl and Win hired a series of talented young associates to work in the office. Among the mainstays were Martin Grady, Hargens, Robert James Sorensen, and Wally Wilcox.[7] Hargens became a principal and owner of Close Associates in 1980 and its sole owner eight years later. He continues to lead the practice today.

RESIDENTIAL DESIGN FUNDAMENTALS

Every Close-designed house was grounded in an understanding of its site's characteristics, realities, and potential, including topography, exposure, and opportunities for privacy and views. "The early work of the firm pioneered the contemporary approach to design, with emphasis on conservation of topography and trees, natural materials, blending of house and site," Lisl stated.[8] "The study of the site and of the relationship to the neighborhood has always been of much concern to us," explained Win. Based on their studies, they concluded there was room for improvement in the way house plans were conventionally designed. "The typical house at that time had a living room on the street side," he said. "Usually you entered directly into the living room. If there was a garage it was usually in the back with a long driveway to it . . . which made it inconvenient for access from the house. We thought there was a better way to use the site than that."[9]

Regarding entrance from the street side of the house, their solution was to design a modestly sized, dedicated entry that opened onto a larger living area toward the back of the residence. This allowed private yard and garden views from rooms where family members often congregated. Moving the garage closer to the street, or integrating it into the house, created more yard and garden space away from public view. Later in their careers, the Closes sent a survey to their clients asking what they liked best and least about their residences. "One [response] that was consistently favorable was the relationship of the house to the site. And that pleased us very much," Win said.[10]

The Closes preferred flat or shed roofs, as opposed to gabled roofs, for practical rather than stylistic reasons. Ice and water problems are "difficult to solve if you have intersecting gables on a roof," explained Win. Sometimes it was not easy to convince a client of the engineering logic behind a flat roof. "People don't believe it when you tell them that's the best roof," said Lisl. "Some don't like the shape, they want to see the shape of the roof as an expression of something." For many people, "it means shelter."[11] The Closes' decisions about materials were not always driven by their modern aesthetic. "I was interested in solving a problem, not being stylistic," Lisl explained.[12] Durability, attractiveness, ease of maintenance, and the ability to serve homeowners well in the long run were also prime considerations. Redwood exemplified those selection criteria. Like many architects of the time, the Closes appreciated the beauty and character of natural materials, especially clear, all-heart redwood, which was readily available and did not require painting. Although it was not inexpensive, "when you omit [the cost] of painting, that makes a difference," reasoned Lisl. "It made sense."

In Lisl's view, many traditional homes were "full of design errors," meaning they included architectural elements that fostered problems, such as gutters that trapped leaves and snow or shingles that loosened over time. For that reason, she shunned unnecessary additions, including decorative trim, ornamentation, and finishes that required upkeep. "That was to me, a starting point. To get rid of the problems. To start with something that is easy to live with," she said.[13]

At the same time, Lisl understood that an architect had to wrestle with many variables to achieve ease of living: "Architectural design must concern itself with heat and cold, water, snow and ice, with all the complex paraphernalia of modern life, underground connections, streets and utilities, with the obstreperous sometimes unpredictable behavior of materials and structures." She argued that "a successful design meets the functional requirements of a building in such a way that proportion, color, texture, visual and acoustical qualities work together to make a single entity."[14] She also knew that the process of architectural design was something of a mystery to the average person. In one of several articles Lisl wrote to demystify the architect–client relationship she said, "People generally don't know about architects, what they do, how they do it, whether their work is really valuable or merely expensive, or if the results of their labors should be classified as Real Estate or Art."[15] The big question many people asked themselves was whether they needed an architect to design their home and, if so, could they afford to hire one? "One use of an architect is to save money and avoid mistakes. . . . Construction is expensive and bad planning can be very costly." Conversely, "a well-designed house will return to its owner the cost of architectural services many times over. It will last longer, look younger and be more trouble free than most homes that are built without professional advice." She stated that the real question clients should ask about an architect's services is "can they afford to be without them?"

UNIVERSITY GROVE

As it had been before the war, the University of Minnesota was a fertile source of clients for the firm in the postwar years. Among those clients were more than a dozen faculty members who wanted to build houses in University Grove.

The Grove, an exceptional neighborhood of 103 single-family homes built on University of Minnesota–owned land in Falcon Heights, was established in 1928 when the university's vice president and comptroller William Middlebrook (a future Grove resident) set aside an attractive and conveniently located parcel of land for an academic housing village. The heavily treed, rolling landscape was within walking distance of the university's St. Paul campus and a streetcar ride away from the Minneapolis campus. The landscape architecture firm of Morrell & Nichols conceived the Grove's original master plan, which responded to the terrain's natural features. The plan rejected the grid and instead platted long blocks between curving streets and avenues, many of which were named for University of Minnesota presidents.[16] Reserved common areas at the center of the deep blocks provided community spaces for recreation and play. Middlebrook astutely reasoned that the appeal of the neighborhood and the advantages it offered would attract faculty to the university and convince them to stay.[17]

At University Grove, Middlebrook instituted a "leasehold arrangement" through which qualified members of the faculty and administration could build homes on land owned by the university. He instituted the leasehold system at the Grove after learning of a similar arrangement at Stanford University in Palo Alto, California.[18] The Grove's land lease required that an architect, rather than a builder or developer, design each new house. To keep prices affordable for its employees and to ensure residences were similarly sized, the university set a cap (which included the architect's fee) on the cost of house construction. The cap escalated over time from $10,000 in the 1920s and '30s, to $18,000 to $27,500 in the '40s and '50s, and $48,500 by 1970. Designs were subject to university approval—a responsibility Win assumed when he became the university's advisory architect.

Middlebrook commissioned the first house built in the Grove, a two-story Tudor designed in 1929 by architect William Ingemann.[19] In addition to Ingemann, many of the state's best-known architects and firms contributed one or more houses to the neighborhood, in a range of historic and modern styles, over the next four decades. Among them were Brooks Cavin, Rollin C. Chapin, Carl Graffunder, Roy Childs Jones, Francis Kerr, Liebenberg and Kaplan, Long and Thorshov, Edwin Lundie, Michael McGuire, Joseph Michels, Norman Nagle, Ralph Rapson, Rhodes Robertson, James Stageberg, Thorshov and Cerny, and Tom Van Housen. The Closes designed fifteen houses in the enclave—more than any other architect or firm—including their own residence completed in 1953.[20] Because multiple architects

Figure 5.3 The Philip and Maria Raup House (1953) is one of fifteen houses designed by the Closes in St. Paul's University Grove. Photograph by William B. Olexy.

Figure 5.4 Ralph Rapson was one of several architects who designed houses for University Grove. The William G. Shepherd House (1956) was his first modern house in the neighborhood. Photograph by William B. Olexy.

designed houses for the Grove over a forty-year period, the neighborhood contains residences in a wide range of styles — Colonial Revival, English Tudor, Bauhaus-inspired, International Style, modern, and California modern. The most unusual kind of house built in the Grove was the prefabricated Quonset hut, a cluster of which was erected in the 1940s to serve as married student housing for GIs returning to school after the war.[21] This diversity of styles prompted the *New York Times* to describe the unique neighborhood as "an architectural time capsule."[22]

The Closes began work on their first Grove house, a residence for Tracy F. Tyler, an associate professor of education at the university, in 1939. Their scheme for the Tyler House took advantage of its site's contours (on the corner of Fulham Street and Hoyt Avenue), which dropped fourteen feet in elevation from the back of the property to street level. Because they viewed mature trees as enhancements, not obstacles, they carefully sited the residence to preserve seven of the eight existing oak trees on the property. "Usually, we tried to orient houses so that the living areas got as much sunshine as possible in the winter and not too much in the summer, so we took advantage of shading devices and trees, particularly foliage," Lisl explained.[23] Their solution for the Tylers was a flat-roof, two-story, three-bedroom house with a tuck-under garage (Plate 11). The exterior was sheathed in brick and horizontal redwood siding on the first floor, and vertical board and batten redwood on the upper level. It was built for $13,000, which included the Closes' 7 percent fee of $850.

The Closes specified birch plywood, brick, and Homasote as primary interior finishes. They experimented with subtle ways to modulate space and bring daylight into rooms. For example, a partial-height wall with built-in seating divides the living room from the entry and provides a measure of privacy. Three sections of translucent panels of glass in the upper portion of the wall allow daylight to enter the living room (Plate 12). In the kitchen and eating area of the house, a full-height glass block wall adds visual interest and daylight in that area. In-ceiling, soffit, and light-shelf lighting was also specified. In addition to built-in seating near the fireplace, a sixteen-foot-long, built-in sideboard runs the width of the east end of the living room. One space-saving feature in the kitchen, a drop-down counter, was lost in a subsequent renovation.

By 1953 Win's faculty and administrative positions at the university had made the Close family, which now included son Bob, born in 1948, eligible to build a home in the Grove. Initially, the Closes were not eager to become Grove residents. "We were very suspicious of it at the start," Lisl said, referring to the restrictive selection criteria for residents. "We thought it might be a company town. It wasn't. It was a very good neighborhood and a very successful one."[24]

Like the Tyler House, the two-story Close House was built into a sloped site on Fulham Street. Because the land rose toward the back of the lot, main living areas were placed on the second floor of the house. As they had done on many of their projects, the Closes wrapped the exterior of the house in redwood siding, which served visually to anchor the house to its wooded site. A horizontal trellis above the entry, which spanned the width of the facade, animated the rectilinear geometry of the house, as did strip windows and a deep roof overhang above the second floor. The ground level comprised a garage, entry, work area, and a space-saving spiral staircase that led to upper-level living spaces. The living room opened onto a private patio behind the house, and wooded community space beyond. *Maya,* a sculpture by prominent Minnesota artist John Rood, for whom the Closes designed a house in 1947, stood in the garden.[25]

Initially, because they were their own clients, the Closes did not think it would be necessary to fill out the same questionnaire of needs, wants, and possessions they required all their clients to complete. "We discovered that was not so," Lisl recalled. The four-bedroom house abounded in practical and cleverly designed elements: an efficient galley kitchen — Lisl did not cook but Esther Bogren, the family's live-in housekeeper, did (Plate 13); Masonite panels used for sliding cabinet doors; built-ins; a storage system for sheet music and art; and a wall-hung vanity that folded away when not in use. Strategically placed skylights infused inner rooms with daylight.[26]

Figure 5.5 In 1953 Lisl and Win Close designed a residence for their family in University Grove. Photograph by William B. Olexy.

The design also included a few elements that gestured to the Loos-designed Scheu House in Vienna, including ample warm wood paneling and a window nook with built-in banquette in the living room that bore a striking resemblance to one in Lisl's childhood home (Plate 14). Other references included the Bechstein grand piano from that house, on which she and her father once played "four-hand," and a 1916 pencil portrait of architect Adolf Loos by Austrian artist Oskar Kokoschka, both of which traveled from the Scheu House in Vienna to the Close House in University Grove.[27]

Win, a talented craftsman, designed numerous pieces of furniture for the house in a variety of materials: he "had a leather phase, a metal phase, and a Plexiglas phase," Lisl said.[28] His designs included several chairs, footstools, beds, end and corner tables, and a dining room table fashioned from a solid-core birch door supported by steel legs. He also fashioned a minimal metal railing, wrapped in clear Plexiglas, to keep children and dogs from tumbling down the spiral staircase while not obstructing view. The Close House was among Lisl's favorite projects for eminently practical reasons: "It's lasted a long time and it's easy to maintain." Ultimately, it suited the Closes well; members of the family lived in it for more than sixty years.[29]

Conceptually, the Wolf House (1959) was perhaps the most unusual Close-designed house in the Grove. It was created for John B. Wolf, a professor of European history at the University of Minnesota, and his wife Theta, a psychology professor at Hamline University in St. Paul. The couple requested a house that had "an appropriate balance between spaciousness and shelter" and provided "an effective background for painting and sculpture." Both John and Theta required a "pleasant study with plenty of work space and book shelves." The Wolfs were in Paris on sabbatical during the

Figure 5.6 A space-saving spiral staircase rose from the ground floor to upper-level living areas. Clear Plexiglas was used for its nearly invisible railing system on the upper floor. Photograph by Jane King Hession.

Figure 5.7 The Close family in the living room of their University Grove home in 1954. Back row from left: Winston, Bob, Roy, Lisl. Front row: Anne and Till Eulenspiegel. Courtesy of Roy M. Close Family Papers.

Figure 5.8 The John and Theta Wolf House (1959) in University Grove. Lisl designed the house and supervised its construction while the Wolfs were in Europe on sabbatical. Gar Hargens/Close Associates and Close Associates Papers (N78), Northwest Architectural Archives, University of Minnesota Libraries, Minneapolis.

planning and construction of the house. For that reason, most of the necessary discussions and negotiations about the project unfolded in letters between architect and clients; it was a laborious enterprise whose challenges cannot be fully appreciated in today's world of instant international communication.[30]

According to the Wolf House design statement, the "limitations of the site," which was one block deep and sandwiched between Burton Street to the west and Coffman Street to the east, "suggested an 'introverted' house." Lisl's response was to modernize an ancient typology: the Roman atrium house. She envisioned a residence "somewhat similar to houses in Pompeii," referring to the courtyard houses built in that Roman city prior to its destruction by a volcanic eruption of Mount Vesuvius in AD 79. Like its historic forerunner, the two-story courtyard at the heart of the Wolf House was both protected from public view and a center for private life and activity. But unlike the earlier Roman houses that were open to the sky, the atrium of the Wolf House required a roof to protect it from Minnesota's climate extremes. Lisl chose the courtyard model not for historic or stylistic reasons but because it solved a problem as effectively in 1959 as it had in an earlier millennium.

The open court on the ground level of the Wolf House was surrounded on three sides by studies for John and Theta, laundry and utility rooms, and a garage. An open-tread staircase connected the two levels of the house. The upper floor consisted of a living room, which overlooked the courtyard, a kitchen, and a dining room. A "bridge" at the top of the stairs linked living areas to two bedrooms

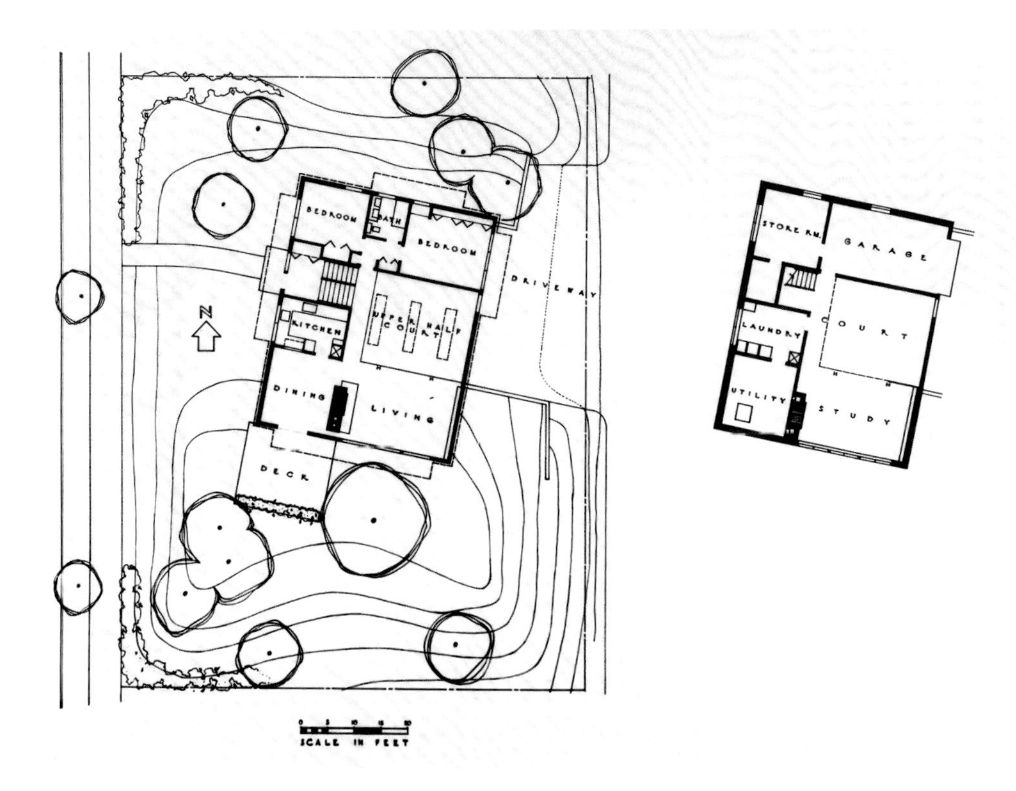

Figure 5.9 As the Wolf House floor plans show, rooms in the residence pinwheel around a two-story atrium. Close Associates Papers (N78), Northwest Architectural Archives, University of Minnesota Libraries, Minneapolis.

Figure 5.10 The two-story atrium space of the Wolf House, circa 1960. A bridge connects upper-level living areas to bedrooms. Close Associates Papers (N78), Northwest Architectural Archives, University of Minnesota Libraries, Minneapolis.

opposite
Figure 5.11 The living room of the Wolf House, circa 1960. A railing, constructed of hollow core doors installed horizontally, cordons off the upper level from the two-story atrium. Close Associates Papers (N78), Northwest Architectural Archives, University of Minnesota Libraries, Minneapolis.

and a bath. Lisl, who excelled at finding unconventional uses for conventional materials, incorporated hollow core doors, installed horizontally, into a railing system on the second floor above the atrium.[31] Daylight entered the house through three long rectangular "skydomes" in the ceiling of the soaring atrium, below which hung a plane of translucent plastic panels that softened and diffused the light.[32] At the Wolfs' request, supplemental electric lighting was also installed in the ceiling. Of the physically challenging task of replacing lightbulbs eighteen feet above the floor, John Wolf vowed "to find a way to service them if I have to learn to fly."[33] When they returned to Minnesota and their newly completed home, the Wolfs thanked Lisl for creating "a thing of beauty and comfort and usefulness and personal satisfaction for us, and, I suspect, for other faculty members who will live there after all of us have gone."[34]

In 1966 the Wolfs left Minnesota for the University of Illinois in Chicago, where both held faculty positions. Subsequent owners of the house included Kenneth Keller, a professor of chemical engineering, who would serve as the University of Minnesota's twelfth president from 1985 to 1988. Pauline Boss, a family psychologist and a professor of family social science at the university, and her husband Dudley Riggs, an improvisational comedian and founder of Minnesota's famed Brave New Workshop, bought the house in 1988 and lived there for more than twenty years.[35] When Boss's doctor recommended she swim to alleviate a back problem—and at the same time Riggs wanted to upgrade their garage—the couple asked the Closes, who had retired by then, to design an indoor pool and a two-car garage. "They came out of retirement for us and we were delighted because we wanted the house to remain a Close house and so it did," said Boss.[36] In what Riggs described as a "separate but equal" division of labor, Win designed the garage, and Lisl—who had researched pool design for her graduate thesis at MIT—planned the pool. She proposed digging a "pool spa" underneath an existing outdoor deck, and rebuilding the deck on top of the room. To retain the illusion that the deck "floated," a feature that originally attracted Riggs to the house, Lisl encircled the top of the sunken pool room with a band of windows placed under the

edge of the deck. So seamless was the addition that "a lot of people in the neighborhood don't even know the pool is there," said Riggs.[37]

Although the Closes were helpful in adapting the house to the specific needs of the couple, Riggs required no outside assistance with one aspect of home upkeep. Unlike Wolf, he did not need "to learn to fly" to change the lightbulbs in the ceiling of the two-story atrium; he already knew how. His early training and world travels as a circus aerialist uniquely qualified him for the acrobatic task.

MODERN HOUSE DESIGNS FOR A NATIONAL MARKET

The Closes never advertised their services. But beginning in the late 1940s, the firm's residential work generated unsolicited press that proved useful in raising its profile both locally and nationally. Unlike features in magazines for the architecture profession that selected projects (such as Skywater or the Interstate Clinic) for their singularity, many trade and general interest publications showcased residential projects for their consumer appeal, livability, and availability. Like many firms in step with the times and doing work that resonated with modern American lifestyles, the Close firm was included in and benefited from such exposure. For example, in 1949 Hedrich-Blessing photographs of a three-level, 1,970-square-foot, Close-designed house in Minneapolis appeared in the "Small Homes Review Issue" of *Popular Homes Magazine*, a publication of the United States Gypsum Company. As was noted of most of the homes featured in the magazine, blueprints for the Close house were available for purchase.[38]

Museums were also beginning to view modern residential design as a subject worthy of serious study. The Walker Art Center in Minneapolis, which at the time identified itself as "a progressive museum of the arts," was one of the first art institutions in the country to explore the topic in depth.[39] At midcentury, Lisl and her firm were invited to take part in two of the museum's most forward-thinking—and well-publicized—shows.

In 1947 the Closes were among five Twin Cities architects and firms invited by the Walker to participate in the Idea House Project, part of the museum's broader initiative to "educate the middle-class consumer about the advantages and availability of modern design."[40] Then Walker director Daniel S. Defenbacher conceived the program in 1941 when Idea House I, a full-scale demonstration house designed by University of Minnesota graduates Malcolm Lein and Miriam Lein, was constructed on land adjacent to the Walker. The exhibition house, the first of its kind in the United States, allowed visitors to experience new ideas in architecture by moving through a model structure.[41] Six years later, during the postwar housing boom, the Walker revisited the concept and built Idea House II, designed by William Friedman, a trained architect and then the museum's director of exhibitions, and Hilde Reiss, the founding curator of the Everyday Art Gallery and first editor of the *Everyday Art Quarterly*. The modern split-level demonstration house was "more aggressive in its modernism" than its predecessor and "offered a prescient glimpse of what would become a dominant style of contemporary housing in the United States."[42] The house was accompanied by *Designs for Idea Houses III through VIII*, an exhibition held in the museum's Everyday Art Gallery of plans and models created by the Close firm and other project participants.[43] Each contributor was assigned the task of designing a contemporary house for hypothetical clients, whose conjectured needs, interests, and budgets were specified in problem statements. Houses were to be "designed for standard construction with readily available materials."[44] Lisl was charged with the design of a $15,000 to $20,000 house for a couple with two children and a live-in mother-in-law. Special requirements of the family, whose hobby was gardening, included a guest room and a garage. It is not known if the German-born Reiss and Lisl knew about each other prior to the exhibition, but the two women shared similar backgrounds and training. Reiss began her architectural studies at the Technical University in the Charlottenburg district of Berlin and received a diploma from the Bauhaus in Dessau in 1932. She immigrated to New York in 1933, the year after Lisl arrived in Boston.[45]

The Idea House II project was ultimately featured in a range of local and national publications, including the Walker Art Center's *Everyday Art Quarterly*, the *New York Times Magazine, Progressive*

Figure 5.12 Architectural models from the 1947 exhibit *Designs for Idea Houses III through VIII* in the Everyday Art Gallery at the Walker Art Center in Minneapolis. Elizabeth and Winston Close, Architects, was one of six firms invited to participate in the show. Rolphe Dauphin for Walker Art Center.

Figure 5.13 Idea House model by Elizabeth and Winston Close, Architects, 1947. Close Associates Papers (N78), Northwest Architectural Archives, University of Minnesota Libraries, Minneapolis.

Architecture, and *McCall's* magazine.[46] Defenbacher attempted to interest *McCall's* in a related "venture" to build all six houses "on one large site as a Walker Art Center project," to be accompanied by a "sizable monograph" on the houses. He acknowledged the enormity of his proposal and noted that while publishing a monograph was "normal procedure" for the museum, "speculating in house building and real estate is not." He claimed to be "deeply interested in carrying it through" and reasoned it made sense for the Walker to "actually build houses rather than merely talk about them." Above all, he believed there was no institution more qualified to do so: "Our leadership in the industrial domestic and design field makes us the logical American museum to carry out this project."[47]

The six houses, plus two additional architect-designed prefabricated houses, were to be built in the Glendale addition to the Tyrol Hills neighborhood in Golden Valley, Minnesota. The Walker hoped to begin construction in the spring of 1948 with financing from the Home Institute of Northwestern National Bank and to sell the houses following their public exhibition.[48] Sadly, none of the modern houses in this unique and visionary proposed collaboration among a design museum, the architectural community, and the construction and real estate industries were built, nor was the anticipated monograph published.[49] According to Andrew Blauvelt, curator of the 2000 exhibition *Ideas for Modern Living: The Idea House Project and Everyday Art Gallery*, had it been realized, "the neighborhood would have been one of the earliest modern suburban developments in the country."[50]

In 1952 the Close firm participated in a second exhibition at the Everyday Art Gallery. *The Architects' Workshop* featured drawings, models, and photographs of houses by nine local architects and firms, including Gerald Buetow, Brooks Cavin, Carl Graffunder, Myron Kehne, Norman Nagle, Harlan McClure and Francis Kerr, and Thorshov and Cerny. In a companion essay published in *Everyday Art Quarterly*, historian Donald R. Torbert wrote of the exhibited houses: "Buildings like those now published by the Walker Art Center can function as guideposts that point to the possibility of a finer urban environment than we have yet developed."[51]

The word "workshop" was included in the title of the show to suggest it was "both an exhibition and a program," as well as "a forum of [public] opinion, and a means of airing attitudes that go into the creation of a product."[52] The "product" in this case was modern architecture, about which the Walker hoped to clear up "existing confusion" through the exhibition and two museum-sponsored clinics led by participating architects. Norman Nagle, Walker curator of design and architecture, led a session on building, and Lisl and Win presented the clinic on house remodeling. Win used the forum to discuss the advantages and disadvantages of purchasing a "big, old house," while Lisl described ways in which design could make an old house more livable, efficient, and functional for modern lifestyles. Although her suggested renovations, such as "knocking out the colonnade between dining and living rooms, taking out the butler's pantry and using the space as a breakfast area," would not be unusual today, they were pushing the envelope in the early 1950s.[53]

Five years later, *House & Home* magazine selected a prototype house designed by Lisl as one of "57 Houses for a Better '57." The stated single purpose of the article, which featured selected custom and tract homes from around the country, was to offer readers "the quality of design, the economy of construction, the ease and graciousness of living, that will make the new houses of '57 irresistible."[54] Lisl's contribution was a 1,725-square-foot, three-bedroom house with carport created for the Hayes-Winston Company. The featured house was constructed in 1956 in Garden City, a 700-acre, mixed-use, planned community in Brooklyn Park, Minnesota. Coincidentally, Win did the site planning for the project on behalf of the University of Minnesota, which at one point owned the land.[55] *House & Home* selected Lisl's design for a pair of ideas that "make this two-story house a Minnesota pioneer." The article claimed the split-level house was "the first two-story tract house of its kind in the Minneapolis area" to feature cost-saving "below-ground-level space" housing the kitchen, dining, and family rooms. "The second new idea the house introduces to Minneapolis is the use of a glue-nailed truss in a second-story house," the prefabrication of which saved

Figure 5.14 In 1949 *Popular Homes Magazine*'s "Small Home Review Issue" published plans for this house as built for the Dalzell family of Minneapolis. Blueprints were available for purchase. HB-11522-B, Chicago History Museum, Hedrich-Blessing Collection.

Figure 5.15 In 1964 Lisl designed the "Atrium Contemporary," a prefabricated house for national distribution for the Weyerhaeuser Company. Seen here as built in Lawton, Oklahoma. Photograph by O. Philip Roedel. Close Associates Papers (N78), Northwest Architectural Archives, University of Minnesota Libraries, Minneapolis.

lumber and controlled costs. In addition to the split-level house featured in the magazine, Lisl designed six additional "attractive and distinctive models" for Garden City.[56]

In 1964 Lisl was commissioned to design a prefabricated house for national distribution that was promoted in both trade and popular magazines. That year the Tacoma-based Weyerhaeuser Company was the nation's largest producer of lumber, but sales were declining. To "reverse the ten-year trend of diminishing profits" and to "keep the homebuilding market for the forest industries," the company established the Registered Homes program.[57] The idea behind the initiative was to work directly with retail lumber dealers to produce "simple component-construction system" houses to be nationally marketed to builders and consumers. To make the program more attractive, Weyerhaeuser spearheaded marketing efforts and offered both financing plans and twenty-year warranties on its wood products.[58] The goal was to give the lumber dealer "a more profitable role in homebuilding by helping him become an efficient prefabricator and a strong merchandiser," which would also mean greater profits for Weyerhaeuser.[59]

To create designs that would appeal to regional builders and buyers across the United States, Weyerhaeuser hired a group of architects to produce sixty varied house plans, each under 2,200 square feet.[60] With more than two decades of experience designing prefabricated houses, Lisl was well qualified for the job. As an example of the kind of house they were looking for, the architectural coordinator for the Registered Homes program referred Lisl to a modern house designed by the California-based firm of Jones & Emmons for Eichler Homes that had appeared in *Sunset* magazine.[61]

Lisl responded by designing a one-level contemporary with a low-slope roof and a cost-saving "compact mechanical core."[62] The defining feature of the house, which was planned for jig fabrication by the lumber dealer, was an outdoor atrium wrapped on three sides by interior rooms and a one-car garage (Plates 15 and 16). A wood grille screened the courtyard from the street. Weyerhaeuser branded the house the "Atrium Contemporary" and promoted it as being "designed especially for the Southwest."[63]

Although it was intended for warm-weather living, the 1,206-square-foot (not including garage or courtyard), air-conditioned house proved attractive to builders in other regions. In September 1965, *House & Home* featured the three-bedroom house as built in Lawton, Oklahoma, by the Currell Lumber Company, one of fifty-seven lumber dealers participating in the program. It further stated that Currell had introduced the house as the sales model for a fifty-lot subdivision it was developing.[64] Promotional material stressed the unique relationship between the interior and the private garden court around which it wrapped, as well as its clean lines, flexible plan, beamed ceilings, clerestory windows, and integrated lighting. The house was available in five color schemes and with several "furnishing schedules." One versatile feature Lisl suggested—a retractable cover over the atrium—was not included in the final design.[65]

In addition to marketing the house to the building trade, Weyerhaeuser advertised it directly to consumers, including "6-million potential home buyers—the readers of *Good Housekeeping* magazine."[66] In October 1965 that women's magazine published a ten-page, lavishly illustrated spread in vivid 1960s-era color on the Lawton contemporary atrium. It found the residence to be ideal for the busy American family and added, "Because the house is thoughtfully planned, it runs smoothly even at the fast pace of modern life."[67]

WORKING WITH THE SITE

Unlike the prototype tract houses she designed for Garden City or the prefabricated atrium house for Weyerhaeuser that were intentionally designed to be adaptable to many lots and locations, most of Lisl's work was site specific. Perhaps because of the firm's solid reputation for the sensitive integration of a house with its site, clients often approached Lisl with spectacular and/or potentially difficult lots. As someone who viewed the design of a house as a complex puzzle to be solved, she welcomed the challenges. To realize the full potential of a site, she often consulted with landscape architects—Herb Baldwin, Roger Martin, and, later, her son Bob Close among them—and valued their complementary skills and knowledge. "They were very important and lined up right away," said Hargens. "There was never just foundation planting at the end of the job."[68]

One of the trickiest sites the firm encountered also came with a unique building program—a double house for two families. The Arthur Naftalin (a future mayor of Minneapolis) and A. Boyd Thomes (a physician) families bought adjoining properties with lofty city views for the affordable price of back taxes owed. But the lots they purchased in the hilly Prospect Park neighborhood of Minneapolis were extremely steep. The solution was an eight-floor, split-level structure, completed in 1948, that was built into the incline; the Naftalins occupied the four lower floors and the Thomeses the four upper floors. Each residence featured a layout uniquely suited to its occupants, but both utilized the same carpeting, woodwork, cabinetry, and drapery, which resulted in cost savings. Dark shingles and yellow trim unified the exteriors of the double house.[69] The unusual nature of the project piqued the interest of the press; photographs of it appeared in several local newspapers. Almost seventy years after the residence was constructed, new owners of one half of the house hired Hargens and Close Associates to renovate living areas and add a sheltered outdoor deck, from which enhanced views of the Minneapolis skyline can now be enjoyed.

In 1947 John and Dorothy Rood possessed one of the most impressive lots in Minneapolis: a one-acre, sloping site on Lowry Hill that fell off precipitously to the east and offered enviable views of the city beyond. They also had an ambitious building program for their new residence. In addition to living and sleeping quarters for the couple, guests, and two servants, requirements included a gallery for their contemporary art collection and a studio and workshop for John Rood, a noted sculptor. The socially well-connected Roods also requested entertaining space for "various types of parties from supper for four to cocktails for three hundred" and landscaped outdoor spaces, including "terraces, grass courts, and settings for outdoor sculpture at various scales."[70] An extant stone retaining wall and carriage house, once part of Minneapolis developer Thomas Lowry's estate, were to be incorporated into the design. Architect Rhodes Robertson collaborated with the Closes on the project.

Entry to the house on Dupont Avenue South was via a paved automobile court, in the center of which stood a large, circular fountain. The main two-story, L-shaped portion of the house, which wrapped around the court, comprised living and dining rooms, a large kitchen and pantry, and accommodations for two maids on the ground floor. Upstairs, an owner's suite, consisting of two bedrooms, dressing rooms, a sitting room, and deck were in the larger of the two wings, and guest quarters and a sewing room in the smaller. On the ground level, a central hallway with flagstone flooring stepped down to the living room and extended outdoors to a terrace on the north. To the west, it continued from the main house to become a long, curved gallery. One wall of the gallery allowed for the display of art, while the other side featured an expanse of glass, access to an outdoor sculpture court, and views. The curve of the gallery played off an existing curved stone wall that defined the outdoor sculpture court. The gallery also served to connect the house to the stone stable, which was converted into a spacious studio for Rood. Several of Rood's artworks were displayed on the property. The Closes, who admired Rood's work, accepted *Jeremiah*, a sculpture carved in lignum vitae, as part of their fee.[71] In 2014 architect James Dayton renovated and updated the house for new owners—a family with four children—but did so in the spirit of the original design.[72] "The spaces are scaled well and flow just right," Dayton said. "It's done in a very sensitive and subtle way that you don't often see in contemporary construction."[73]

In the early 1960s, Lisl took on the challenge of designing a house for an "impossible" site for Hendrik J. Oskam, a University of Minnesota physicist, and his wife, Marri.[74] Shortly after they moved from their native Holland to Minneapolis in 1958, the Oskams were introduced to the Closes' architecture as guests in the home of fellow Netherlanders Willem and Willemina Luyten. For this reason, when it was time to design their own residence they asked Lisl to be their architect. Marri had grown up in a fourteen-room Jugendstil house near Utrecht, but she and Hendrik had no children and did not want to build a large or traditional house. Instead, they

Figure 5.16 The John and Dorothy Rood House (1947) on Lowry Hill in Minneapolis. HB-14358-A, Chicago History Museum, Hedrich-Blessing Collection.

Figure 5.17 View from the terrace of the Rood House to Rood's studio. HB-14358-F, Chicago History Museum, Hedrich-Blessing Collection.

Figure 5.18 View from the Rood studio, along the gallery, to the main house. HB-14358-C, Chicago History Museum, Hedrich-Blessing Collection.

desired a comfortable modern house with a feeling of "space and light," she explained.[75]

Their chosen lot was a steeply sloped, heavily wooded piece of land on Indianhead Lake in Edina. Because of its location (well below Dakota Trail, a main road in what is now the Indian Hills neighborhood), it presented both design and access issues. The Oskams adamantly resisted bulldozing or flattening the site: "Filling would kill the land," said Hendrik.[76] Therefore, it was necessary to install 198 treated cedar poles to retain the precipitous land on either side of the long entry drive and garage.[77] From the drive, a flight of steps led farther down the hill to the two-story, walk-out house and a "dog's suite" for the couple's Irish setter.

The plan of the 1,731-square-foot house, completed in 1964, was somewhat unorthodox but perfectly suited to the couple's needs. Except for an enclosed kitchen and bathroom, the entry level of the house was completely open—no walls divided the dining area, living room, and Hendrik's study/library. In the center of that floor, an open stair led down to two bedrooms, utilities, and an outdoor terrace on the lower level. The butterfly roof that rose on the lake side of the house framed large stretches of glass and views to the water. Access to the upper-level deck and lower-level patio was through a pair of sliding glass doors produced by the Andersen Corporation of Bayport, Minnesota. The doors (and the Oskams' Irish setter) appeared in a national advertisement for the company that was published in *Newsweek* magazine in 1970.[78]

The materials used on the interior of the house reflected the architect's and clients' shared modern design preferences and European roots. They employed glazed Dutch brick for hall and kitchen flooring, the fireplace, and terrace, and natural redwood for the beamed ceiling. According to Marri, Lisl "loved what we did with the house in the way of furniture; obeying the architecture instead of having great big pieces or whatever you wanted in the

Figure 5.19 The Rood House gallery, featuring art by John Rood. HB-14358-K, Chicago History Museum, Hedrich-Blessing Collection.

house" (Plate 17). However, "it was very difficult at that time" to find modern lighting and furniture, she said. Most of it was sourced through Barrett Pohl, a store in Dinkytown near the University of Minnesota that once sold modern home furnishings.[79]

Lisl chose redwood boards to sheath the exterior of the house. Unconventionally, she had the vertical siding installed "wrong side out" because she liked the textural, long grooving that was produced on that side during the milling process. She would employ this technique on other houses, too (Plate 18).

The Oskams lived together in the house until Hendrik's death in 2001. In 2015, fearing the escalating value of land in her neighborhood could put her house at risk of being a teardown, Marri led a successful campaign to have it designated an Edina Heritage Landmark. As the only modern house among eleven protected properties in that city, it is recognized as "one of the outstanding residential examples of the International Style in the Twin Cities area" and as a significant work by Elizabeth Close, "an influential force in regional architecture [whose work is] demonstrably

Figure 5.20 The Hendrik and Marri Oskam House (1962) in Edina, Minnesota, had a steep building site that was characterized as "impossible." Photograph by William B. Olexy.

Figure 5.21 The open plan of the upper level of the Oskam House included a living room, kitchen, dining area, study, and bathroom. Sliding doors at right open on a deck with lake views. Photograph by William B. Olexy.

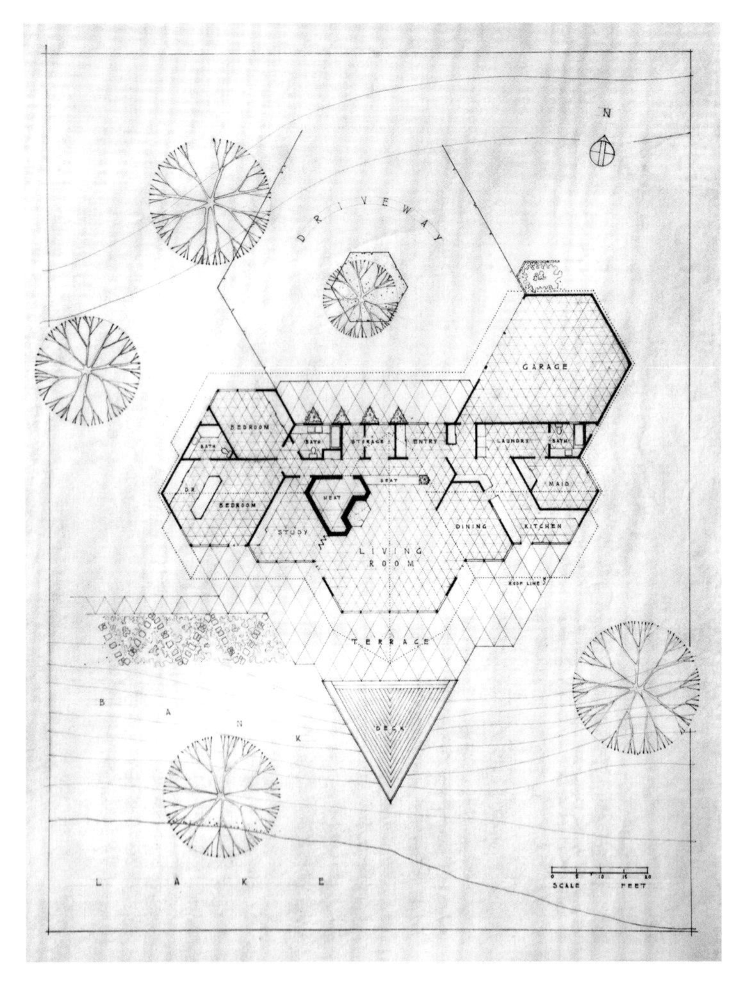

Figure 5.22 Philip and Helen Duff requested their house be planned with nonrectilinear geometry, as evidenced in the floor plan. Courtesy Gar Hargens/Close Associates and Close Associates Papers (N78), Northwest Architectural Archives, University of Minnesota Libraries, Minneapolis.

important in women's history and architectural history."[80] Marri believes today, perhaps more than ever, Lisl's smart, efficient design for the house has valuable lessons to teach. "You don't have to own an enormous house in order to have it spacious in feeling and comfortable. A small house can be very practical and pleasant."[81]

In 1955, when Philip and Helen Duff decided to build a retirement home, they chose a sylvan, multiacre lot on Lake Marion in Wayzata, Minnesota. The Duffs, who were friends of the Closes, knew they wanted a one-story house that was easy to maintain. They also desired access to terrace and garden areas and a guesthouse for visitors, including their six grown children and grandchildren. The couple specifically requested that "non-rectilinear geometry" be used to generate the design. According to Gar Hargens, the Duffs knew the Closes and their architecture well enough to ask, "Can you do something special with the grid?"—referring to the underlying geometry on which plans were often based. "And so, they skewed it. It's a diamond grid, which gives the house all sorts of wonderful angles," Hargens explained.

As built, the house comprised two bedrooms, three baths, living and dining rooms, a study, kitchen, maid's quarters, and a two-car garage. The dynamic roof, which is composed of flat, shed, and low-slope gable portions, animates both the exterior and interior spaces of the house. "There is a spirit to it that's just hard to get in a flat-roofed, more conventional modernist Close project," said Hargens. As they often did, the Closes used a generous amount of redwood in the house and utilized Flexi-core precast concrete slabs over a crawlspace "to distribute in the core the heating and cooling" systems for the house, he added. The living room, which stood at the heart of the house, had a massive, Crab Orchard stone fireplace and flagstone floors, built-ins, and a glass wall on the marsh and lake side of the room, as well as access to a stone terrace and triangular deck.[82]

In addition to providing architectural services, the firm was asked by the Duffs—as it was by many clients—to design interiors and secure suitable modern furnishings, lighting, fabrics, and other

Figure 5.23 The Philip and Helen Duff House (1955) on Lake Marion in Wayzata, Minnesota, received an AIA Minnesota 25-Year Award in 1989. The house was demolished in 2012. Photograph by George Miles Ryan Studios, Inc. Courtesy of Gar Hargens/Close Associates and Close Associates Papers (N78), Northwest Architectural Archives, University of Minnesota Libraries, Minneapolis.

Figure 5.24 Crab Orchard stone was used to construct the massive fireplace surround in the living room of the Duff House. Photograph by George Miles Ryan Studios Inc. Courtesy Gar Hargens/Close Associates and Close Associates Papers (N78), Northwest Architectural Archives, University of Minnesota Libraries, Minneapolis.

opposite
Figure 5.25 In 1948 Lisl designed a house for Dr. Ruth Boynton and Prudence Cutright in Bloomington, Minnesota. Boynton was director of the Student Health Service at the University of Minnesota. Photograph by Lucian H. Brown. Close Associates Papers (N78), Northwest Architectural Archives, University of Minnesota Libraries, Minneapolis.

decorative items. "Lisl would always say, make it warm, make it comfortable, and she was very, very sensitive to which fabric to use. . . . She was very good with color," said Hargens.[83] Owing to the limited number of companies in Minnesota that served the modern design market, these items were principally sourced from now legendary midcentury creative talents who had showrooms in New York and other U.S. cities. Furnishings for the Duff house were purchased from Jens Risom Design, Dan Cooper Design, F. Schumacher & Co., Knoll Associates, and Herman Miller. Other sources Lisl frequently tapped were Jack Lenor Larsen, Charles Stendig, Baldwin Kingrey, and Design Imports.

The Duff House was one of the firm's most celebrated projects. It received an Honor Award honorable mention from the Minnesota Society of the American Institute of Architects (now AIA Minnesota) in 1959. The project also earned the firm its only AIA Minnesota 25-Year Award, given by that organization for "the best of Minnesota architecture built a quarter-century ago." The judges noted that "the design is resolved at each level from the siting to the window mullions. It does everything: modulates the views and absorbs the landscape. The outcome is fresh and wonderful."[84] A write-up for the award observed the house was designed to improve with age: "The redwood cladding has softened in hue as the landscape has matured in anticipating the Organic ideal whereby building perimeter and environment embrace creating the single perfect composition."[85] In Hargens's view, the Duff House was "a masterpiece."[86]

The house would not survive another twenty-five years. The property was put on the market in 2012, and the house and guest-house were demolished for new construction. In an increasingly prevalent preservation conundrum, the fate of the Duff House—and many other architecturally significant properties in Minnesota and across the country—was sealed by the continuing allure of the very site that inspired its design in the first place.

During the 1950s, '60s, and '70s, the firm designed scores of finely crafted houses in Minnesota and beyond. The Closes credit their success and enjoyment of their work, in part, to the people who sought their services, including many high-profile individuals.

Figure 5.26 The Paul Dennison House (1950) in Edina's Rolling Green neighborhood was designed for the president of the Minnesota Rubber and Gasket Company. The large two-story, L-shaped house had five bedrooms and a three-car garage and was sheathed in stone and striated wood. It was demolished in 1990. Close Associates Papers (N78), Northwest Architectural Archives, University of Minnesota Libraries, Minneapolis.

Figure 5.27 The Gove and Elsie Hambidge House (1958), Roseville, Minnesota. The 4,700-square-foot house was set low in its heavily treed site to screen it from view and noise from a nearby highway. Photograph by Walter Zambino. Close Associates Papers (N78), Northwest Architectural Archives, University of Minnesota Libraries, Minneapolis.

"Our clients were people who were interested in architecture and knew enough about it to make it fun," said Lisl.[87] They included: Jason and Lorentina Quist (1947, Edina, Plate 19); Dr. Ruth Boynton and Prudence Cutright (1948, Bloomington); Howard and Ruth Brin (1948, Minneapolis); Bruce Dayton (1949, Excelsior); Paul Dennison (1950, Edina); Lyndon King (1950, Minneapolis); Elmer and Eleanor Andersen (1956, Deer Lake); James and Plina Bennett (1956, Wayzata); Wallace and Mary Lee Dayton (1956, Shorewood); Marion and Robert Fry (1956, St. Paul, Plates 20 and 21); Dr. Gove and Elsie Hambidge (1958, Roseville, Plate 22); Dr. Harold and Ingeborg Ulvestad (1959, Edina); Jared and Catherine How (1966, Mankato); Bruce and Martha Atwater (1970, Wayzata); Conley and Marney Brooks (1976, Long Lake); and Stanley and Karen Hubbard (1981, St. Marys Point).

HOUSES ON WHEELS

Lisl enjoyed house design because it presented a variety of challenges. Until 1968, all the homes she designed had at least one thing in common: they were built to stay in one place. When the Iseman Corporation of Sioux Falls, South Dakota, asked her to create a series of prototypes for factory-built mobile homes, she found herself in new territory.

In 1920 Charles Iseman founded the Sioux Tire and Battery Company. Some years later, when he noticed cars were making Americans increasingly mobile, he "recognized the need for portable quality housing for people on the move." To capitalize on this opportunity, he changed the focus of his business to the sale and production of mobile homes.[88] In 1968 the company offered Lisl an initial investment of five hundred dollars to develop "mobile home floor plans, exterior design, and/or any other creative ideas you might have which you feel would be of benefit to us."[89] Company president Lloyd L. Reaves was looking for innovative concepts, but he didn't offer her much direction: "I really don't know what I had in mind other than I am searching for new ideas." Likening his pursuit to finding the next "Mustang just around the corner," referencing the Ford Motor Company's then wildly popular car, he wrote, "I want to discover it before the competition does."[90]

A little over two weeks later, Lisl responded with ten drawings of "various possibilities." The studies, she explained, "attempt to express the mobile homes as permanent structures rather than trailers. . . . They contribute a modern residential character."[91] Noting that most mobile home communities lacked effective site planning, she added, "There is no reason why the estates should not offer the same degree of amenity as any well planned residential community."

The designs ranged from efficiency units to a one-bedroom home with a shed roof to a four-bedroom, four-section house. A one-piece vacation house and a motel unit were also proposed. For each design, she calculated the truck-bed size required for shipping. For cost and efficiency reasons, she recommended that "conventional materials be used until better ones are developed." Lisl proposed striated plywood, offered in multiple colors, for exterior walls and stained plywood for interior surfaces. "We have not tried to design the cheapest possible units, but rather to explore arrangements which could provide greater amenity, thus increasing the appeal of mobile homes and their market potential," she added. Unfortunately, the project never gained traction.

HOUSING

Lisl began her professional career working on public housing, and her interest in multiple-family projects never waned. Although the firm's first efforts in the 1930s to design housing, notably University Terrace and "Trotsky Heights," were unrealized, it successfully completed several projects in later decades.

Golden Age Housing in Minneapolis was designed for the Minneapolis Housing and Redevelopment Authority in 1959. The low-rent, public housing project consisted of twenty-four apartments for seniors. To humanize the scale of the building, units were massed in six clusters of four one-bedroom apartments each. Clusters were spaced on the site to allow the creation of private courts, gardens, and off-street parking.[92] The project was one of fourteen award-winning apartments and townhouses nationwide selected by the "Homes for Better Living" program sponsored by the AIA and *American Home* and *House & Home* magazines. In a national study in 1967 on "design and its relationship to livability" in multiple-dwelling housing, Golden Age was one of four projects in the Twin Cities singled out for skillful planning and site organization.[93]

St. Paul's Cleveland Terrace Apartments, completed in 1969, has the distinction of being the first condominium project in Ramsey County. According to James I. Brown, one of its developers, the architects faced a "difficult three-fold challenge with amazing perceptiveness." The first task was to design a large, fourteen-apartment building in such a way that it fit "appropriately" into the quiet, residential neighborhood in which it stood. The solution was a single building that appeared to be three smaller ones: skillful use of color and setbacks contributed to the illusion. Second, the developers wanted units to feel "like a home not an apartment," so privacy, soundproofing, and multiple exposures were factored into the

Figure 5.28 Golden Age Housing (1959), Minneapolis, designed for the Minneapolis Housing and Redevelopment Authority. Lisl grouped the twenty-four housing units into six clusters to create space for private terraces, gardens, and off-street parking. Close Associates Papers (N78), Northwest Architectural Archives, University of Minnesota Libraries, Minneapolis.

design. The final requirement, minimal maintenance, was achieved through the selection of easy-upkeep materials, including windows that did not require painting or storms, fiberglass doors, and siding with a durable, baked-on finish. In an unusual but successful arrangement, owners prepaid the $400,000 cost of the project, so no construction financing was necessary.[94]

In 1969 Close Associates was part of a consortium that developed Windslope, a moderate-income housing project sponsored by the Minneapolis Chapter of the American Institute of Architects.[95] The federally funded project, located in The Preserve, a 1,200-acre planned development in Eden Prairie, Minnesota, was "believed to be the first public housing project in the country sponsored by a nonprofit professional organization."[96] Close Associates was chosen for its "skill in design and expertise in the housing field" to serve as architects and planners for the project.[97] A goal of the 10.8-acre, 168-dwelling-unit development was to "integrate the townhouse units into the natural environment while at the same time providing a general sense of community for the residents."[98] Although neighbors vehemently objected to—and threatened legal action over—the Closes' selection of white, yellow, and green exterior siding to "further enhance the natural building environment," the project was realized in its original polychromatic glory.[99]

Lisl never tired of designing houses and housing and continued to design residences throughout her long architectural career. For her, the problem-solving aspect of planning a house to suit a family's unique needs was "the interesting part." In the process, she met "many interesting people" who became lifelong friends. "I am really sometimes touched by how long they remember," she said. One set of clients sent "a Christmas card every year and they always say how well the house has adapted to their various stages of life. That's the kind of relationship you don't get from the commercial building industry."[100]

Figure 5.29 At the Cleveland Terrace Apartments (1969) in St. Paul, Lisl used several strategies, including setbacks and color, to make the fourteen-apartment complex appear to be three smaller buildings. Close Associates Papers (N78), Northwest Architectural Archives, University of Minnesota Libraries, Minneapolis.

Figure 5.30 A goal of Windslope, a moderate-income housing project in Eden Prairie, Minnesota, was to integrate townhouse units into the natural environment. Saari and Forrai Architectural Photography.

6

BUILDINGS FOR WORK AND PLAY

When the Closes moved from their home on Dell Place to University Grove they needed to find a new location for their office. Instead of looking for space to rent, in 1952 they purchased a lot on the corner of East Franklin Avenue and Thirty-first Avenue South in the Seward neighborhood of Minneapolis, a little more than four miles from their new house. There they built a dedicated office for the firm. The flat-roofed, rectangular, one-story building was constructed of the same attractive, practical, low-maintenance materials they favored in their residential work: redwood, Homasote, and concrete block. "It also employed many of the design features they became known for: chassis framing, concrete plank heating and cooling, split-level design, cement board soffits, and untreated redwood siding," noted Gar Hargens. On the interior, "heavy lampshade paper on wooden frames" was used in the ceiling to cover lights and provide "warm, ambient lighting."[1] The building at 3101 East Franklin Avenue has been the firm's headquarters for more than sixty-five years.[2]

Figure 6.1 In 1953 the Closes designed a new office building in Minneapolis for their firm. It remains the home of Close Associates today. Close Associates Papers (N78), Northwest Architectural Archives, University of Minnesota Libraries, Minneapolis.

It was also one of many commercial buildings Elizabeth and Winston Close, Architects (later Close Associates), designed over the years. Although most of their work was residential, the firm had considerable expertise in the design of medical, technical, laboratory, educational, and corporate facilities.

CLINICS AND HOSPITALS

The first commercial structure Lisl and Win designed, and one of their earliest realized projects, was a small flower stand for J. D. Holtzermann of Minneapolis, built in 1940. The following year they completed their first medical building, the Interstate Clinic in Red Wing, Minnesota, discussed in chapter 3. The modern aesthetic and efficient planning of the clinic—and the publicity it received—led to several medical office commissions, including the Kaufman Clinic (1941), designed for a physician in Win's hometown of Appleton, Minnesota; the Sigford (1954) and Trezona (1956) dental clinics; and the Nicol Clinic (1958), all in Minneapolis.

In 1957, the firm was hired to design an addition for the Lake Phalen campus of the Gillette State Hospital for Crippled Children. Soon after, Lisl embarked on what would be a series of projects for St. Barnabas Hospital in the Elliot Park neighborhood of Minneapolis, including a nurses' residence and classroom wing in 1958, a general service building and laundry facility in 1960, and coronary care unit, laboratory, and X-ray department expansions in 1964.

Six years later, St. Barnabas merged with nearby Swedish Hospital, a union that would soon be rebranded as the Metropolitan Medical Center.[3] For the new organization, Lisl formed what Hargens described as "a legal architectural joint venture" with the Minneapolis firm of Horty, Elving & Associates, which had previously handled architectural services for Swedish Hospital, to design a combined facility, parking structure, and medical office building.[4] The two boards "couldn't decide whether to hire Tom Horty, who was doing the Swedish Hospital, or hire me, who was doing St. Barnabas," recalled Lisl. "So, they came to us and asked, 'Could you

Figure 6.2 The first commercial building completed by Close and Scheu was a flower stand in Minneapolis for J. D. Holtzermann (1940). Courtesy of Roy M. Close Family Papers.

Figure 6.3 Lisl designed several small medical offices and clinics in the 1950s, including the Trezona Dental Clinic (1956), Minneapolis. Close Associates Papers (N78), Northwest Architectural Archives, University of Minnesota Libraries, Minneapolis.

work together?' We said sure, no problem."[5] The collaboration was a productive one. "He was very nice and [I] got to be good friends with him as well," she added. Hargens, who worked with Lisl and her team on the commissions, said the two firms divided the design work. "We worked on the patient care areas, and Horty did the laboratories and surgery spaces."[6] According to Hargens, it was "a great project," but it was far from being an easy one. "It went on forever . . . but she kept her cool and soldiered on."

A distinguishing feature of Lisl's planning for the Elliot Park complex was the introduction to a Minneapolis hospital of the Friesen system of patient care, developed by Canadian health care consultant Gordon Friesen. The fundamental idea behind Friesen's system was the availability of a nurse to the patient at all times. To facilitate this, he advocated a supply distribution system that made everything a patient needed accessible from a single cabinet in or near the patient's room.[7] Cabinets were efficiently stocked in a central location, hung on a rail system, and transported to the desired destination. Lisl's design utilized products from the Herman Miller Company's recently introduced Co/Struc system, which "streamlined hospital services with mobile and modular containers, carts, frames, and rails."[8] This rethinking of the nurse/patient relationship "put nurse servers in the hallways, which decentralized the staff so that the staff could be in the room [with the patient] and in audio contact with the nursing center. That was revolutionary," Hargens explained. "Everything was there: the chart, medication, the food, linen, even soiled linen which was under negative pressure in the lower part of the cabinet."[9]

In Hargens's view, it's not surprising that Lisl approached planning from the perspective of the patient and the caregiver. Because of her extensive experience designing houses (and reliance on questionnaires to elicit clients' needs), "Lisl brought a residential sensitivity to that project," he said. "That residential sensitivity to where does your bag go, where do you hang your coat, what's the lighting doing to the feeling in this room, all of that informed the bigger public spaces and was a characteristic of this firm."[10] For this

Figure 6.4 As part of an architectural joint venture with the firm of Horty, Elving & Associates, Lisl worked on several projects for Metropolitan Medical Center in Minneapolis, including the design of this Medical Office Building in 1967. Close Associates Papers (N 78), Northwest Architectural Archives, University of Minnesota Libraries, Minneapolis.

Figure 6.5 The Metropolitan Medical Center Combined Facility (1967), Minneapolis. Close Associates Papers (N78), Northwest Architectural Archives, University of Minnesota Libraries, Minneapolis.

Figure 6.6 Lobby, Metropolitan Medical Center (1967), Minneapolis. Close Associates Papers (N78), Northwest Architectural Archives, University of Minnesota Libraries, Minneapolis.

Figure 6.7 The Ice Center, Golden Valley, Minnesota. When it opened in 1957, the Ice Center was one of few indoor ice arenas in the western suburbs of Minneapolis. Close Associates Papers (N78), Northwest Architectural Archives, University of Minnesota Libraries, Minneapolis.

reason, even her largest, most complex public projects functioned well at the human level.

Over the years, the firm worked on numerous medical commissions. They included multiple projects for the Meeker County Hospital (1960s); a doctors' building for Abbott Northwestern Hospital (1971); a clinic and several remodelings for the Bethesda Lutheran Medical Center (1970s); a chemical dependency center for Anoka State Hospital (1976); the Ronald McDonald House in Minneapolis (1977); Northeast Community Clinic (1977); additional projects for Metropolitan Medical Center (1980s); and multiple remodelings for the Children's Hospital of St. Paul.

BUILDINGS FOR RECREATION

Lyman E. Wakefield Jr., a vice president of Minneapolis First National Bank, had more than a casual interest in figure skating when he and his wife, Elizabeth, commissioned Lisl's firm to design the Ice Center in Golden Valley, Minnesota, in 1957. Wakefield, who was known as the "father of figure skating in Minnesota," was a four-time national intercollegiate skating champion while an undergraduate at Dartmouth College and a judge of figure skating at the world championship level.[11]

Originally, the project was to be "a small studio rink for figure skating," according to Lisl. But plans were expanded when it became clear that "there was a great demand for general recreational skating facilities and also hockey practice space." For this reason, spectator seating was added to one side of the rink and the ice sheet enlarged to 85 feet by 185 feet. Lisl took advantage of the sloping site by "lowering the rink level a full story below the entrance," thereby allowing the lobby and other public spaces to overlook the ice below. One-hundred-foot-long bowstring trusses spanned the interior of the steel-framed building, eliminating the need for interior columns. To permit multiple uses, such as hockey and recreational and figure skating at the same time, a movable partition was installed. The partition, which was suspended from an overhead trolley system, could be positioned anywhere along the length of the rink. To keep "summer air conditioning costs to a minimum," large areas of

Figure 6.8 A movable partition, suspended from an overhead trolley system, allowed the Ice Center's rink space to be adapted to multiple uses at the same time. Close Associates Papers (N78), Northwest Architectural Archives, University of Minnesota Libraries, Minneapolis.

Figure 6.9 In 1959 the Minneapolis Park and Recreation Board hired Lisl to design a shelter for Bossen Field Park. She responded with this small but dynamic building. Courtesy of Gar Hargens/Close Associates and Close Associates Papers (N78), Northwest Architectural Archives, University of Minnesota Libraries, Minneapolis.

glass were avoided in exterior walls. Instead, light was brought into the building through "glass blocks set in a pattern into the concrete block exterior walls."[12]

When it opened, the building, located at 5800 Wayzata Boulevard, was one of few indoor ice arenas in the western metropolitan area. In addition to serving the public, the Ice Center was used by several local high schools, including Golden Valley, St. Louis Park, Edina, and Breck (which later acquired the arena). In turn, Breck sold the land and building to the city of Golden Valley, which eventually demolished the Ice Center as part of commercial redevelopment of the area along what is now Interstate 394.

In its heyday, the Ice Center was well used by the Minneapolis skating community, and on occasion it found its way into the local and national press. A February 1959 photograph and item in *Sports Illustrated* showed Lyman Wakefield and his daughter Louise, also a competitive skater, on the ice at "Minneapolis' new Ice Center."[13] Later that same year, the *Minneapolis Star* focused on the hot weather advantages of the refrigerated building in "Brother, It's Cold INSIDE . . ."[14] The article touted the arena as a destination for summer youth recreation programs and a place where a "refreshing winter world" could be enjoyed on the hottest summer day—a welcome pleasure in an era when air conditioning was not prevalent. The Ice Center was the firm's first and only skating arena.

Two years later, in 1959, Lisl designed an outdoor recreational facility: a park building for the Minneapolis Park and Recreation Board for Bossen Field Park. The small but striking modern building comprised three freestanding wings linked by a triangular roof. It housed an office, restroom facilities, and a storage area.

FDR MEMORIAL COMPETITION

Neither Lisl nor Win was in the habit of designing memorials, but in 1960 they collaborated on an entry for the Franklin Delano Roosevelt Memorial Competition for a site in Washington, D.C. They did so primarily for idealistic reasons. "We were very interested in this because we were admirers of Roosevelt. We listened to all his speeches. He was a wonderful man," Lisl said.[15]

Figure 6.10 Model for the Closes' entry for the Franklin Delano Roosevelt Memorial Competition (1960), Washington, D.C. The design was organized as a serpentine progression through a series of outdoor rooms, each dedicated to one aspect of Roosevelt's "Four Freedoms" speech. Close Associates Papers (N78), Northwest Architectural Archives, University of Minnesota Libraries, Minneapolis.

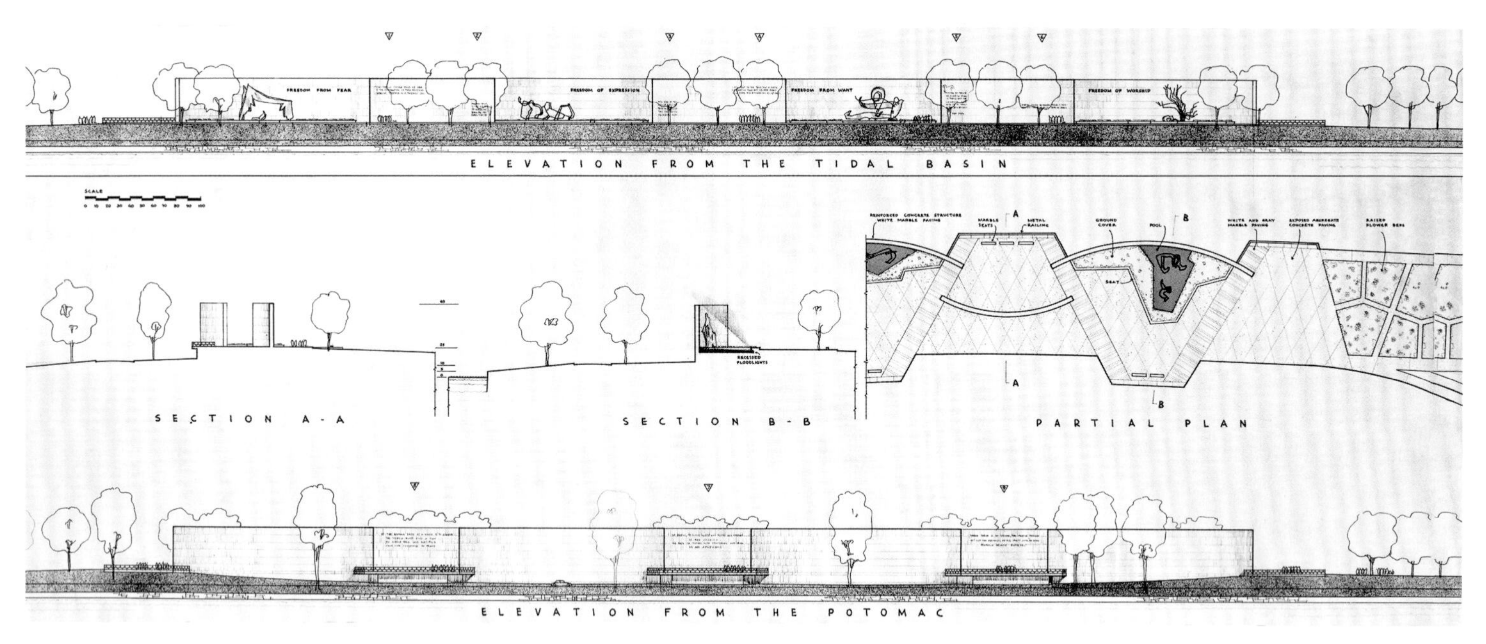

Figure 6.11 Sections and elevations of the Closes' entry for the Franklin Delano Roosevelt Memorial Competition. They proposed a low, horizontal memorial to visually complement other monuments in view. Close Associates Papers (N78), Northwest Architectural Archives, University of Minnesota Libraries, Minneapolis.

In 1955, ten years after Roosevelt's death, Congress authorized the FDR Memorial commission and four years later set aside a parcel of land between the Potomac River and the Tidal Basin as its future site. The competition drew 574 entries, most by "sizable teams, not individuals," which alone set Lisl and Win's design apart.[16]

The Closes rooted their concept in Roosevelt's 1941 State of the Union address, known as the "Four Freedoms" speech, in which he declared people the world over were entitled to four freedoms: freedom of speech and expression; freedom of worship; freedom from want; and freedom from fear. Spatially, their design — a serpentine progression of fountains and curved walls — was divided into four sections, each bearing an inscribed freedom text. "The curved slabs provided an interesting light and shade pattern and a good background for the pools and sculptures representing the four freedoms," they wrote in the project statement.[17]

The Closes believed the site had a "serene beauty," and their design considered its proximity to the Washington Monument and Jefferson and Lincoln Memorials — all within view — to be an important element of their concept. For this reason, they kept the monument low and strove for "an extended horizontal composition, which would incorporate the other monuments in the overall composition and create pleasant vistas to and from them." When it was lit at night, they anticipated their sculptural remembrance and its reflections in the water would create a "luminous light pattern [that] would be an effective link between the Jefferson and Lincoln memorials." When viewed from across the Potomac, the overlapping curved walls would "form a simple base for the Washington Monument without competing in any way."[18] Furthermore, they believed "the pedestrian way between the Lincoln and Roosevelt memorials should be an integral part of the site development." In a nod to the roots of Roosevelt's Dutch surname, meaning "rose field," they designed the memorial's approach to pass through a rose garden.

A significant and singular aspect of the Closes' design was that it recognized Roosevelt's disability. "It seemed at the time that [the memorial] should be easily maneuverable because he was in a wheelchair," Lisl said. Most of the designs "had steps, big dramatic ones. [Ours] was the only one that didn't, and I think that would have made a nice memorial."[19]

A panel of jurors, chaired by architect Pietro Belluschi, selected six projects to advance to the finals. Although the Closes' design was not among them, it was selected as one of twenty-two honorable mentions — a remarkable achievement for a firm of its size — and was published in both *Architectural Record* and *Architectural Forum* magazines. With characteristic candor, Lisl later stated, "I thought it was a successful project and I was sort of annoyed when we didn't get it."[20]

Ultimately, the Boston-based firm of William F. Pedersen and Bradford S. Tilney won the competition. Their monumentally scaled design consisted of eight reinforced concrete monoliths, one of which was 172 feet high, each inscribed with excerpts from Roosevelt's speeches. Although award judges praised the scheme for "giving a clear image of Mr. Roosevelt's greatness," it proved to be much less popular with the public and the Roosevelt family.[21] Critics dismissed it as "instant Stonehenge" and "a cemetery of broken dreams," among other disparagements. Ultimately, it was not built.[22] In 1966 a second competition was held and a design by architect Marcel Breuer declared the winner. Subsequently, it too was roundly criticized and not constructed. In 1974 landscape architect Lawrence Halprin was commissioned to create the tribute. More than two decades would pass before Halprin's memorial to FDR was constructed in 1997 — thirty-seven years after the initial competition.

PEAVEY TECHNICAL CENTER

In 1966 the Peavey Company, a Minneapolis-based grain merchandising and processing firm, hired Close Associates to design a new, modern research facility.[23] Lisl led the multiyear project, which involved programming, site selection, and the design of a 50,000-square-foot building dedicated to the company's diversification and product development initiatives.

Initially the site search centered on several existing industrial park complexes that were "high on accessibility" and closer to

Peavey's headquarters in Minneapolis, but "low in amenity." Those were rejected in favor of a site in the planned community of Jonathan in Chaska, Minnesota, which was chosen for its "great natural beauty, overlooking Hazeltine Lake and golf course."[24] Lisl worked with landscape architect Roger Martin, then a professor and chair of the Department of Landscape Architecture at the University of Minnesota, to place the building on the hilly, bucolic property and to develop site access, parking, and planting layouts and specifications. Bob Sorensen, an architect with Close Associates, was Lisl's "right-hand person" on the project.[25]

In addition to aspiring to create a "building of distinction appropriate to the corporate image of the Peavey Company," the firm focused on efficiency, flexibility, and economy as key factors in the design's evolution. Specifically, the complex consisted of research, development, and quality control laboratories, a pilot plant, offices, conference rooms, a demonstration kitchen, library, and numerous support and mechanical spaces. The floor plan for the two-level, L-shaped building clustered offices and laboratories in one wing, with the offices placed along the building's exterior walls and corresponding laboratories at its core. A glazed link connected the pilot plant to the laboratory wing. Labs were designed on a twelve-foot by twenty-four-foot module to "provide optimal flexibility" and to "permit incorporation of moderate-sized, freestanding equipment." Characteristically, Lisl brought color to the project by using plastic laminates to face cabinetry and doors. "Everyone likes the colorful labs," she later wrote.[26]

The simple masses of the research facility were constructed of poured-in-place concrete, a material Lisl chose because it provided the "stability essential to laboratory requirements." Vertical structural fins not only gave rhythmic interest to the building's facade but also efficiently functioned as shading devices to protect offices from excess sunlight and "skybrightness."[27] In 1982 the Peavey

Figure 6.12 The Peavey Technical Center (1966), Chaska, Minnesota, was designed as a research and laboratory facility. Photograph by Phillip MacMillan James & Associates. Close Associates Papers (N78), Northwest Architectural Archives, University of Minnesota Libraries, Minneapolis.

Figure 6.13 The Peavey Technical Center's concrete fins functioned as shading devices to protect interior spaces from excess sunlight. Photograph by Phillip MacMillan James & Associates. Close Associates Papers (N78), Northwest Architectural Archives, University of Minnesota Libraries, Minneapolis.

Figure 6.14 Lisl designed Peavey's laboratories to be flexible and adaptable to evolving uses. Photograph by Phillip MacMillan James & Associates. Close Associates Papers (N78), Northwest Architectural Archives, University of Minnesota Libraries, Minneapolis.

Company was acquired by ConAgra Inc., which eventually sold the building. Today the former Peavey Technical Center is owned by the Eastern Carver County Schools and serves as its district education center.

For Lisl the experience gained in programming and designing a highly specific, technical facility for the Peavey Company proved valuable a few years later when she designed an equally complex but very different building for scientific investigation: a laboratory for freshwater research.[28]

Figure 6.15 Lisl Close, circa 1972, on-site during the construction of the Freshwater Biological Institute in Navarre, Minnesota. Courtesy of Freshwater.

FRESHWATER BIOLOGICAL INSTITUTE

Richard Gray had known the Closes for almost thirty years when he asked their firm, in 1968, to design a state-of-the-art research lab for the Freshwater Biological Research Foundation—a nonprofit organization "dedicated to basic research on problems relating to freshwater in lakes, rivers and marshes," which he cofounded.[29]

Gray first commissioned the Closes in 1941 to design a house for his family in Minnetonka Mills. Eighteen years later, he hired the firm a second time to transform the family's summer retreat and boathouse on Lake Minnetonka in Mound, Minnesota, into a year-round residence. On May 6, 1965, the Grays' lake house was among six hundred residences destroyed by one of five twisters that struck during the "worst tornado outbreak in Twin Cities history."[30] Only the foundation was spared. When the Grays, who were in Europe when the storm hit, returned to Minnesota they asked Lisl to redesign and rebuild their home; they moved into the house in March 1966.

Although the tornadoes had passed, Gray, who had a lifelong interest in natural science, noticed that "Lake Minnetonka was suffering [from] the drastic disturbance." To better understand the lingering effects, he "established a small freshwater laboratory" in the basement of his house. There he conducted weekly studies of water samples drawn from the lake. In 1968, when his testing revealed a red algae bloom, "a sure sign of bad pollution," he discovered to his dismay that there was "no major freshwater laboratory facility in the United States" to offer advice.[31] To rectify this omission, he

Figure 6.16 The Freshwater Biological Institute (1974) in Navarre, Minnesota, was dedicated to the research of problems related to freshwater lakes, rivers, and marshes. In her design, Lisl broke the mass of the building into loosely connected pavilions. Saari and Forrai Architectural Photography.

cofounded the Freshwater Biological Research Foundation, raised $4 million to build a modern laboratory to house it, and hired Lisl to design the building. In a 1972 statement the organization said of its architect selection: "The women's lib movement had nothing to do with our choice of 'Lisl' Close. . . . She is merely one of the best." Of her architecture it wrote: "Her buildings are modern, powerful, beautiful yet practical. The Freshwater Biological Institute facility will be no exception."[32]

Lisl enlisted Wally Wilcox, an associate in her office and "a very good man," to supervise the construction of the project.[33] Wilcox worked diligently on the building and contributed significantly to the quality of its construction, said Hargens. "Part of its excellence is because he worried about every nail."[34] Landscape architect Herb Baldwin handled the site development for the complex that would become known as the Freshwater Biological Institute.

The five-acre site for the FWBI—on a marshy inlet off Lake Minnetonka's Lafayette Bay in Navarre—was undeniably beautiful and ideally situated for its purpose. But it was located within a residential zone, which was a concern. For this reason, Lisl sought to "maintain appropriate character and scale" by designing the building low to the ground and breaking its mass into four loosely connected pavilions built into the hillside.[35] Planted earth berms further screened the building and parking areas from the road and made the structure appear even lower than it was. Ultimately, residents did not object to the plan because "it was respectful of the neighborhood," she said.[36]

In her scheme, Lisl sought to balance the many technical requirements of the research facility with her interest in creating a building that "look[ed] pleasant and inviting and not like most laboratories."[37] Both highly specific and flexibly designed spaces were key to the successful functioning of the building. "Any research program is certain to involve new areas of study and unpredictable requirements. Therefore, the laboratories must be extremely adaptable," she explained.[38] The program called for twelve laboratories—for microbiology, chemistry, and algae—to be used by resident scientists, and six additional labs for visiting researchers. Shared laboratory functions and areas for "multidisciplinary interaction" were placed in the "groin" spaces that linked the pavilions.[39] The facility also comprised offices, seminar rooms, a library, lounges, and a reception area, many of which faced the marsh and lake (Plates 23 and 24).

Poured-in-place concrete was used for the structure, as it had been at the Peavey Technical Center, because of its "inherent stiffness and resistance to vibration," an important consideration in a laboratory setting.[40] Exterior walls were faced with grayish-pink brick and dark-stained, rough-sawn cedar. The firm also designed housing for visiting faculty and a boathouse for the site, neither of which was built.[41]

Upon completion of the building, ownership was transferred to the University of Minnesota. For twenty years it administered the complex, conducted research, and trained doctoral students on the premises. In the mid-1990s, the university returned the facility to the Freshwater Society, as the nonprofit was then known. The building was subsequently leased to the Cargill Corporation, which continued to use it as a laboratory until November 2015. The following year the society sold the property, which is now being operated as the Freshwater Business Center.[42]

The Freshwater Institute was one of Lisl's favorite projects because she worked with "an excellent board. . . . It had a good program . . . and it was an exciting project all the way through."[43] The building received the firm's only AIA Minnesota Honor Award, in 1975. One of the Freshwater Institute jurors noted, "The challenge of a most exceptional site has been met with a quiet building, of angular plan, adapting to the land. The scheme adjusts to changing research needs. It is a human's environment for study, thought and accomplishment."[44]

A SCHOOL FOR MUSIC

During his twenty-one years as advisory architect, Win was deeply involved in facilitating the University of Minnesota's expansion across the Mississippi River and the planning of its West Bank campus. After his retirement from the university in 1971, he and Lisl had the opportunity to work together to design the Donald N. Ferguson Hall—a new home for the university's School of Music

Figure 6.17 Donald N. Ferguson Hall (1986), home to the music school at the University of Minnesota, was the only building Close Associates designed for the university. Courtesy of the University of Minnesota Archives, University of Minnesota–Twin Cities.

Figure 6.18 Landscape architects Herb Baldwin and Bob Close worked with the Closes to carve amphitheater seating into the building's sloped site. Photograph by Alexius Horatius, Wikimedia Commons.

Figure 6.19 Ferguson Hall's interior spaces included a recital hall; orchestra, chorus, and band rooms; a music library; and numerous practice rooms. Saari and Forrai Architectural Photography.

on the West Bank. It would be their first and only campus building. As musicians (Lisl played cello and Win was a violist), they were eager to collaborate on a building dedicated to music education and performance.

For decades the music department had occupied a series of "buildings, rooms, and nooks and crannies" on the campus and beyond, all of which eventually proved inadequate for a program that was growing in enrollment, scope, and repute.[45] As early as 1959, the university began submitting funding proposals for a new building to the Minnesota legislature. In 1974 lawmakers approved $100,000 for planning, and three years later an additional $500,000 for architectural drawings. Nine years passed before "the legislature approved a bonding bill that appropriated $15,990,000 for a new music building to be constructed on the banks of the Mississippi River."

As is often true, the chosen site for the building presented both advantages and challenges. Primary among its pluses was its location: on a ridge above a bluff of the Mississippi River with a view to the East Bank campus. One of its potential drawbacks was the near heroic scale of the brick and concrete buildings that already stood in that quadrant of the West Bank campus, including the O. Meredith Wilson Library, Heller Hall, Anderson Hall, the Social Sciences Building, and the Rarig Center for Performing Arts and Radio–Television Facility. Rarig, designed by Ralph Rapson in 1972, directly abutted the music school site and was a particularly commanding presence on the plaza. Win explained, "Our main consideration was not touching the river bluff . . . [but] we also wanted to relate the building to the plaza and Rarig Center, the other performing arts building on the West Bank campus."[46]

The Closes kept the brick-and-concrete building relatively low, but referenced Rarig by rimming Ferguson's various roof planes with thinner, lighter versions of the dominant cornice that topped Rapson's building. As Lisl had done at the Peavey Technical Center, rhythmically placed vertical (nonstructural) concrete fins both enlivened the building's facade and functioned as sun shades. According to Win, there was a musical method to the melodic arrangement of the screens—and a logic to the office widths (sixteen feet on the second floor and twelve feet on the first) and window placements. The configuration visually "sets up a four-three ratio, a rhythm. It gives the facade a time signature and a musical motif I kind of like," he said.[47]

Although the building, completed in 1986, comprises mainly rectilinear volumes, the Closes broke the rigid geometry utilized by the surrounding buildings in two ways. First, they worked with landscape architects Herb Baldwin and Bob Close to carve an outdoor amphitheater in a hillside at the north end of the building; curved tiers of seating wrapped the performance area. Second, they added a whimsical touch to a rooftop terrace by cutting a circular hole in the brick privacy wall that bordered it, thereby creating a framed view of the West Bank campus from that space.

The larger of the building's two wings housed classrooms and faculty offices on the main floor and numerous practice rooms of varying sizes on the lower level. The facility also included a recital hall; orchestra, chorus, and band rooms; and a music library. Win and Lisl worked closely with California-based acoustical consultant Paul Veneklasen and Associates on the building's sound properties. Large rehearsal rooms were equipped with a "back wall" of acoustical panels. "The wall absorbs and reflects the music the same way an audience would," which enabled students to better anticipate performance conditions. Practice rooms were acoustically insulated using "clubhouse sandwich-type, combination of gypsum and fiberglass over twelve inches thick." Win later quipped, "It's the most gypsum-intense building I've ever seen." When the music school came in $1 million under budget, Close Associate architect Jim McBurney led the team that designed an underground music library, which was illuminated by a large light well, on the front of the building.[48]

A concert hall intended as a venue for "the school's concerts, recitals, master classes, and lecture/demonstrations and a permanent home for the school's opera workshop program" was an integral part of the larger vision for the music school complex.[49] In 1984 the

Figure 6.20 Lisl, a cellist, tested the acoustics in a practice room at Ferguson Hall. Courtesy of the University of Minnesota Archives, University of Minnesota–Twin Cities.

legislature approved $1.6 million toward its planning and construction, but an additional $3.4 million (at that time) was needed to move forward. According to Hargens, the concert hall "was part of the original Music School commission. We worked on it through schematics."[50] Because full funding was delayed, "by the time it was ready to go ahead, the state decided they needed to re-interview," he explained. "Some architects, like Ed Sovik, argued that the job should stay with the Closes" and declined to interview for the competition, Hargens said. Not everyone agreed. In the end, members of the state selection board deadlocked over the Closes' submission and one by Curt Green of HGA; ultimately HGA was awarded the commission to build what became known as the Ted Mann Concert Hall, completed in 1993. Although the Closes accepted the defeat with gracious professionalism, "losing as we did was a crushing blow," said Hargens.[51] "That was going to be one of their seminal projects."[52]

THE INTERNATIONAL SCHOOL

The design of a Minnesota campus for the International School was one of the last major projects on which Lisl and Win worked (in collaboration with Hargens). Although the firm became involved with the project in 1986, the International School organization began one hundred years earlier and six thousand miles away.

The first International School was founded in 1886 as a girls' school in Choueifat, Lebanon, by Tanios Saad, a Lebanese pastor, and Louisa Proctor, an Irishwoman dedicated to social welfare. They recognized the importance of educating young girls and shared a determination to create a school to that end "in a society that was very resistant to the education of women."[53] The school soon became coeducational and, following World War I, attracted students from around the world. Its primary mission was to provide students with "the highest standard of academic excellence within a global context."[54] By 1956 the International School was being run by Saad's daughter-in-law, Leila Saad, and Ralph Bistany, a businessman, who turned the financially struggling organization into a profit-making enterprise. In 1976 the bilingual school opened its first branch school in Sharjah in the United Arab Emirates. Over the next seven years, three additional schools opened in Abu Dhabi and Al Ain in the UAE, and at Ashwicke Hall, near Bath, England. Saad and Bistany selected Minnesota as the site of the sixth school because "it is in the heart of America, is a [center] of high technology, and its people have a great concern for excellence in education."[55]

During its first year of operation, the school served twenty-two students in primary grades in a temporary location in New Brighton. In 1987 it purchased a fifty-five-acre parcel of land near Bryant Lake in the Minneapolis suburb of Eden Prairie as the site of the new campus. In addition to being "physically beautiful," the site was chosen because of Eden Prairie's emphasis on "planned growth" and its proximity to local and interstate highways, thereby ensuring easy access for students from multiple Twin Cities locations.[56] The firm of Close Associates was hired to design the complex because it was "well-known for working with a site, not against it, and for fitting buildings into surroundings in an unobtrusive way," a value shared by the school.[57]

The school, which was to be planned and built in two phases, anticipated an optimal enrollment of two thousand students to be accommodated in fifty-six classrooms. Phase one amenities included a library, cafeteria, gymnasium, swimming pool, administrative and multipurpose areas, and playing fields. Phase two would add a performance space, hockey rink, and dormitories for boarding students.

From the viewpoint of the architects, the site, with its south-sloping ridge and views to Bryant Lake, a local natural resource, offered a "distinct advantage with compelling design implications." To minimize the structures' visual impact on neighboring residential areas and the lake, the architects designed the buildings to "meld into the hillside, becoming part of the ridge rather than an imposition upon it." They proposed breaking the buildings into low, two-story, flat-roofed "units of residential dimension" and stepping them down the hillside. In this way, most of the buildings would have a southern exposure, as well as access to view and breezes. Although the city objected to the specified flat roofs, and instead proposed mansard roofs, the firm "strongly disagreed" and successfully

Figure 6.21 In 1987 the Closes designed the International School in Eden Prairie—the first United States campus for the institution, which was founded in Lebanon in 1886. Close Associates Papers (N78), Northwest Architectural Archives, University of Minnesota Libraries, Minneapolis.

argued that the latter would create the much higher building profile they sought to avoid.[58] To further mitigate the institutional feel of block-like rectangular structures, each building was subdivided into three components linked by wedge-shaped transitional areas with glass curtain wall facades, around which the outer sections angled. Building exteriors were sheathed in cast stone and face brick. Brick, gypsum board, Homasote, and wood were used as interior finishes. Bob Close, of Close Grant Design Company, served as landscape architect on the project.[59]

One interesting and unusual feature of the plan—and a decidedly residential one—was the inclusion of balconies off classrooms on the second floor, which served to open interior spaces to the landscape beyond. Balconies were the very same feature that Lisl had unsuccessfully attempted to include in Sumner Field—the first project she worked on as a young architect in Minnesota fifty years earlier.

In 1988 Close Associates celebrated its fifty-year anniversary. It was a time of transition for the office and for Win and Lisl personally. That year, Hargens became president and sole owner of the firm they had established in 1938. The Closes continued to work with Hargens, on a variety of projects, for the next four years. In 1992 they retired as architects.

A LONG LIFE, WELL LIVED

EPILOGUE

Elizabeth and Winston Close made history in May 1969 when they were elected Fellows of the American Institute of Architects (FAIA). Although they were the first married couple to be simultaneously elevated, each was considered on individual merits. Prior to their election, only ten Minnesota architects had received the honor, which recognizes "exceptional work and contributions to architecture and society."[1] Lisl was the eleventh woman in the country to be named an AIA Fellow.[2]

An American Institute of Architects (AIA) press release identified the Closes as "pioneers of the contemporary house" and "an important contributory force to the development and acceptance of modern architecture" in the region.[3] Win was "recognized for his long-time influence on the planning and architecture of the University of Minnesota," and Lisl was singled out as being "well-known for her outstanding residential designs."[4] Among the people who wrote personal letters of support for Lisl's nomination was Viennese-born architect Victor Gruen. Renowned as the designer of Southdale Center in Edina, Minnesota, the first indoor shopping mall in America, Gruen had known Lisl since the 1930s and was a close friend of her brother, Friedl. "I have followed with great interest [her] unique career as a woman in architecture. On my visits to Minneapolis I had the opportunity to see some of her executed work and I was deeply impressed by it."[5] Gruen also noted that the Closes largely pursued diverging, individual careers for more than twenty-five years. He said of Lisl during that time: "Most design work has been hers and she has received numerous awards and recognitions for the excellence of the results."[6] Former Minnesota governor Elmer Andersen, for whom Lisl designed two projects, also voiced his support, writing, "I have had occasion to work with many architects in my life, public and private, and I know of no one who combines all the attributes of professional skill and personal effectiveness as does Mrs. Close."[7]

In addition to the strength of their architectural work, "what made them easily accepted into the College of Fellows was that they had done a lot for the profession," said Gar Hargens.[8] "For a firm this size, they spent a great deal of time in leadership roles." Win served as president of both the Minnesota Society of Architects (MSAIA, now AIA Minnesota) and the Association of University Architects. Lisl chaired several chapter committees, including those on home building, urban design, residential architecture, and hospital and health care. In 1983 she was elected president of MSAIA, becoming the first woman to hold the office. Nationally, she served on AIA committees on housing and architectural building information services, and on a Federal Housing Administration advisory panel on residential design. Both Closes contributed numerous articles on residential design and urban planning to local and national publications, thereby helping to educate the public on architectural subjects.

The practice and performance of music consumed many of the Closes' leisure hours. For years, they were involved with the Civic Orchestra of Minneapolis, performed with string quartets and other chamber groups, and were board members of the Minnesota Opera. Friends and family note that Lisl and Win always made time after work to enjoy a glass of sherry, have dinner with family, and practice the cello and viola, respectively. Architect and educator Georgia Bizios, FAIA, who worked for the firm in the 1970s, believes Lisl's (and Win's) downtime was well earned. "She worked eight and eight and a half hours a day, seriously in a concentrated manner, no nonsense. She made very little small talk . . . but she knew how to take time to do the things that were important to her—family, cultural events, friends."[9]

Win and Lisl officially retired from Close Associates in 1992, fifty-four years after they founded the firm as the state's first architectural practice dedicated to modern design. Hargens believes their architectural legacy is a collection of buildings that are "elegant, beautiful, durable, and practical," as well as "very honest, very Minnesota, very Midwestern, in a way, in [their] openness, relying on materials and simple forms to tell the story and to provide the functional spaces." They were "proud of their abilities and proud of their work . . . but there was humility there. It was unprofessional to brag or show off," he said. "That was part of who they were."[10]

On June 15, 1997, Win died from complications of a stroke. He was ninety-one. He was remembered as "one of the pioneers of

Figure E.1 Lisl Close, circa 1966, at Peavey Technical Center. Close Associates Papers (N78), Northwest Architectural Archives, University of Minnesota Libraries, Minneapolis.

modern architecture in Minnesota" and as "an advocate for housing for all income groups." Architect Leonard Parker described Win, in his capacity as university advisory architect and campus planner, as "a patient and effective administrator who was able to form consensus among many groups that needed facilities in the fast-growing postwar era."[11] Another colleague believed Win "took on a tremendous responsibility in leading the University towards a development that would serve it well into the coming years."[12]

In 2002 Lisl once again made history by becoming the first woman to receive the AIA Minnesota Gold Medal in "recognition of a lifetime of distinguished achievement and significant contributions to architecture." The award cited her "exceptional design work" characterized by its "strikingly unique appearance," skillful site integration, light-filled, spacious interiors, and "always a rich landscape."[13] The *Minneapolis Star Tribune* later reported that Lisl gave "the most gracious acceptance speech in the history of the awards," with her final thank you going to Esther Bogren, her housekeeper for thirty years. She acknowledged Bogren for helping to raise her three children and for running the household. Bogren's service allowed Lisl to pursue the work for which she was being honored that night.[14] The following year, the University of Minnesota bestowed its highest honor on Lisl when it presented her with a Doctor of Humane Letters degree for her "contributions to Modern Architecture in America."[15] Other architects so honored by the university include Florence Knoll Bassett, Frank Gehry, Cesar Pelli, Antoine Predock, and David Salmela.[16]

Soon after she received these lifetime honors, Lisl's health began to decline. With the assistance and attention of her children, she moved out of University Grove in 2004 and into the Jones-Harrison Residence, a care facility near Cedar Lake in Minneapolis, where she would remain for the rest of her life. She died on November 29, 2011, at the age of ninety-nine. Lisl's memorial service, "A Centenary Celebration," was held on June 4, 2012, her one-hundredth birthday. Family, friends, and colleagues eulogized her and a string quartet played. In recognition of her Austrian Social Democratic roots, everyone in attendance was invited to sing (in German) the *Lied der Arbeit,* or "Work Song," composed by her grandfather Josef Scheu for the party in 1868.

Tributes spoke of her strong will and the independent streak that as a young woman allowed her to envision a career in architecture and cross an ocean to make it happen; of the determination and single-mindedness with which she pursued employment during the Depression; of her refusal to work in any arena other than modern design; of her long, successful partnership with Win, her children and grandchildren, her many friends, and her love of music. And above all, of her work and the professionalism and dignity with which she performed it.

Lisl was always too busy creating architecture to consider her role in the broader context of the discipline. She didn't think herself remarkable for becoming an architect in the early 1930s. She didn't give much thought to being a pioneering woman in a male-dominated profession, nor did she congratulate herself for forging a highly successful career in that field. She seemed unaware of being an exemplar for other aspiring women architects. And yet she was all those things. Although Lisl rarely shirked a responsibility, she left it to others to shine a light on her life and legacy.

In the view of architect and educator Julia Robinson, FAIA, as an architect "Lisl was more interested in good design than high design. She had a special talent for taking ordinary materials and making them into architecture," she said. "She was such an important part of the architectural community. She gave it dignity and gravitas."[17]

"Lisl was ahead of her time in so many ways, not only being an architect . . . being committed to good design, being a good citizen of her community, and a good family member," said Georgia Bizios. "Many things architects and people consider new or novel [today], Lisl was thinking them and practicing them many decades ago."[18]

Minneapolis architect Joan Soranno, FAIA, observed, "She was a role model for me not only because she was a successful woman architect but because she fully embraced modernism and never wavered from that conviction. She showed the rest of us how it could be done with talent, grace, and wisdom."[19]

Today there are many architects who happen to be women. While the pursuit of a career the caliber of Lisl's still requires extraordinary dedication, perseverance, talent, hard work, and resilience, most women who are currently in the field — and those who will enter it in the future — will not have to negotiate the same obstacles Lisl encountered on her journey. In part, they have Lisl, and other pioneering women in architecture, to thank for smoothing the way.

It's a gift that Bizios, for one, does not take for granted. "By the time I worked with Lisl she was very well established. I valued that because it made it easier for me that I didn't have to be the first. I didn't have to prove to them that women can be architects. Lisl had already done that."[20] And she did it well. The fact that so many Close-designed buildings still stand and now serve a new generation of owners and users is an architectural testament to one remarkable woman's professional expertise and artistic vision.

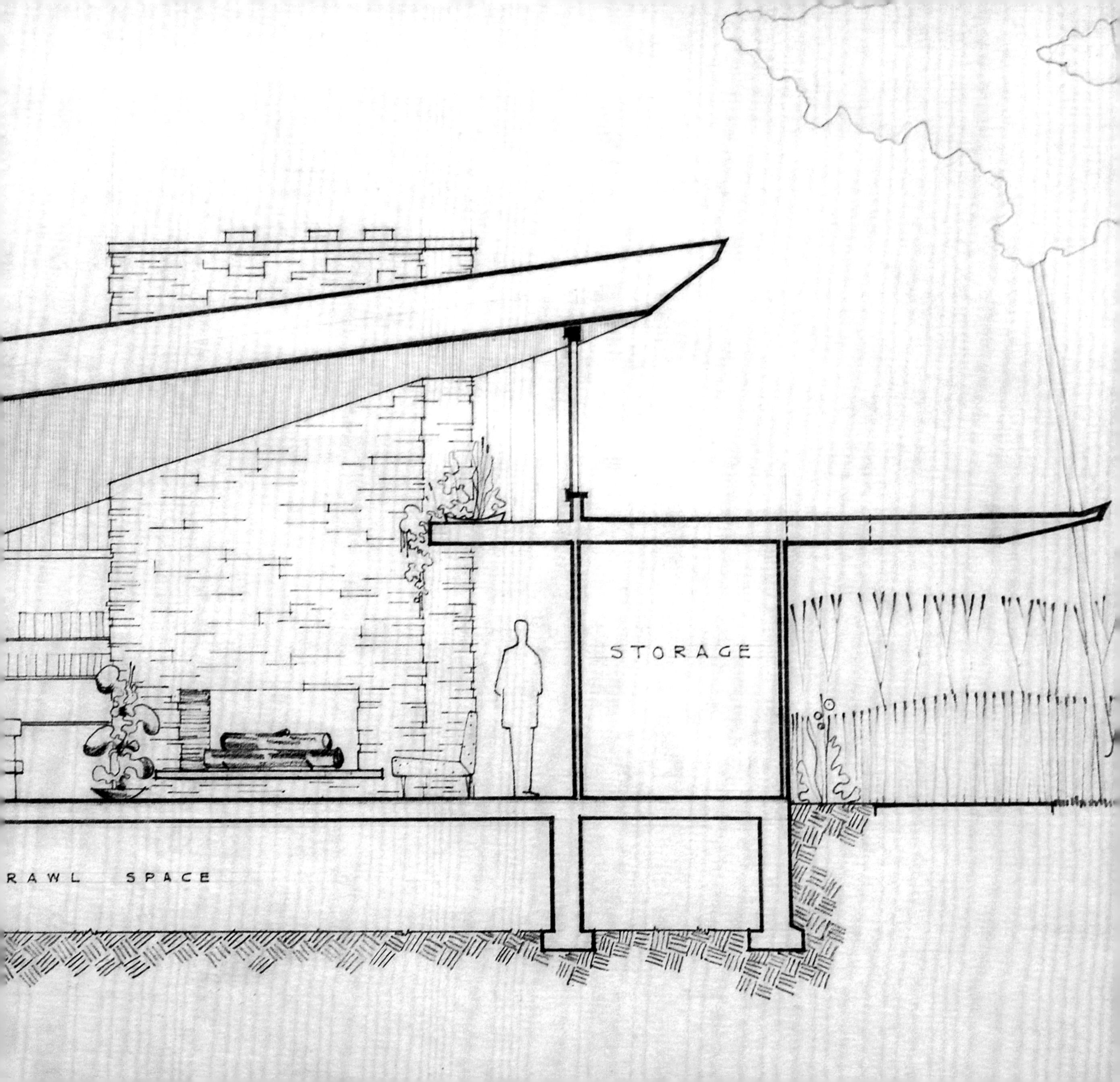
STORAGE
RAWL SPACE

Acknowledgments

The motivation to write this book grew out of a series of oral history interviews I conducted with Lisl Close beginning in 2000. Admittedly, I knew little about her when we embarked on a year-long exploration of her life and career, but it quickly became clear that both merited additional research and documentation. The interviews, two of which are archived in the "Voices of Minnesota" collection at the Minnesota Historical Society, were made possible by a grant from that institution. I am grateful to the Minnesota Historical Society and indebted to historian Patty Dean for suggesting I apply for the grant and for introducing me to Lisl. Above all, I thank Lisl for sharing many afternoons—and her remarkable life—with me.

I never had the privilege of meeting Winston Close, but his and Lisl's three children, Anne Ulmer, Roy Close, and Bob Close, supported the project in several ways. I thank them for agreeing to be interviewed and for thoughtfully answering all the questions I posed. Special appreciation goes to Roy for sharing the considerable resources of the Scheu/Close family archive with me; for his timely, critical, and often humorous editorial review of the manuscript; and for taming my tendency to overuse commas. Thanks also go to Veronica Kothbauer and Caroline Gotschy, daughters of Lisl's brother Friedrich, for providing valuable information on the Scheu House and family in Vienna.

Over the years, three organizations dedicated to fostering research in the arts, architecture, and design supported the project. In 2001, "The Houses of Lisl Scheu Close" received a Milka Bliznakov Prize honorable mention. The prize, an initiative of Virginia Tech's International Archive of Women in Architecture, recognizes "research that advances knowledge of women's contributions to architecture and related design fields." In 2008, the New York–based Beverly Willis Architecture Foundation, which strives to advance "the knowledge and recognition of women's contributions to architecture," awarded a fellowship to the project. Those funds helped support a portion of the writing. A 2010 research grant from the Graham Foundation for Advanced Studies in the Fine Arts underwrote travel to Vienna, Austria, to research Lisl's roots in that city and to visit the Scheu House, a seminal influence in her life and career. I am grateful to these remarkable organizations for recognizing the significance of Lisl's architecture and for their respective contributions toward making this book possible.

Several people in Vienna provided valuable assistance. Adolf Loos scholar Ralf Bock enhanced my understanding of Loos's architecture through his own published work. He kindly drove me around Vienna to visit sites and buildings germane to my research. Most significant, he arranged access to the Scheu House at 3 Larochegasse. I am grateful to Sigrid Leodolter, then owner of the house, who welcomed us into her home and permitted Bill Olexy to photograph it. Red Vienna expert Dr. Christa Veigl offered valuable insight into the Scheu family's Social Democratic roots in Vienna and guided me through important buildings from that era. Thank you to Elfriede Pokorny of the VGA for providing information on American Relief Administration's Children's Fund in Vienna and the Scheu family's involvement with it.

Vienna-based architect Judith Eiblmayr and I connected over a shared interest in Lisl and a determination to document her story on two continents. I thank Judith for sharing her knowledge of Vienna, the Scheu family, and Austrian modernism. I am grateful to her and Benjamin Petri LaFirst for translating incomprehensible (to me) German texts.

Writing is a solitary pursuit, but few writers manage to complete a manuscript without the support and assistance of others. Among those who merit special appreciation are Gar Hargens, principal of Close Associates, who worked with the Closes for decades and freely shared his knowledge and the firm's archives with me; Cheryll Fong, assistant curator at the Northwest Architectural Archives, who responded to every research request with good nature and efficiency; Joan Soranno for providing a thoughtful foreword for the book; and architect Dale Mulfinger for his belief in this project, gentle prodding to keep it moving along, and active efforts to make it happen. A very big thank you to all those people who responded generously to funding requests: you made this book possible.

Nearly twenty years ago Todd Orjala, then acquisitions editor at the University of Minnesota Press, was the first to express an interest in a book on Lisl Close. I am grateful to him and to senior editor Pieter Martin, who subsequently shepherded this book with skill and diplomacy through editing and production at the Press. Additional thanks go to Laura Westlund, Eric Lundgren, Anne Carter, Rachel Moeller, Heather Skinner, Emily Hamilton, Jeff Moen, and Jena Sher.

The act of asking someone to critically read a lengthy manuscript puts even the best relationships—personal or professional—at risk. I am deeply appreciative to the following individuals for catching my errors and remaining my friends: Roy Close, Judith Eiblmayr, Tommy Everson, Gar Hargens, Linda Mack, Maria Manion, Dale Mulfinger, Bill Olexy, and Fran Siftar. My words are far better for your careful attention to them. I extend my appreciation to two anonymous peer reviewers of the manuscript, whose suggestions deepened the manuscript's content in several ways. Thank you, whoever you are.

In addition to those individuals previously mentioned, dozens of people played key roles in the realization of this book by opening doors, sharing memories, sitting down for interviews, providing photographs, scanning images, answering questions, or simply showing an interest in the project. They include Rolf Anderson, Christine Avery, Georgia Bizios, Bette Blakeney, Su Blumentals, Mathias Böhm, Pauline Boss, Jessica Buelow, Greg Castillo, Linda Close, Caroline Constant, Judy Cornelius, Brent Dalzell, Ellen Demerath, Nicole Dittrich, Simon Elliott, Afton Esson, Bill Faulkner, Tom Fisher, Phil Freshman, Doreen Frost, Eric Galatz, Jane Gorence, Dan Hedlund, Sara Branson Homstad, Josue Hurtado, Lynda Jacobsen, Kathryn Keefer, Kathleen Kulberg, Gayla Lindt, Jhna Lundin and Rick Lundin, Paul Madsen, Anne Maple, Kate Maple, Tom Maple, Alli Mertins, Lin Nelson-Mason, Jennifer Komar Olivarez, Marri Oskam, Rebekah Padilla, Cindy Peltier, Brian Peterson, Jean Peterson, Robin Preble, Chris Prok, Gladys Reiling and Roger Reiling, Dudley Riggs, Julia Robinson, Bob Roscoe, Karen Rue, Denes Saari, Maria Forrai Saari, Mary Salisbury, Jeff Scherer, Pete Sieger, Steve Sikora, Kate Solomonson, Lauren Soth, Susan Stafford, Dianne Steinbach, Teri Swanson, Jenny Terrell, Tom Trow, Christopher True, Lynn Underwood, Lisa Von Drasek, Jill Vuchetich, John Waggener, John Wareham, Steve Woods, and Marina Yolbulur-Nissim. A word of thanks to the Minnesota Chapter of the Society of Architectural Historians for giving me the opportunity to present my research at an annual "Works in Progress" event. All authors benefit from early feedback.

This list would be incomplete without mentioning the late Leon Satkowski, former professor of architectural history at the University of Minnesota. When I entered architecture school in the late 1980s, Leon's masterful lectures ignited in me a love of architectural history. The grace and lucidity of his writing inspired me to strive toward that elusive ideal. His mentorship and encouragement set me on the architectural path I now travel.

It is doubtful that this project would have happened without the good-natured support and considerable creative talents of my husband, Bill Olexy. His photographic gifts are evident in many illustrations included in this book. Less obvious are the fruits of the countless hours he spent graciously reading chapters, catching typos, scanning photographs, doing research, walking dogs, making dinners, bolstering my spirits, and keeping our lives afloat while I wrote this book. *Merci pour tout, mon amour.*

Donors

The University of Minnesota Press gratefully acknowledges generous contributions provided for the publication of this book from the following individuals:

Georgia Bizios

Lynda and Darel Jacobsen

Edward J. Kodet, Jr., FAIA

Mark Larson and
Jean Rehkamp Larson

Michaela Mahady

Rosemary McMonigal

Lea Babcock Scherer
and Jeffrey Scherer

With special thanks to:

The children of Elizabeth
and Winston Close:
Anne Close Ulmer,
Roy M. Close, Bob Close

James and Megan Dayton

Dale and Jan Mulfinger

Gladys and Roger Reiling

Chronology

1912
Elizabeth "Lisl" Hilde Scheu born on June 4, Vienna, Austria

1930
Begins architectural education at the Technische Hochschule in Vienna

1932
Leaves Austria for the United States

1934
Receives bachelor of science in architecture from the Massachusetts Institute of Technology (MIT)

1935
Receives master of architecture from MIT

1935
Employed by Kastner & Stonorov in Philadelphia

1936
Moves to Minnesota, employed by Magney and Tusler

1938
Cofounds Close and Scheu with Winston Close

Marries Winston "Win" Arthur Close (born 1906)

1940
Name of firm changes to Elizabeth and Winston Close, Architects

Daughter, Anne Close, born

1944
Son Roy Close born

1948
Son Robert Close born

1969
Name of firm changes to Close Associates

1969
Becomes Fellow in the American Institute of Architects

1983
President of the Minnesota Society of the American Institute of Architects (AIA)

1992
Retires from practice

1997
Winston Close dies in Minneapolis

2002
Receives AIA Minnesota Gold Medal

2003
Receives Doctor of Humane Letters degree from the University of Minnesota

2011
Dies in Minneapolis

2012
Memorial service held on June 4, one-hundredth anniversary of her birth

Selected Projects

Unless otherwise noted, all building locations are in Minnesota. Asterisks denote projects that were not built.

1936

B. F. Skinner, house*
Falcon Heights

Ray Swarthout, house*
(for Close & Scheu Architects, of the Office of Magney and Tusler)
Hennepin County

1938

Cooperative Housing*
St. Paul

Ray Faulkner, house
Minneapolis

William Knutson, house*
Minneapolis

Erling Muller, house*
Minneapolis

Guy A. Nelson Tourist Camp*

University Terrace*
St. Paul

1939

Frank Ernst, house
Bloomington

Charles Hoffman, house
Golden Valley

Willem and Willemina Luyten, house
Minneapolis

Otto Werness, house
St. Louis Park

1940

Arthur Allen, house alterations
Minnetonka

William Campbell, house
Minneapolis

Oliver Field, house
Bloomington

J. D. Holtzermann, flower stand
Minneapolis

Interstate Clinic (demolished)
Red Wing

Benjamin and Gertrude Lippincott, addition
Minneapolis

Earl Mora, house
Minneapolis

Leslie Smith, house
Minnetonka Mills

Hjalmar Storlie, house renovations
Minneapolis

Robert and Helen Sullivan, house
St. Paul

Tracy and Helen Tyler, house
Falcon Heights

Russell Wilder Jr., house
Rochester

James and Mildred Wood, house
Minneapolis

1941

"Skywater," Joseph and
Dagmar Beach, cabin
Osceola, Wisconsin

Richard Gray, house
Minnetonka Mills

Starke and Jinny Hathaway, house
Minneapolis

Ralph Helstein, house
Minneapolis

Lee Kalgren, house
Minneapolis

Kaufman Clinic
Appleton

Lennox Mills, house
Minneapolis

William Mitchell, house
St. Paul

Page & Hill Company,
prefabricated house designs
Shakopee

Sawyer and Jane Rank, house
St. Paul

J. M. Starr, house
St. Paul

1944

Gerald Hill, cabin
Lake Vermilion

1946

William Mitchell, house
White Bear Lake

1947

Joseph Bolduc, house*
Golden Valley

Joseph Boran,
speculative housing

Frank Krebs, house
St. Paul

Jason and Lorentina Quist, house
Edina

John and Dorothy Rood, house
Minneapolis

Walker Art Center
Designs for Idea Houses III through VIII exhibition,
model house
Minneapolis

Waterbury Company,
manufacturing building
Minneapolis

Fritz and Helen Wheeler,
house and cabin
Madeline Island, Wisconsin

1948

Ruth Boynton/Prudence Cutright, house
Bloomington

Howard and Ruth Brin, house
Minneapolis

Richard Hoffman, house
Little Canada

Ray Johnson, house
Minneapolis

Donald and Elizabeth Lawrence, house
Minneapolis

Werner Levi, house
Lake Owasso

Naftalin/Thomes, house
Minneapolis

F. G. Wallace, house addition
Mound

Stuart and Mary Wells,
farm remodel
Long Lake

Russell Wilder Jr.,
double house remodel
Rochester

1949

James Brown, house
St. Paul

C. W. Dalzell, house
Minneapolis

Bruce Dayton, house
Excelsior

Richard Dobson, house remodel*
Maple Plain

David and Harriett Fingerman, house
St. Louis Park

Henry and Harriet Hartle, house
Owatonna

Howard and Barbara Kaewer Jr., house
Eden Prairie

Edward and Katherine Meehan, house
Falcon Heights

Rudolf Modley, house
Kent, Connecticut

Harold Stevenson, house remodel
Falcon Heights

Cecil and Mary Watson, house
Minneapolis

Harold Whiting, house
Owatonna

1950

J. Cowan, house
Algona, Iowa

Paul Dennison, house (demolished)
Edina

Harold Deutsch, house
Minneapolis

William and Judy Driscoll, house
Wayzata

Richard Falck, house remodel
Northfield

German International
Industrial Exhibition
"Model American Home"
(demolished)
Berlin, Germany

Lyndon and Betty King, house
Minneapolis

Thomas and Bernice O'Brien, house
Falcon Heights

John and Renee Peck, house
North Oaks

David State, house*
St. Paul

Paul Wendt, house
Minneapolis

1951

Merlin Berg, house
Minneapolis

Frederick Gram, house
St. Paul

Isaac Hoffman, house
St. Paul

Donald Martindale, house
St. Paul

Minnesota Rubber and
Gasket Company, factory

Chester and Janet Simmons, house
Wayzata

1952

Thomas and Leatrice Benson,
farmhouse remodel
Appleton

Lawrence Coe, house
Rice Lake, Wisconsin

Leo Harris, building remodel
Minneapolis

Jug Liquor

Matthew and Jean Leavitt, summer home
Lake Minnetonka

Scott Long, house
Minneapolis

William Mitchell, house remodel
White Bear Lake

Gustave Nubel, house
Minneapolis

John and Renee Pack, house
North Oaks

N. O. and Kathryne Pearce,
house remodel studies
Minneapolis

Orval Perlman, house*
Northfield

Robert and Lois Pflueger, house
Ortonville

Alice Best Rogers,
duplex and garage remodel
Minneapolis

Arnulf Ueland, house
Minneapolis

Walker Art Center
The Architects' Workshop,
exhibition
Minneapolis

1953

J. G. Benner, house
Minneapolis

Brin Glass, office remodel
Minneapolis

Elizabeth and Winston Close,
Architects, office
Minneapolis

Elizabeth and Winston Close,
house
Falcon Heights

Charles and Jean Critchfield,
interiors consultation
Minneapolis

Margaret Crosby, house
Mound

Paul Dennison,
pool studies
Edina

Richard Falck, house
Northfield

Robert and Beulah Hebbel, house
St. Paul

Robert and Betty Ann Jones,
house
Falcon Heights

Jennings Peteler, house
Minnetonka

Robert Peters,
plant expansion*
St. Paul

Philip and Marian Raup, house
Falcon Heights

1954

Walter and Nelly Ashauer, house
North Oaks

James Best, house*
Minneapolis

Lorrie Cavanaugh, house
Minneapolis

Bryce Crawford, house remodel
St. Paul

Gaylord Davidson, house
Wayzata

Howard and Betty Engelman,
house remodel*
Hopkins

George and Jean Fleming, house
Evansville, Indiana

Walter and Johnnie Heller,
house
Falcon Heights

Heidi and Alpha Henriksen, house*
Minneapolis

Wenzel Lindfors, house*
North Oaks

J. R. McIntyre, house
Swift Current,
Saskatchewan, Canada

William Middlebrook,
residence
Deephaven

W. A. Olson, house
Bloomington

Sigford Dental Clinic
Minneapolis

James Slocum, house
Maplewood

Henry Wilding, house remodel
Owatonna

1955

Theodore and Amy Althausen,
house studies
Golden Valley

Ann Arnold, house
Stillwater

Canton Lumber, building
Minneapolis

Philip and Helen Duff, house
(demolished)
Wayzata

Ivan and Vee Frantz, house
Falcon Heights

George and Miriam Freese, house
North Oaks

Hovland Medical Clinic*
Minneapolis

William and Harriet Martin
Falcon Heights

Nelson Drive-in Restaurant*
Minneapolis

Pemble Factory*
River Falls, Wisconsin

Clarence and Patricia Rowe,
house
St. Paul

1956

Lowell Alm, house
Bloomington

Elmer and Eleanor Andersen,
house
Deer Lake

Charles Arnao, house
Wayzata

Henry and Joyce Barbour,
house
North Oaks

James and Plina Bennett, house
Wayzata

Willard Cochrane, house
Falcon Heights

Wallace and Mary Lee Dayton, house
Shorewood

Robert and Marion Fry, house
St. Paul

Fullerton Lumber Company,
"Precision-bilt System" house
Minneapolis

Reynolds and Marjorie Galbraith,
house
Whitefish Lake

James and Geraldine Jenkins, house
Falcon Heights

Scott and Margaret Reardon, house
Sioux Falls, South Dakota

Trezona Medical Clinic,
renovation
Minneapolis

George Willharm, house
Excelsior

1957

Bemidji Church
Bemidji

John and Ida Davies,
house
Roseville

Gillette State Hospital
for Crippled Children,
addition
St. Paul

Richard Gray, house
Mound

Hayes-Winston Company,
model houses
Brooklyn Park

Ice Center (demolished)
Golden Valley

Raymond Nixon, house
Falcon Heights

John Olin, house
Excelsior

O. H. Peterson, house
Minneapolis

Drs. Rowe and Brown
Medical Offices
St. Paul

1958

Gove and Elsie Hambidge, house
Roseville
Tom Nee, house remodel
Minneapolis

Nicol Clinic
Minneapolis

Sara Page, house remodel
St. Paul

Phi Mu Sorority/
University of Minnesota,
remodel
Minneapolis

St. Barnabas Hospital,
classroom wing
Minneapolis

St. Barnabas Hospital,
nurses' residence
Minneapolis

1959

Bossen Field Park, shelter,
Minneapolis Park
and Recreation Board
Minneapolis

Golden Age Housing,
Minneapolis Housing
and Redevelopment Authority
Minneapolis

Richard Gray,
boathouse and house remodel
Mound

Richard Leavenworth, house
Minneapolis

Donald Myers, house
Minneapolis

Harold and Ingeborg Ulvestad,
house (demolished)
Edina

John and Theta Wolf, house
Falcon Heights

1960

Donald and Elizabeth Judkins, house
Wayzata

Franklin Delano Roosevelt
National Memorial, competition*
Washington, D.C.

St. Barnabas Hospital,
general services building
Minneapolis

1961

"Skywater," Dagmar Beach,
guest cabin
Osceola, Wisconsin

Adrian Helgeson, house
Golden Valley

John Moga, house
Anoka

John Olin, house
Christmas Lake

Polystructures, research
and development

Reardon Homes, housing
Sioux Falls, South Dakota

Bernard Sandler, house
Minneapolis

1962

J. F. Madden, house
Rochester

A. C. Menke, house
La Crosse, Wisconsin

Hendrik and Marri Oskam, house
Edina

1963

Afton Coulee Ridge, planning
Afton

Elmer Andersen, house
Turtle Lake

Robert Chaffin, house
Waseca

Thomas Hancock, house
La Crosse, Wisconsin

Stanley Leonard, house remodel
St. Paul

Allen Solem, house
Falcon Heights

Loring Staples, house remodel
Minneapolis

Van Cleve Court Apartments
Minneapolis

1964

Meeker County Hospital, additions
Litchfield

Ruth Roberts, cabin
Grand Marais

St. Barnabas Hospital,
addition
Minneapolis

St. Barnabas Hospital,
laboratory expansion
Minneapolis

St. Barnabas Hospital,
X-ray expansion
Minneapolis

Weyerhaeuser Registered
Homes Program,
Atrium Contemporary
prefabricated
model home

1965

Frederick and Mary Rose Goetz,
cabin
Bayfield, Wisconsin

Richard Gray, house
Mound

1966

Richard Bond, house remodel*
Grand Marais

Alicia and John Falck, remodel
Northfield

Hazeltine Development
Corporation, master plan
Chaska

Jared and Catherine How, house
Mankato

Richard and Freda Jordan,
house interiors
Falcon Heights

Richard and Helen Kain, remodel
Falcon Heights

Henry McKnight, property studies
Minneapolis

Minneapolis Housing
and Redevelopment Authority,
elderly housing*
Minneapolis

Joseph Olson, house
Falcon Heights

Peavey Technical Center
Chaska

Redleaf Medical Office, remodel
St. Paul

St. Barnabas Hospital,
laundry room addition
Minneapolis

Elsie Worch, house
St. Paul

1967

John Carney,
middle-income housing studies
Minneapolis

Daniel Joseph, house remodel*
Arden Hills

Meeker County Hospital, kitchen remodel
Litchfield

Metropolitan Medical Center,
combined facility, power station
(with Horty, Elving & Associates Inc.)
Minneapolis

Metropolitan Medical Center,
medical office building
(with Horty, Elving & Associates Inc.)
Minneapolis

Metropolitan Medical Center,
parking structure
(with Horty, Elving & Associates Inc.)
Minneapolis

D. K. and Dorothy Millett,
house remodel
Edina

Drs. Nelson, Jerome, Subak,
and Lund,
medical office remodel
Minneapolis

Frank Preston Jr.,
townhouse feasibility study
Minneapolis

Scott Reardon,
office building and warehouse
Northfield

Paul Schilling, house remodel
St. Paul

St. Barnabas Hospital,
kitchen remodel
Minneapolis

1968

Iseman Company,
mobile home prototypes*
Sioux Falls, South Dakota

Tom Reardon, speculative housing
Sioux Falls, South Dakota

St. Barnabas Hospital,
laboratory expansion
Minneapolis

1969

Cleveland Terrace Apartments
St. Paul

Close Associates Office, addition
Minneapolis

Drs. Gross, Charnley, and Berg,
medical office
Minneapolis

Hambidge and Associates,
office renovation
Minneapolis

Donald Lawrence, garage
Minneapolis

Robert Muller, house
Maple Grove

Nelson Drive-In, remodel
Minneapolis

Windslope, housing,
for MSAIA
Eden Prairie

1970

Martha and Bruce Atwater Jr.,
house
Wayzata

Brave New Workshop, theater remodel
Minneapolis

Cedar Riverside Association,
medical building feasibility study
Minneapolis

Bryce Crawford, house remodel
St. Paul

Wallace Dayton, house
Christmas Lake

Walter DeMars, house
St. Paul

Reynold Jensen, house remodel
Minnetonka

Edgar Johnson, house
Waseca

Morton Kane, house
Golden Valley

Milwaukee Avenue Housing,
housing study
Minneapolis

Tracy Tyler, house remodel
Falcon Heights

1971

Abbott Northwestern Hospital,
doctors' building
Minneapolis

Paul Dieperink, house*
Afton

Harold Muller,
house addition
Minneapolis

1972

Dakon II, warehouse addition
Sioux Falls, South Dakota

Wallace Dayton,
house remodel
Excelsior

Hiawatha YMCA, remodel

Edgar Johnson,
house remodel
Waseca

Bill King, cabin
McCall, Idaho

R. H. Lutes, house remodel*
Mankato

Robert Megard,
house remodel
St. Paul

Snowcrest Ski Lodge, remodel
Somerset, Wisconsin

USDA, grain laboratory
Beltsville, Maryland

1973

Lawrence and Alex Boies,
house
North Oaks

Robert and Janet Herr, house
Prescott, Wisconsin

Roswith Lade, house
Afton

Dan and Shirley Maxwell, house
Plymouth

Seward West Housing,
site development*
Minneapolis

Shubert Outdoor Advertising,
warehouse remodel
Minneapolis

Richard and Ella Slade,
vacation house
Lutsen

Maurice Soberg, house remodel*
Kensington

Walter and Jane White, house
Orono

1974

Dakota Iron,
warehouse remodel
Bloomington

Freshwater Biological Institute
Navarre

Wally Green, house remodel
Golden Valley

William King, cabin guesthouse
McCall, Idaho

Leonard, Street & Deinard,
office remodel
Minneapolis

James Leslie, house*
Deephaven

Allen Milligan, house
Minnetonka

George Peterson, house
Mankato

Saganaga Lodge*
Gunflint Lake

Richard Slade,
kitchen remodel
St. Paul

St. Barnabas Hospital,
power station
Minneapolis

Cynthia and Eric Stokes,
house remodel
Minneapolis

Sidney and Adele Zeitlin,
studio addition
St. Paul

1975

Robert Bromschweig,
house alterations*
Minneapolis

Don and Ivy Celander, house*
North Oaks

Farmington City Hall,
alterations and additions
Farmington

Firehouse Restaurant/Theater
Minneapolis

Homeward Bound Project,
residential facility
New Hope

Norwood and Muriel Nelson, house
Anoka

Nicklow Liquor Store,
architectural services
Minneapolis

Adrian Swanson, house remodel*
Minneapolis

Wapasha Resort,
addition and remodel
Wabasha

1976

Anoka State Hospital,
chemical dependency center
Anoka

Doris Brooker, house
Grand Rapids

Conley and Marney Brooks,
house
Long Lake

Frederic Cook, house remodel*
Wayzata

Wallace Dayton,
house remodel
Excelsior

Edwin and Ellen Elwell,
house remodel
Minneapolis

Robert O. Erickson, house*
Edina

William Gregory, house
Wayzata

John Huseth, house*
Minneapolis

Jones-Harrison Residence,
comprehensive study for
Minneapolis

Minneapolis Opera Company,
alterations and remodel
St. Paul

North Chalet Liquors, remodel
Crystal

Prospect Park Methodist Church,
remodel
Minneapolis

Riverbluff Housing
Minneapolis

Robert Swanson,
house remodel
Deephaven

1977

Bethesda Lutheran
Medical Center, NE clinic
Vadnais Heights

Lawrence and Alex Boies,
house remodel
North Oaks

Brooker-Lund, house
Eden Prairie

Ray Fuhrman, condominiums*
Jordan

Barbara and Frank Heffelfinger,
house
Eden Prairie

Leonard, Street & Deinard,
office renovations
Minneapolis

Northeast Community Clinic
Minneapolis

Ronald McDonald House
Minneapolis

Erland and Elaine Persson, house
Chanhassen

Robyn Peterson, house remodel
Minneapolis

Polish Cultural Center, remodel*
Minneapolis

Richard Poppele, house
Minneapolis

Psychological Testing Center,
office remodel
Minneapolis

Paul Redleaf, house
White Bear Lake

Richard Slade, house remodel
St. Paul

1978

Bethesda Lutheran Medical Center,
remodel
St. Paul

Lawrence and Alex Boies,
kitchen remodel
North Oaks

Francis and Marge Bradley,
house remodel
St. Louis Park

Michael Favero, house
Minneapolis

Robert and Lucy Mitchell, house*
Wayzata

John and Jacqueline Nelson, house
Flossmoor, Illinois

Seward West Re-Design,
earth-sheltered townhouses
Minneapolis

1979

H. B. Fuller Company,
research labs
Vadnais Heights

John and Elizabeth Guthrie, house
Wayzata

William and Chrysmarie Isaacson,
house
Afton

Lyman Lodge,
property improvement
Excelsior

Robert and Carol Owens, house
Tonka Bay

Pratt School, renovations
Minneapolis

Tuttle School, renovations
Minneapolis

Beryl Wright, condominiums*
St. Paul

1980

James Brown, house remodel
Prescott, Arizona

Caswell-Massey,
store remodel
Minneapolis

Joe Giganti, house addition
Eagan

Richard Helgeson, house*
Hopkins

Viola Kanatz,
house addition
Brooklyn Center

Lowertown Redevelopment
St. Paul

Donald Mayberg,
house remodel
Minneapolis

Prince of Peace Lutheran Church,
sanctuary remodel
Roseville

Peter and Peggy Rejto, house remodel
Minneapolis

Ronald McDonald House,
Phase II
Minneapolis

St. John's University,
dormitory studies
Collegeville

Lewis and Hollie Wannamaker,
house addition
St. Paul

Robert and Nettie Warwood
North Oaks

Byron Webster, house addition
Afton

1981

Bruce Atwater,
kitchen renovation
Wayzata

Anne Barnum, house addition
Minneapolis

Brooks and Bowman,
retail store
Minnetonka

Bruce Dayton, house remodel
Wayzata

Ernst and Josephine Eckert,
house addition
St. Paul

Richard Gray, cabin
Minnetrista

Stanley and Karen Hubbard,
house
St. Marys Point

William Kennedy,
house alterations
St. Paul

Arlan and Bev Mercil, house
East Bethel

Metroplace, condominiums
Minneapolis

Minnetonka Inc.,
planned residential development*

Powderhorn Community Council,
town court housing
Minneapolis

Redfield Homes, housing
Minnetrista

Robert Warwood, residence
North Oaks

1982

Brooker-Lund, house addition
Eden Prairie

Wallace Dayton, remodel
Excelsior

Richard and Alice Falck, remodel
Northfield

Donald Mayberg, remodel
Minneapolis

Ed Stanko, house*
Minneapolis

James Sullivan, house
St. Paul

1983

Brian and Susan Anderson,
house addition
Minneapolis

Caswell-Massey, store design
Minneapolis

Al and Neva Feiler, parking lot
Bloomington

Starke Hathaway, remodel
Minneapolis

John and Anne Hughes, house
Sioux Falls, South Dakota

Janssen Development Company,
rental housing*
Minneapolis

Greg and Sarah Kruger, house addition
Minneapolis

Leonard, Street & Deinard,
office remodel
Minneapolis

Richard McGehee, house addition
Roseville

Muller Mortuary, remodel
St. Paul

George and Noel Nelms, remodel
Edina

Louis Safer, house remodel
St. Paul

George Shaw, house addition
Minneapolis

St. Lawrence Church, basement remodel
Minneapolis

Stempf Alignment Supply,
building expansion
Minnetonka

Tuttle-Marcy Elementary School,
art room remodel
Minneapolis

1984

Caswell-Massey, store remodel
St. Paul

Wallace and Mary Lee Dayton,
house
Wayzata

Tom and Shirley Ludlow,
house renovation*
Mounds View

Prior Lake City Hall,
addition
Prior Lake

1985

Titus and Carol Belleville,
house addition
Minneapolis

Jackson and Gayle Crose,
house addition
St. Louis Park

Robert and Elizabeth Galloway,
house
Plymouth

John and Vivian Newmann,
house addition
Brooklyn Park

Bill and Diana Nordrum,
house remodel
Minneapolis

Scoliosis House
Minneapolis

Katie Trotsky,
house renovation
Minneapolis

Wasserman and Baill Attorneys,
office renovation
Minneapolis

1986

Betty Anderson, garage addition
St. Paul

Oliver Arrett, house
Deephaven

Bruce Atwater,
house remodel
Wayzata

Boy Scouts Viking Council,
facilities remodel
Various

Conley and Marney Brooks,
house addition
Long Lake

Bye-Wicklund,
porch remodel
Minneapolis

Camp Tanadoona, shelter
Chanhassen

David and Sigrid Coats,
house addition
Minneapolis

Concordia Lutheran Church
St. Paul

Donald N. Ferguson Hall,
University of Minnesota
Minneapolis

Girl Scout Headquarters, addition
Brooklyn Center

Girl Scouts of Greater Minneapolis,
property study
Minneapolis

Jeffrey and Mary Hicken, house addition
Anoka

Metropolitan Medical Center,
information services
Minneapolis

Metropolitan Medical Center,
neurology office remodel
Minneapolis

Metropolitan Medical Center,
Unit 5A
Minneapolis

Minnesota Memories,
storefront
Minneapolis

Ron and JoAnne Moquist, house*
Sioux Falls, South Dakota

Oneida Education Center
St. Paul

Niles Schulz, house addition
Minneapolis

Tri-County Hospital
Wadena

Tulips Restaurant, renovation
St. Paul

1987

The International School
Eden Prairie

1990

Children's Hospital of St. Paul,
cart design
St. Paul

Children's Hospital of St. Paul,
fourth-floor remodel
St. Paul

Children's Hospital of St. Paul,
laboratory remodel
St. Paul

Children's Hospital of St. Paul,
signage
St. Paul

Children's Hospital of St. Paul,
third-floor remodel
St. Paul

Children's Hospital of St. Paul,
waiting room interiors
St. Paul

Robert and Carolyn Hedin,
house
Red Wing

Minneapolis Friends Meeting,
church renovation
Minneapolis

Minneapolis Public Schools/
Marcy Elementary
Minneapolis

Twin Cities Housing Development,
new construction
St. Paul

Twin Cities Housing Development/
909 Selby Commons
St. Paul

Twin Cities Housing Development,
office
St. Paul

Twin Cities Housing Development,
remodel
St. Paul

1991

Gillette/Children's Hospital, addition
St. Paul

Children's Hospital of St. Paul,
elevator remodel
St. Paul

Children's Hospital of St. Paul,
play structure
St. Paul

The International School of Minnesota,
classroom (pod) design
Eden Prairie

The International School of Minnesota,
fine arts building
Eden Prairie

The International School of Minnesota,
kitchen/cafeteria remodel
Eden Prairie

The Loft, elevator feasibility study
Minneapolis

Powderhorn Community Council,
in-fill housing prototype
Minneapolis

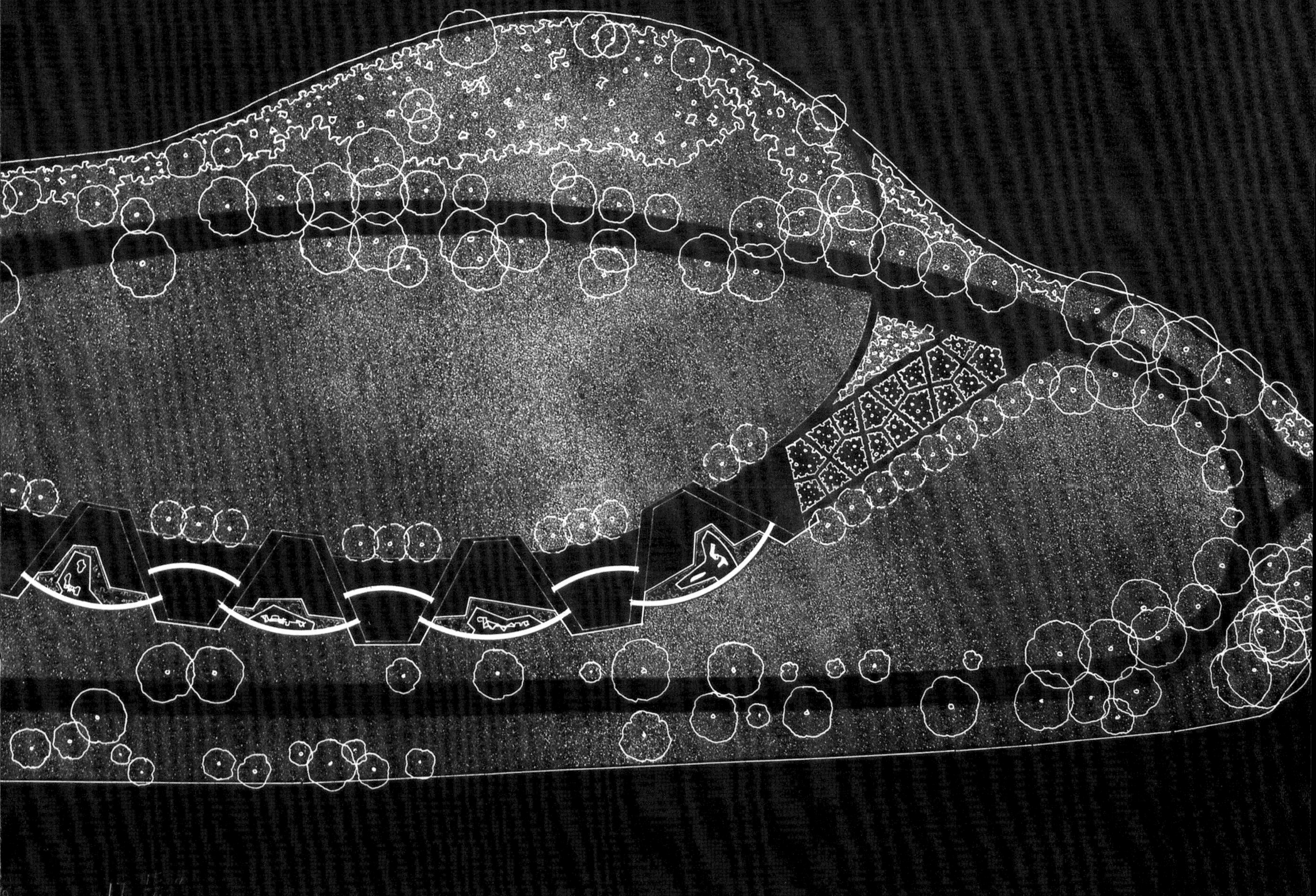

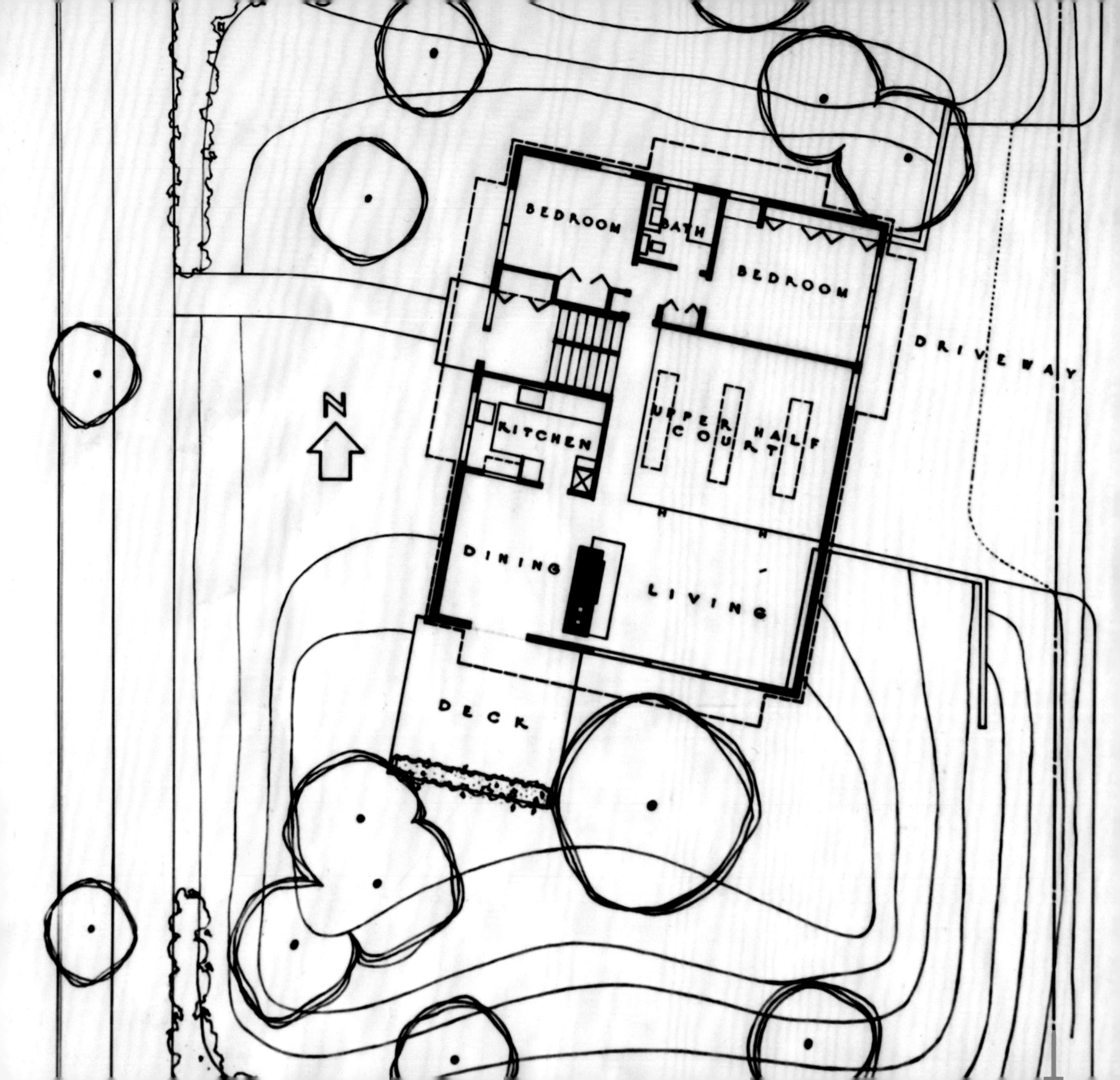
BEDROOM
BATH
BEDROOM
DRIVEWAY
N
KITCHEN
UPPER HALF COURT
DINING
LIVING
DECK

Notes

INTRODUCTION

1 "Gold Medal," www.aia-mn.org. Previous recipients were Ralph Rapson, Thomas Ellerbe, Edward Sovik, Robert Cerny, Leonard Parker, Richard Hammel, James Stageberg, George Rafferty, Curtis Green, Frederick Bentz, Bruce Abrahamson, and John Rauma. It would be another twelve years before a second woman, Julie Snow, received the Gold Medal in 2014.

2 Roy Close remarks at Lisl Close memorial service, June 4, 2012.

3 Elizabeth "Lisl" Scheu Close, FAIA, Oral History Interview with Jane King Hession, April 17, 2000; Minnesota Historical Society, St. Paul, Minnesota.

4 *Modern Architecture: International Exhibition*, exhibition catalog (New York: Museum of Modern Art, 1932), www.moma.org.

5 *Modern Architecture.*

6 Other planned venues were the Pennsylvania Art Museum, Philadelphia; the Carnegie Institute, Pittsburgh; Wadsworth Athenaeum, Hartford, Connecticut; Fogg Art Museum, Cambridge, Massachusetts; the Art Museum, Worcester, Massachusetts; Buffalo Fine Arts Academy; the Rochester Memorial Art Gallery, Rochester, New York; Cleveland Museum of Art; Cincinnati Art Museum; Toledo Museum of Art; Milwaukee Art Institute; and Bullock's Wilshire gallery, Los Angeles. Museum of Modern Art press release, January 17, 1932, www.moma.org.

7 The Vienna Werkbund, which reached its height with the Werkbundsiedlung, was a later phase of the Austrian Werkbund founded in 1913. It sought a productive "collaboration between art, crafts, and industry." "Werkbundsiedlung Wien," www.werkbundsiedlung-wien.at/en.

8 *Werkbundsiedlung Wien 1932: A Model for New Living*, exhibition brochure, Wien Museum.

9 *Werkbundsiedlung Wien 1932.*

10 Judith Eiblmayr, interview with author, December 4, 2017, Edina, Minnesota.

11 Judith Fawcett, "Dual Homebuilder," *Ivory Tower*, March 10, 1958.

12 Close Oral History, April 17, 2000.

13 Sarah Allaback, *The First American Women Architects* (Urbana: University of Illinois Press, 2008), 97.

14 Allaback, 233–35. Allaback acknowledged that her list "Female Graduates of Architecture Schools, 1878–1934" remains incomplete.

15 Information and quotes in this paragraph from "A Thousand Women in Architecture, Part I," *Architectural Record*, March 1948, 105.

16 It took a while for some official documents to acknowledge two sexes in the profession. In 1954, when Lisl received certification from the National Council of Architectural Registration Boards (NCARB), the preprinted certificate text referred to her as "he." Elizabeth S. Close NCARB certificate, November 19, 1954, from the collection of Close Associates.

17 Susana Torre, ed., *Women in American Architecture: A Historic and Contemporary Perspective* (New York: Whitney Library of Design, 1977), 90. The data are based on a 1958 survey conducted by Rose Connor, AIA, using "lists of women architects sent by the Architectural Examining Boards of the various states."

18 Despina Stratigakos, *Where Are the Women Architects?* (Princeton, N.J.: Princeton University Press, 2016), 30.

19 Edna Kathryn Croft (BS, 1921) is listed as the first woman graduate of the university's School of Architecture, which was established in 1913. Twenty-three of the forty-eight graduates earned bachelor's degrees in "architecture and decoration" or "interior architecture." "Class Lists by Year," University of Minnesota School of Architecture | College of Design, https://arch.design.umn.edu.

20 Brink, who earned a BS in architecture and decoration, collaborated with Ingemann on the design

of the Lowell Inn (1927) in Stillwater, Minnesota. Prior to opening their firms, Parker and Brunson worked in the offices of Purcell and Feick (later Purcell and Elmslie) and Augustus Gauger, respectively. Information from the Emma F. Brunson Papers (N123) and Marion Alice Parker Collection (N130), Northwest Architectural Archives, University of Minnesota Libraries, Minneapolis. Also, Allaback, *The First American Women Architects*, 56, 165–66.

21 "Will Speak," undated clipping from an unknown newspaper. The use of Lisl's maiden name, and the location of the talk, dates the clipping to between February 1936 and April 1938. Roy M. Close Family Papers.

22 In addition to Lisl, the article featured Dorothea F. Radusch, DDS, an associate professor at the University of Minnesota; Jane Kavanagh, a lawyer with Bonham and Kavanagh in Mound, Minnesota; and Dr. Ruth Boynton, director of student health at the University of Minnesota. In 1948 Lisl designed a house for Boynton in Bloomington, Minnesota. "Doctor, Lawyer, Dentist, Architect Agree: Women Are Own Worst Enemy," *Minneapolis Star*, December 6, 1949.

23 "Here's a Quick Look at: Mrs. Elizabeth Close," *Minneapolis Star*, September 18, 1952.

24 Jacqueline Larkin, "Woman behind the Man: Her Blueprint for Living Calls for Architectural Teamwork," *Minneapolis Star*, July 4, 1956.

25 Close Oral History, June 26, 2000.

26 Linda Mack, "Women Architects Make Their Way in an Old Boys' Profession," *Minneapolis Star Tribune First Sunday*, April 6, 1992.

CHAPTER 1
VIENNA, 1912 to 1932

1 The author thanks Elfriede Pokorny of the Verein für Geschichte der Arbeiterinnenbewegung and Dr. Christa Veigl, both of Vienna, for identifying the date and providing context for the Augarten event. The event is more fully documented in the booklet *Wiens Kinder und Amerika: Die amerikanische Kinderhilfsaktion 1919*, by Friedrich Reischl.

2 Close Oral History, May 1, 2000.

3 Mayor Jacob Reumann, a friend of Scheu, made the appointment. Scheu held the post until 1923. Eve Blau, *The Architecture of Red Vienna, 1919–1934* (Cambridge, Mass.: MIT Press, 1999), 91.

4 According to Lisl, it was O'Neal (whom she called "Brownie"), not her mother, who raised her. O'Neal was living with the Scheus in Vienna at the outbreak of World War I. As a British citizen, she was regarded as an enemy alien and was forced to remain in Austria until the end of the war.

5 The World Heritage nomination states that the palace and gardens together comprise a "remarkable ensemble and a perfect example of *Gesamtkunstwerk*," or a "masterly fusion of many art forms," http://whc.unesco.org.

6 Benedetto Gravagnuolo, *Adolf Loos: Theory and Works* (London: Art Data, 1995), 146.

7 Loos did more than sign the book—he wrote a two-page essay titled "Die kranken Ohren Beethovens" ("The Sick Ears of Beethoven"), in which he compared his feelings of being misunderstood as an architect to Beethoven's perceived struggle to be understood as a composer. The Scheu House Guest Book, unpublished artifact in the collection of the Wien Museum, Vienna, Austria, and Close Oral History, March 20, 2000.

8 Close Oral History, March 20, 2000.

9 Ulrich Conrads, *Programs and Manifestoes on Twentieth-Century Architecture* (Cambridge, Mass.: MIT Press, 1993), 20. In 1898 Loos attempted to ally himself with the artists and architects of the Viennese Secession movement by offering to design, pro bono, some interior furnishings for the newly completed Secession Building by Joseph Maria Olbrich. His offer was rejected.

10 Untitled article in the *Nation*, July 9, 1914. Robert Scheu was also the author of *Travels through Bohemia, 1919*, a book that chronicles his journey through that region between the world wars.

11 The living room and inglenook from Loos's apartment are now in the collection of the Wien Museum Karlsplatz in Vienna.

12 In addition to maintaining an enduring friendship with Loos, Gustav Scheu served as his friend's defense attorney in 1928 when Loos was arrested on child molestation and indecent act charges. Although Loos was acquitted of the two most serious charges, he was found guilty of "causing [the girls to commit] obscene acts." He was sentenced to four months in prison, but given credit for jail time served. Christopher Long, *Adolf Loos on Trial* (Prague: Kant, 2017), 129–30.

13 Josef Scheu's contributions to the Austrian Social Democratic Party, as well as those of other members of the Scheu family, are documented at the Red Vienna Museum (*Das Rote Wien im Waschsalon*) in Karl-Marx-Hof in Vienna, and on that organization's Web-based Dictionary of Viennese Social Democracy (*Weblexikon der Wiener Sozialidemokratie*, www.dasrotewien-waschsalon.at). The Josef-Scheu-Hof, a 212-apartment complex in Vienna, was named for Scheu, and a street in the tenth district bears the name Scheugasse.

14 Information in this paragraph is from Andreas Scheu Papers, International Institute of Social History, Amsterdam, www.iisg.amsterdam/en.

15 Howard published his ideas in 1898 in *Tomorrow: A Peaceful Path to Real Reform*, retitled *Garden Cities of Tomorrow* in the 1902 edition. Fundamentally, Howard argued that the ideal condition was neither the town nor the country, but a "town–country magnet," or Garden City, which offered all the advantages but none of the disadvantages of town or country alone.

16 Scheu served as housing adviser for a little more than a year, resigning in June 1920. He remained on the city council until 1923. Blau, *Red Vienna*, 91, 92, 94. Ultimately, the Social Democrats abandoned Scheu's Garden City–inspired proposals in favor of massive, multiblock apartment complexes.

17 Gravagnuolo, *Adolf Loos*, 168.

18 Generally, Susanne Blumesberger, ed., *Helene Scheu-Riesz (1880–1970): Eine Frau zwischen den Welten* (Vienna: Präsens Verlag, 2005). The author thanks Judith Eiblmayr and Benjamin Petri LaFirst for providing translated portions of Blumesberger's book. Opinions differ as to whether Helene joined the party. Blumesberger claims "she joined the Social Democratic Organization of Women," but daughter-in-law Herta Scheu stated that although Helene was active in peace and humanitarian movements, she was "a nonpolitical" person and did not join the party. Herta Scheu interview in the unpublished manuscript "Helene Scheu-Riesz (1880–1970): A Biography of an Austrian Woman and Publisher," compiled by O. M. Drekonja and Anne Close Ulmer, n.d., Roy M. Close Family Papers.

19 Scheu-Riesz related her association with Cadbury in her 1947 book *Open Sesame: Books Are Keys*, published by Island Press Cooperative, a company she founded in New York. No doubt the Scheus were also aware of Cadbury's dedicated efforts to improve living conditions for workers and the poor. In 1879 Cadbury and his brother established the Bournville housing estate around their chocolate factory outside Birmingham, England. The concept, which predated Ebenezer Howard's Garden City plan, featured dwelling units with individual gardens as well as access to public spaces—notable amenities, at the time, for working-class housing. "The Garden City Conference: A Visit to Bournville," *Manchester Guardian*, September 23, 1901.

20 Volumes in the Sesame series included *Ali Baba and the Forty Thieves, A Midsummer's Night Dream*, and English, French, Norwegian, Chinese, and Czech stories. In 1934 she wrote *Gretchen Discovers America*, a loosely veiled, fictionalized account of Lisl's move to the United States, published by the London-based firm of J. M. Dent and Sons. In 1944 Helene edited *Will You Marry Me?*, a collection of marriage proposals by famous writers and historic figures over the centuries. The book remains in print today.

21 Sesam-Verlag's edition of the German-language *Alice im Spiegelland* is rare and highly collectible today. Lisl inherited the original watercolor paintings Birnbaum created for the edition. She later donated them to the Kerlan Collection of the Children's Literature Research Collections at the University of Minnesota, Minneapolis.

22 General Loos background from Ralf Bock, *Adolf Loos: Works and Projects* (Milan: Skira, 2007). Loos was a fastidious dresser who favored bespoke clothing. As such, he had many opinions on the relationship between a well-cut suit and cultural advancement. He frequented the finest tailors in Vienna, including Ebenstein, Kniže, Goldman and Salatsch, and Mandl, for whom he designed retail spaces.

23 They include the Steiner House (1910) for manufacturer Hugo Steiner and his wife, Lilly, an artist; the Horner House (1912) for Andreas Horner, a hotel concierge, and his wife, Helene; the Stoessl House (1913), for author and literary critic Otto Stoessl and his wife, Annette, an educator. All three houses stand within a three-mile radius of the Scheu House. Generally, Bock, *Adolf Loos*.

24 A photograph from the 1950s shows the first-floor terrace enclosed in glass. It was not original to the house and has since been removed. Roy M. Close Family Papers.

25 To address food shortages during World War I, Lisl's mother attempted to raise chickens and goats on the property. Lisl later recalled the enterprise was amusing but unsuccessful because her mother purchased a rooster instead of a hen, and the goats were "unpleasant animals." Close Oral History, June 5, 2000.

26 Gravagnuolo, *Adolf Loos*, 146.

27 Gravagnuolo, 148.

28 Historian Eve Blau has described the building's profile and use of terraces in the housing unit as an "adapt[ation of] the Scheu House type to proletarian purposes." Blau, *Red Vienna*, 300. Prior to designing the Scheu House, Loos proposed a terraced scheme for a 1910 "Project for a Department Store," in Alexandria, Egypt, and later for several projects, including "A Group of Twenty Houses with Terraces" for the Côte d'Azur, France, and the Grand Hotel Babylon for Nice, France, both dating from 1923, and the 1931 Fleischner House in Haifa, Israel. None of the projects were built. Gravagnuolo, *Adolf Loos*, 177–79.

29 Close Oral History, June 26, 2000.

30 Bock, *Adolf Loos*, 71.

31 Bock, 34.

32 Gravagnuolo, *Adolf Loos*, 139.

33 Loos was an admirer of English tailoring and furniture, and he believed Chippendale chairs to be "the most comfortable and perfect chairs for the dining room." He employed a craftsman to produce copies of Chippendale furniture for his clients, including the Scheus. Bock, *Adolf Loos*, 37.

34 Close Oral History, March 20, 2000.

35 Bock, *Adolf Loos*, 81.

36 Lisl and Madi "were inseparable" until 1927, when Madi was killed in a rock-climbing accident in Grundlsee, Austria. She was fourteen. Tragically, Madi was the third of the Rosenfelds' four children to die at a young age. Close Oral History, June 5, 2000.

37 Marvin Trachtenberg and Isabelle Hyman, *Architecture from Prehistory to Postmodernity*, 2nd ed. (New York: Harry N. Abrams), 492, and generally.

38 Trachtenberg and Hyman, 492.

39 Kathleen James-Chakraborty, *Architecture since 1400* (Minneapolis: University of Minnesota Press, 2014), 348.

40 Close Oral History, June 26, 2000.

41 Blau, *Red Vienna*, 93.

42 The entries between 1937 and 1954 chronicle visitors to Helene's residences in New York City and Chapel Hill, North Carolina, where she lived after she left Vienna. She returned to Vienna, and the Scheu House, in 1954.

43 Addams, an ardent feminist, shared the 1931 Nobel Peace Prize with peace activist Nicholas Murray Butler. The Illinois-born Addams was the founder and international president of the Women's International League for Peace and Freedom. www.nobelprize.org.

44 All quotations in this paragraph from Close Oral History, June 26, 2000. Late in life Lisl remained "astonished" by the signatures recorded in the guest book, concluding, "I think somebody could write a book about it—a book about the book."

45 Lisl later attributed her interest in and study of the cello to hearing Niedermann practicing on the instrument in the Scheu House.

46 According to Lisl's son Roy Close, Gustav Scheu was the attorney for Universal Edition, a music publisher founded in Vienna in 1901. Among the composers the company published were Berg and Webern, as well as Gustav Mahler and Arnold Schoenberg. Roy Close interview with author, August 28, 2017, Osceola, Wisconsin.

47 *Calliope Austria: Women in Society, Culture, and the Sciences*, exhibition catalog of the Federal Ministry for Europe, Integration and Foreign Affairs Cultural Policy Division (Austria: GRASL FairPrint, 2016), 65.

48 Carmen Espegel, *Women Architects in the Modern Movement* (New York and London: Routledge, 2018), 166.

49 Elizabeth and Winston Close interview with Lauren Soth, 1987, Falcon Heights, Minnesota.

50 Close Oral History, January 25, 2001.

51 Mathilda McQuaid, *Lilly Reich: Designer and Architect*, exhibition catalogue (New York: Museum of Modern Art, 1996), www.moma.org/calendar/exhibitions/278.

52 "Flora Steiger-Crawford," *Dictionnaire historique de la Suisse*, www.his-dhs-dss.ch.

53 Quotations and information in this paragraph from *Calliope Austria*, 65–71.

54 Generally, Espegel, *Women Architects*.

55 Even today, despite her Viennese pedigree, famous childhood home, and significant career as a modern architect in the United States, Elizabeth Scheu Close remains almost entirely unknown in Europe—even in Austria.

56 Sources referenced include *Calliope Austria* and Tanja Poppelretuer, "German-Speaking Refugee Women Architects before the Second World War" (unpublished manuscript, University of Salford, Manchester, 2018).

57 Close Oral History, March 27, 2000.

58 Close Oral History, June 26, 2000.

59 Close Oral History, January 25, 2001.

60 Close Oral History, March 20, 2000.

61 Close Oral History, March 20, 2000. According to Roy Close, his mother did not have a religious upbringing despite Helene's rejection of Judaism and embrace of Quakerism. "Lisl never thought of herself as a Quaker—she was an atheist to her boots, and in any case, if her mother was for it, Lisl was probably against it." Roy Close email to author, December 19, 2018.

62 Ulmer is the daughter and eldest child of Lisl and Win Close. Anne Ulmer interview with author, May 3, 2010, Cannon Falls, Minnesota.

63 Close Oral History, January 25, 2001.

64 According to Roy Close, this was the "unofficial version of the story." Roy Close interview.

65 Roy Close interview.

66 Close Oral History, June 1, 2001.

67 When Lisl first arrived in the United States on August 29, 1932, she was granted entry to study for one year at MIT. In July 1933, she was granted an extension until October 29, 1934. Filene signed the affidavit on August 23, 1934. No doubt Lisl needed the document to secure an immigration visa under the 1924 U.S. Immigration Act, which set quotas on immigration from certain countries, including Austria. Roy M. Close Family Papers.

68 Lisl, then fifteen, served as one of Barbara Nolen's bridesmaids.

69 Blumesberger, *Helene Scheu-Riesz.*

70 Roy Close interview.

71 Blumesberger, *Helene Scheu-Riesz.* Blumesberger added that Blanche C. Weill, "a wealthy child psychologist," helped fund the Island Workshop Press, which was also called Island Press Cooperative at one time. Later the name was shortened to Island Press.

72 Anne Ulmer interview.

73 Six months passed before Friedl and Herta's two-year-old daughter, Helga, was permitted to join them in London. According to Veronica Kothbauer, Helga's younger sister, the Scheus initially thought it was safer to leave her in Vienna with her maternal grandmother. However, the Nazis "wanted to 'confiscate' Helga thinking that her parents would return to collect her," and thereby use her as a pawn. When they did not return, the Nazis issued a passport to Helga and allowed her to travel to England. Veronica Kothbauer email to author, March 28, 2018.

74 Veronica Kothbauer email to author. The house remained in the possession of members of Herta's family, including her mother, brother Walter (who "had joined the Nazis"), and his wife, during the war.

75 Lisl's son Roy and daughter-in-law Linda accompanied her on the trip. Close Oral History, March 20, 2000.

76 Close Oral History, March 20, 2000.

CHAPTER 2 BECOMING AN ARCHITECT IN AMERICA

1 Caroline Shillaber, *Massachusetts Institute of Technology School of Architecture 1861–1961: A Hundred Year Chronicle* (Cambridge: Massachusetts Institute of Technology, 1963), 34. Women were first accepted to the university in 1883.

2 Generally, from MIT History, https://libraries.mit.edu/mithistory/research/schools-and-departments/school-of-architecture-and-planning/department-of-architecture.

3 Lawrence B. Anderson, "The Rogers Building, 1866–1938," *Places: A Quarterly Journal of Environmental Design* (Massachusetts Institute of Technology) 1, no. 4 (1984): 38.

4 Anderson, 39.

5 Close Oral History, March 27, 2000.

6 Close Oral History, August 22, 2000.

7 Close Oral History, August 22, 2000.

8 Close Oral History, March 27, 2000.

9 Close Oral History, April 17, 2000. The Boston Architectural Club existed until 1944, when it became the Boston Architectural Center and, later, the Boston Architectural College.

10 That same year, German architect Ludwig Mies van der Rohe moved to the United States and a year later became head of the School of Architecture at the Armour Institute of Technology (later the Illinois Institute of Technology) in Chicago. Hungarian-born László Moholy-Nagy, an influential avant-garde designer, painter, and photographer, also immigrated to America to become the director of the New Bauhaus in Chicago. Both men had previously held leadership and teaching positions at the Bauhaus in Germany.

11 Close Oral History, April 17, 2000.

12 Lawrence B. Anderson, "Architectural Education at M.I.T.: The 1930s and After," *Architectural Education and Boston: Centennial Publication of the Boston Architectural Center, 1889–1989* (Boston: The Center, 1989), 87–90. Jacques Carlu was the "guru" at MIT, and Jean-Jacques Haffner had that role at Harvard.

13 Oral history interview with Lawrence Anderson, January 30–March 30, 1992, Smithsonian Archives of American Art, Washington, D.C., www.aaa.si.edu/collections/interviews.

14 Oral history interview with Lawrence Anderson.

15 Oral history interview with Lawrence Anderson. In addition to his role in shifting MIT's curriculum away from classicism toward modernism, Anderson practiced what he preached. In 1937 he and MIT colleague Herbert Beckwith cofounded Anderson & Beckwith, an influential modern architecture firm in Cambridge.

16 Shillaber, *Massachusetts Institute of Technology*, 75.

17 Shillaber, 75.

18 Shillaber, 75.

19 The name of the fellow student with whom Lisl traveled has been lost. Lisl did identify her as a woman who was engaged to the son of the head of the Bureau of Indian Affairs, which motivated the drive to the Southwest. Lisl Close Oral History Interview/Idea House Project, April 18, 2000. Walker Art Center Archives, Minneapolis.

20 Close Oral History, March 27, 2000.

21 Close Oral History, June 26, 2000.

22 Elizabeth Hilde Scheu, "A Production Plant for Pre-Fabricated Houses" (undergraduate thesis, Massachusetts Institute of Technology, October 3,

1934), author's collection. It is not surprising that she would approach a problem from that vantage point. According to Lisl's son Roy, "There's a long socialist tradition in my family. . . . My mother was a third-generation socialist. Shake the family tree where you will, a socialist is likely to fall out." Roy Close email to author, February 3, 2018.

23 Roy Close interview.

24 Elizabeth and Winston Close interview.

25 Among the projects Win worked on for Thomas Ellerbe & Company was St. Paul City Hall and Ramsey County Courthouse in St. Paul, completed in 1932. Roy Close interview.

26 In 1930, while at MIT, Anderson received the prestigious Paris Prize for postgraduate study at the École des Beaux-Arts in Paris, the only University of Minnesota alumnus to do so. His competition drawings, as well as those of other Paris Prize winners, are now in the collection of the Metropolitan Museum of Art in New York. Anderson was instrumental in turning MIT's curriculum toward modernism. "Lawrence Anderson: Architect and Dean at MIT Was 87," obituary, *New York Times*, April 12, 1994, and *100 Years of Student Drawings: Celebrating the School of Architecture's Centennial, 1913–2013*, a publication of the Goldstein Museum of Design and the University of Minnesota College of Design.

27 Lawrence Anderson Oral History. Bunshaft also earned his undergraduate degree at MIT in 1933. A partner in the firm of Skidmore, Owings & Merrill (SOM), he designed the Lever House (1952), an early International Style skyscraper that is now a New York City landmark. Weese is perhaps best known for his design of the Washington Metro system in Washington, D.C. Netsch, also a partner at SOM, was the lead designer of the U.S. Air Force Academy Cadet Chapel in Colorado Springs.

28 Close Oral History, May 1, 2000,

29 Amalienbad, completed in 1926 in Vienna's Tenth District, is an architecturally spectacular example of such a facility. Unfortunately, no record exists of Lisl's graduate thesis project.

30 Roy Close interview.

31 Founded in 1933 and originally named the Federal Emergency Administration of Public Works in 1933, it became the Public Works Administration, or PWA, in 1935. The PWA focused primarily on the construction of large-scale projects and infrastructure.

32 Close Oral History, June 26, 2000.

33 Close Oral History, June 26, 2000.

34 Close Oral History, June 26, 2000.

35 Close Oral History, June 26, 2000.

36 General information and all quotations in this paragraph from the Carl Mackley Houses National Register of Historic Places (NRHP) registration form, May 6, 1998. The project was named for Carl Mackley, a union member who was killed during a strike in 1930.

37 Press release, June 9, 1936, Museum of Modern Art, www.moma.org. Westfield Acres was demolished in 2001.

38 Federal Writers' Project of the Works Progress Administration for the State of New Jersey, *New Jersey: A Guide to Its Present and Past* (New York: Viking Press, 1939), 236.

39 Oral History interview with Marion Greenwood, January 31, 1964, Archives of American Art, Smithsonian Institution, www.aaa.si.edu/collections/interviews. Greenwood studied mural and fresco painting in Mexico and later taught fresco painting at Columbia University.

40 Close Oral History, June 5, 2000.

41 Carl Mackley Houses NRHP.

42 Press release, Museum of Modern Art, July 9, 1936, www.moma.org/documents/moma_press-release_325054.pdf.

43 Close Oral History, August 22, 2000.

44 Anthony Alofsin, ed., *Frank Lloyd Wright: Europe and Beyond* (Berkeley: University of California Press, 1999), 18.

45 Roy Close interview.

46 Roy Close interview. Stonorov maintained a lifelong interest in and ties with labor unions. He was a longtime friend of United Automobile Workers president Walter Reuther and designed the UAW headquarters building in Detroit. In 1970, while traveling together to inspect the construction of the UAW's Black Lake Conference Center in Onaway, Michigan, Stonorov and Reuther were killed in a plane crash. Oscar Stonorov Papers, 1912–1970, American Heritage Center, University of Wyoming, Laramie, https://rmoa.unm.edu.

47 "Historic Wind Chill Temperatures in Minnesota," Minnesota Department of Natural Resources, www. dnr.state.mn.us. This number is based on the "new formula" for calculating wind chill. According to the old formula, the wind chill was -87°F. "Heatwave of July 1936," National Weather Service, www.weather.gov.

48 National Housing Conference Inc. records. Social Welfare History Archives, University of Minnesota, Minneapolis, https://archives.lib.umn.edu.

49 This was the first of three annual European housing tours Alfred led between 1936 and 1938. Daniel T. Rodgers, *Atlantic Crossings: Social Politics in a Progressive Age* (Cambridge, Mass.: Harvard University Press, 2009), 465, and International

Federation for Housing and Planning, IFHP History, www.ifhp.org.

50 "Engineer Backs Slum Project," *Minneapolis Star*, August 1935.

51 According to University of Minnesota associate professor Katherine Solomonson, "They had particular parts of Sumner Field Homes that were for African- Americans. Another section, a larger section for what they called 'mixed whites,' " *Cornerstones: A History of North Minneapolis | Sumner Field*, Twin Cities PBS: TPT documentary, www.mnvideovault.org.

52 Close Oral History, June 5, 2000. Sumner Field Homes were demolished in 1998.

53 Among them was a 1936 house in Hennepin County for client Ray Swarthout. The house was not built when bids for its construction exceeded estimates "by approximately one hundred percent." Letter to C. A. Bardwell Co. from Close and Scheu, of the Office of Magney and Tusler, January 27, 1937. Close Associates Papers, Northwest Architectural Archives, University of Minnesota Libraries, Minneapolis.

54 Close Oral History, March 27, 2000.

55 Mack, "Women Architects Make Their Way in an Old Boys' Profession."

CHAPTER 3 MINNESOTA'S FIRST MODERN ARCHITECTS

1 Mack, "Women Architects Make Their Way in an Old Boys' Profession."

2 Roy Close interview.

3 Roy Close interview.

4 *Minneapolis Journal*, undated clipping, Roy M. Close Family Papers.

5 Possibly the first woman to "have the temerity" to open her own firm was architect Louise Blanchard Bethune (1856–1913), who did so in Buffalo, New York, at the age of twenty-five. Bethune was the first female architect to become a Fellow of the American Institute of Architects (FAIA) in 1889. Susana Torre, ed., *Women in American Architecture: A Historic and Contemporary Perspective* (New York: Whitney Library of Design, 1977), 61–62.

6 Gar Hargens interview with Jane King Hession and Rolf Anderson, for the Minnesota Modern Masters program of the Minnesota Chapter of the Society of Architectural Historians, November 8, 2015.

7 Georgia Bizios interview with author, June 3, 2012, Minneapolis.

8 Hargens interview, November 8, 2015.

9 Bizios interview.

10 Julia Robinson telephone interview with author, September 28, 2018.

11 Hargens interview, November 8, 2015.

12 "Sponsor" to the American Institute of Architects College of Fellows, 1969. Roy M. Close Family Papers. Although the identity of the "sponsor" is not known, this person did identify himself or herself as the Closes' "associate for twelve years."

13 Oral History with Lawrence Anderson.

14 Oral History with Lawrence Anderson.

15 "Werkbundsiedlung Wien," www.werkbundsied lung-wien.at.

16 Linda Lee, "St. Paul's Architectural Time Capsule," *New York Times*, January 5, 1989.

17 Alan K. Lathrop, *Minnesota Architects: A Biographical Dictionary* (Minneapolis: University of Minnesota Press, 2010), 184.

18 The Closes also knew and admired Jones. They named their first son, Roy, after him.

19 Gwendolyn Wright, *USA: Modern Architectures in History* (London: Reaktion Books, 2008), 10.

20 "Eight Houses for Modern Living," *Life*, September 26, 1938.

21 "Eight Houses for Modern Living."

22 The Blackbourns, who had an annual income of $5,000 to $6,000, could not afford to build Wright's extravagant scheme. A version of the house, minus the pool Wright originally proposed, was built two years later, at a cost of roughly $20,000, for Bernard Schwartz in Two Rivers, Wisconsin. The other "modern" architects who created designs were Edward Durrell Stone, William Wurster, and Wallace K. Harrison and J. André Fouilhoux. The "traditional" architects were Richard Koch, H. Roy Kelly, Aymar Embury II, and Royal Barry Wills.

23 "*Life* Presents Landscapes and a Garden Calendar for *Life*'s Houses," *Life*, March 20, 1939.

24 Winston Close to [B. F.] Fred Skinner, July 1, 1941, Close Associates Papers. Almost certainly, the "Feigls" in question were Herbert Feigl, a philosophy professor and later Regents Professor at the University of Minnesota, and his wife, Maria. Herbert Feigl was born in Bohemia (today in the Czech Republic) and earned his doctorate at the University of Vienna in 1927. Herbert Feigl Papers, University of Minnesota Archives, https://archives.lib.umn.edu.

25 Yvonne Skinner to Lisl Close, undated, Close Associates Papers.

26 The 1936 house, at 2297 Folwell Avenue, was designed by Wessel, Brunet, and Kline. Brent Dalzell email to author, May 8, 2018.

27 B. F. Skinner, *Walden Two* (Toronto: Macmillan, 1948), 21, 213.

28 Among the sites considered for the project was one near the intersection of Como and Cleveland Avenues in St. Paul and another on the corner of Fulham Street and Hoyt Avenue in Falcon Heights. The latter proposed site is now a part of University Grove. Close and Scheu to William Middlebrook, April 5, 1938, and William Middlebrook to W. A. Close, June 3, 1938, Close Associates Papers.

29 Recruitment letter from the Temporary Committee of Coop Housing Study Group, n.d., Close Associates Papers. The letter lists seven principles essential to the success of the proposed cooperative housing. Those principles are slightly altered versions of the 1844 Rochdale Principles, the organizing tenets of the Rochdale Society of Equitable Pioneers, a group of weavers in Rochdale, England, who founded the "first successful cooperative in documented history." The principles became the organizational model for cooperatives worldwide. "A History of Housing Cooperatives," National Cooperative Law Center, www.nationalcooperativelawcenter.com.

30 In some documentation, the project is referred to as "Kain Coop Housing." The project did not go ahead because "the equity required per family was more than many of the group could afford." Close and Scheu to Mr. B. Frank Crane, June 6, 1938, Close Associates Papers.

31 Winston and Elizabeth Close interview with Lauren Soth, August 18, 1988, Falcon Heights, Minnesota.

32 Close Oral History, March 27, 2000.

33 Also in the group were Hap and Christy Christensen, B. F. and Yvonne Skinner, and Starke and Jinny Hathaway, for whom the Closes designed a 1941 residence in Minneapolis. "Cooperative Housing Group" list, n.d., Close Associates Papers.

34 Ray Faulkner to Win and Lisl Close, undated. Close Associates Papers. Faulkner, who was at Northwestern University during the late design and construction phase of the house, was the sole signer of the contracts and the primary correspondent on the project. He may have borne the lion's share of the cost of the house. In a 1938 document, witnessed by Ziegfeld, Faulkner agreed to pay Close and Scheu 7 percent "of the cost of construction of the house designed by them for me, plus two water color [*sic*] paintings." Document dated September 14, 1938, Close Associates Papers.

35 Winston and Elizabeth Close interview. The author could find no documentation on this project.

36 The once expansive view from the house to the valley below was blocked when Interstate 94 was built in the late 1960s and a highway sound barrier was constructed at the end of the cul-de-sac. The view from the Faulkner House was similarly compromised.

37 Close Oral History, April 17, 2000.

38 The first of Wright's Usonian houses to be built was the Herbert and Katherine Jacobs House (1936) in Madison, Wisconsin.

39 Quotations in this paragraph and the next are from Sarah Faulkner to Lauren Soth, November, 18, 1988. Roy M. Close Family Papers.

40 Ray Faulkner, Edwin Ziegfeld, and Gerald Hill, *Art Today: An Introduction to the Fine and Functional Arts* (New York: Henry Holt, 1941), xx.

41 General background information, Lauren Soth, "The Art Today House and Its Aftermath: A Case History in Architectural Patronage," an unpublished, undated paper. Ray Faulkner would go on to earn his doctorate in educational psychology at the University of Minnesota in 1937. *Bulletin of the University of Minnesota Register of Ph.D. Degrees*, May 22, 1939, University of Minnesota Archives, www.lib.umn.edu/uarchives.

42 Winston Close to Ray Faulkner, July 15, 1938, Close Associate Papers.

43 Quotations in this paragraph, Winston and Elizabeth Close interview.

44 *Minnesota Daily*, undated clipping. An item in the October 22, 1938, issue of the *Bulletin of the Minneapolis Institute of Arts* took a slightly different view. Of the incident it said: "Over near the University an unknown man dropped dead on looking his first at a recently completed modern house." Roy M. Close Family Papers.

45 Close Oral History, May 15, 2000.

46 According to Gar Hargens, the Closes "loved Homasote and used it for ceilings and soffits." Although it later became available in four-by-eight-foot sheets, originally it was produced in less-modular friendly five-by-ten-foot sheets. Gar Hargens email to author, October 9, 2018.

47 Winston and Elizabeth Close interview.

48 Adjusted for inflation, $12,000 in 1938 is roughly equivalent to $219,000 in 2019.

49 Mrs. Ben J. E. Lippincott to Lauren Soth, November 13, 1989, Roy M. Close Family Papers.

50 Undated, untitled clipping from the *Minnesota*

Daily, and "Open House to Aid Spanish Children," *Minnesota Daily*, January 4, 1939. Roy M. Close Family Papers.

51 Soth, "The Art Today House," 2.

52 "Willem Jacob Luyten (1899–1994)" obituary, American Astronomical Society, https://aas.org.

53 Elizabeth and Winston Close interview.

54 Kathleen James-Chakraborty, *Architecture since 1400*, 350. The movement was founded in Leiden in 1917, the city in which Willem Luyten completed his PhD in 1922.

55 James-Chakraborty, *Architecture since 1400*, 350.

56 Charlotte Fiell and Peter Fiell, *The Story of Design: From the Paleolithic to the Present* (New York: Monacelli Press, 2016), 263.

57 Cardboard model information from Willem and Willemina Luyten interview with Lauren Soth, August 18, 1988, Minneapolis. Sun exposure calculations from Willem Luyten to Win and Lisl Close, February 18, 1939, Close Associates Papers. Willem figured the savings based on the 1939 rate of two cents per kilowatt hour.

58 Close Oral History, June 26, 2000.

59 Tyler Stewart Rogers, *Plan Your House to Suit Yourself* (New York: Charles Scribner's Sons, 1938), 1.

60 Close and Scheu inventory form for "House for Willem Luyten, Minneapolis," n.d., Close Associates Papers.

61 Quotations in this paragraph from Close Oral History, May 15, 2000.

62 Quotations in this paragraph from Elizabeth and Winston Close interview.

63 Plot plan for the Luyten House, April 6, 1939, Close Associates Papers.

64 Quotations in this paragraph from Elizabeth and Winston Close interview.

65 Lydia E. Hedin et al., "Alexander P. Anderson, 1862–1943," www.andersoncenter.org.

66 Quotations in this paragraph from Elizabeth and Winston Close interview.

67 Quotations and general information from Interstate Clinic project statement, n.d., Close Associates Papers.

68 "New Clinic to Open Here," *Red Wing Daily Republican*, August 30, 1940.

69 "New Clinic to Open Here."

70 "Demolition Smash," *Red Wing Republican Eagle*, July 25, 1985.

71 Close Oral History, September 25, 2000.

72 Skywater project statement, n.d., Close Associates Papers.

73 Close Oral History, September 25, 2000.

74 Originally, Win built three sets of Skywater furniture. In 1996 the Closes donated one complete original set to the Minnesota Historical Society.

75 Dagmar originally asked the Closes to design a guest cabin at Skywater in the fall of 1943, but knowing it was unlikely to happen at that time owing to wartime restrictions on materials she wrote, "Some day . . . after the war . . . we want you to build us upon it a snug home for our old age." Dagmar Beach to Lizel [*sic*] Close, October 18, 1943, Close Associates Papers.

76 Today Roy and Linda Close own Skywater.

CHAPTER 4 DESIGNS FOR PREFABRICATION AND THE COLD WAR

1 Generally, "Records of the War Production Board," WP[B], National Archives, www.archives.gov.

2 Winston Close to "Grays," December 29, 1942, Close Associates Papers.

3 Winston Close to "Fields," n.d., Close Associates Papers.

4 Lisl Close to Dagmar Beach, June 6, 1942, Close Associates Papers.

5 Close to "Grays."

6 Close was honorably discharged on October 9, 1950. Winston Close Naval Reserve Papers, Roy M. Close Family Papers.

7 Win was also stationed in Washington, D.C., where his family joined him.

8 Lisl Close to Dagmar Beach, October 23, 1943, Close Associates Papers.

9 "Real Log Houses," Page & Hill Company, promotional brochure, Close Associates Papers.

10 Generally, from "Page & Hill: Pioneer PF Home Builder," *PF—The Magazine of Prefabrication*, August 1956, Roy M. Close Family Papers. One "North Shore" model, designed for the company by Minnesota architect Chilson D. Aldrich, was built in 1935 on the shore of Lake Superior north of Duluth. It is recognized as a "Historic Property" by the Duluth Preservation Alliance, https://duluthpreservation.org.

11 The company continued to thrive by securing government contracts to produce grain storage structures, as well as ammunition boxes and loading pallets needed for the war effort. "Page & Hill: Pioneer PF Home Builder."

12 Scheu, "A Production Plant for Pre-Fabricated Houses."

13 H. Ward Jandl, *Yesterday's Houses of Tomorrow: Innovative American Homes 1850 to 1950* (Washington, D.C.: Preservation Press, 1991), 12.

14 Generally, *Home Delivery: Fabricating the Modern Dwelling*, exhibition catalog (New York: Museum of Modern Art, 2008).

15 Irving Bowman, "An Industrial Approach to Housing," *Architectural Forum*, July 1932, 73–75, 78–79. Significantly, two of the Bowman Brothers' projects, including a "Project for a Pre-Fabricated Small House," were featured in the exhibition catalog for MoMA's *Modern Architecture: International Exhibition* in 1932.

16. Jandl, *Yesterday's Houses of Tomorrow*, 12.

17 Robert Bailey, "Plastics: Building Material of the 20th Century," *Modern Materials*, November 2003, 5.

18 Unless otherwise noted, all quotations in this paragraph from Scheu, "A Production Plant for Pre-Fabricated Houses."

19 Even today, "plastics and systems combining plastics and other materials continue to be introduced into the construction scene." Robert Bailey, "Plastics: Building Material of the 20th Century," *Modern Materials*, November 2003.

20 Later in Minnesota, she worked with company engineer Dan Park to facilitate the process. Tom Maple Jr. interview with author, March 17, 2009, Wayzata, Minnesota. Maple is the son of Thomas S. Maple Sr., a developer of Acorn Ridge, a neighborhood of Page & Hill prefabricated homes in Minnetonka, Minnesota.

21 *PF—The Magazine of Prefabrication*, August 1956. It is unknown if other architects produced designs for Page & Hill at the time. In 1957 the company's main production plant in Shakopee was destroyed by fire and with it the company's records.

22 Elizabeth and Winston Close interview.

23 "Minneapolis Builders Erect PF Homes with Pride and Profit," *PF—The Magazine of Prefabrication*, October 1956.

24 "Minneapolis Builders Erect PF Homes."

25 The company also had factories in Albert Lea and Waterville in Minnesota.

26 Today, some of these houses are recognized as architecturally significant. In 2012, the city of Shakopee designated two Page & Hill prefabs, constructed in 1948, as historic properties. Shannon Fiecke, "More Shakopee Houses Deemed Historic," *Shakopee Valley News*, July 20, 2012.

27 "Page & Hill: Pioneer PF Home Builder."

28 Office Memorandum United States Government from Paul A. Shinkman to Henry J. Kellermann, November 3, 1950. CDF 1950–54, box 5225, National Archives and Records Administration (NARA), College Park, Maryland. Archival information for NARA given here applies to subsequent citations in this chapter's notes.

29 Greg Castillo, "Domesticating the Cold War: Household Consumption as Propaganda in Marshall Plan Germany," *Journal of Contemporary History* 40, no. 2 (2005): 261–88, www.jstor.org/stable/30036324.

30 Castillo, "Domesticating the Cold War."

31 Department of State telegram from Berlin to Secretary of State, July 29, 1950, NARA.

32 Wagner was the son of Martin Wagner, a Harvard professor and former municipal planning chief for Weimar-era Berlin. Castillo, "Domesticating the Cold War."

33 Letter from identified sender to General Sarnoff (Radio Corporation of America), September 12, 1950, NARA.

34 Department of State telegram to HICOG (High Command of Occupied Germany) Frankfurt from Acheson, August 18, 1950, NARA.

35 Department of State telegram from Berlin to Secretary of State, October 15, 1950, and United States Government Office Memorandum from Paul A. Shinkman to Henry J. Kellermann, November 3, 1950, NARA.

36 Department of State telegram from Berlin to Secretary of State, October 15, 1950, NARA.

37 Department of State telegram from Berlin to Secretary of State, September 30, 1950, NARA.

38 Department of State telegram from Berlin to Secretary of State, October 5, 1950, NARA.

39 United States Government Office Memorandum from Shinkman to Kellermann.

40 "Model U.S. Home at West Berlin Fair No. One Attraction for Awed Germans," undated clipping from an unidentified newspaper, NARA.

41 Department of State telegram from Frankfort [*sic*] to Secretary of State, September 22, 1950, NARA.

42 Department of State telegram from Berlin to Secretary of State, September 25, 1950, NARA.

43 Department of State telegram from HICOG to Frankfort [*sic*] , September 26, 1950, NARA.

44 Greg Castillo email to author, January 24, 2019.

45 Department of State telegram from Berlin to Secretary of State, October 18, 1950, NARA.

46 Herb Paul, "Shakopee House Goes to Berlin," *Minneapolis Star*, September 7, 1950.

CHAPTER 5
HOUSES AND HOUSING

1 Close also led planning for an early unbuilt version of the Washington Avenue Bridge, which connects the East and West Bank campuses of the university today. As originally envisioned, the double-decked bridge featured a moving sidewalk on the covered pedestrian level. Close predicted that if built, it would be "one of the great bridges of the world." Herm Sittard, "River Span May Rank with Great," *Minneapolis Star*, November 7, 1957.

2 Close Oral History, March 27, 2000.

3 Close Oral History, March 27, 2000.

4 "Sponsor" letter to the American Institute of Architects College of Fellows, 1969. Roy M. Close Family Papers.

5 Hargens interview, November 18, 2015.

6 Hargens interview, November 18, 2015.

7 Other employees at the firm included Maria Ambrose, Mark Bengstrom, Vickie Berg, Georgia Bizios, Dione DeMartelaere, Mike Dunn, Ollie Foran, John Harriss, Sarah Branson Homstad, Paul Karlson, Kemper Kirkpatrick, Fred Kirshmann, Jim Lammers, Chuck Levine, Jean Levy, Anna Mathis, Jim McBurney, Dick Morrill, Rolf Oliver, Joel Otto, Bekah Padilla, Julia Robinson, Bob Roscoe, Debbie Schramel, Scott Stanton, Jens Vange, Lloyd Wannis, Richard Wayment, and Chris Zagaria. Alex Gray Boies, Jill Fuhrman, Helen Lofstrom, Susan Olson, Rachel Wiest, and Betty Wiklund provided able administrative assistance. The author thanks Gar Hargens for providing this list.

8 Elizabeth Scheu Close résumé, undated, Close Associates Papers.

9 Quotations in this paragraph, except as otherwise noted, from Elizabeth and Winston Close interview.

10 Elizabeth and Winston Close interview.

11 Except as noted, all quotations in this paragraph from Elizabeth and Winston Close interview.

12 Close Oral History, June 5, 2000.

13 Close Oral History, June 5, 2000.

14 Elizabeth Close, "Architecture: Art within Restrictions," *Minneapolis Tribune*, September 28, 1966.

15 Elizabeth Close, "So You Want to Build the Taj Mahal," *Architecture Minnesota*, August 1977.

16 They include (George) Vincent Street, (Cyrus) Northrop Street, (Marion) Burton Street, (Lotus) Coffman Street, and (William) Folwell Avenue.

17 Among those advantages was financing available through the university.

18 Judy Woodward, "University Grove: An Architectural Time Capsule," *Park Bugle*, September 24, 2013. The leasehold arrangement was necessary at Stanford because upon founding the university in 1885, Leland and Jane Stanford specified that campus lands could never be sold. They so specified to ensure "the land endowment to the University would exist in perpetuity." "Residential Ground Lease," Stanford faculty housing brochure, http://fsh.Stanford.edu.

19 In 1954 the Closes designed a house for Middlebrook on Lake Minnetonka in Minnesota.

20 In addition to the houses mentioned in this section, the Close-designed residences in the Grove are the Meehan House (1949) and the O'Brien House (1950) on Northrop Street; the Nixon House (1957) on Burton Street; the Raup House (1953) on Fulham Street; the Martin House (1955) on Hoyt Avenue; and the Jones House (1953), the Heller House (1954), the Frantz House (1955), the Cochrane House (1956), the Jenkins House (1956), the Solem House (1963), and the Olson House (1966) on Folwell Avenue.

21 The Quonset huts were dismantled in the 1960s. Woodward, "University Grove."

22 Linda Lee, "St. Paul's Architectural Time Capsule," *New York Times*, January 5, 1989.

23 Close Oral History, June 26, 2000.

24 Close Oral History, June 26, 2000.

25 Roy Close email to author, July 2, 2018.

26 An elevator was installed in the house in the early 1990s when Lisl experienced a health problem that affected her mobility.

27 The portrait bore an inscription in German from Loos that Lisl explained translated to "This looks more like me than I do."

28 Close Oral History, May 15, 2000. Win and Lisl used Plexiglas to wrap the spiral staircase after the family's Weimaraner ("Till Eulenspiegel" or "Till" for short) slid across the floor and tumbled down the stairs. The safety feature proved a wise investment when grandchildren later came to visit. Also, "Furniture and Small Items," unpublished booklet of "furniture and other items designed and built by the Closes over a period of several years," Roy M. Close Family Papers.

29 Quotations in this paragraph from Close Oral History, May 15, 2000.

30 Quotations and general information in this and the following paragraph from "Statement of the Problem" for the John and Theta Wolf House, n.d., Close Associates Papers.

31 "The Closes loved to use inexpensive hollow core doors wherever they could." Gar Hargens email to author, October 7, 2018.

32 The suspended ceiling panel was later removed

and new insulated skydomes and LED lighting installed. Gar Hargens email to author.

33 John Wolf to "Lisl, ma chèrie," n.d., Close Associates Papers.

34 John and Theta Wolf letter to Lisl Close, September 8, 1960, Close Associates Papers.

35 Riggs also founded Café Espresso on East Hennepin Avenue in Minneapolis in 1958, which he believes was the "first espresso shop between Chicago and San Francisco." Over the years, Lisl planned renovations for two Riggs properties: Café Espresso and the Brave New Workshop in the Uptown neighborhood of Minneapolis. Dudley Riggs interview with author, August 1, 2014, Falcon Heights, Minnesota.

36 Pauline Boss interview with author, August 1, 2014, Falcon Heights, Minnesota.

37 Riggs interview.

38 The article identified the house as "owned by Mr. and Mrs. C. W. Dalzell, Minneapolis, Minn.," but there is no record of the project in the Close Associates Papers. A house designed by Robert Cerny of the Minneapolis firm of Long and Thorshov was also featured in the magazine, but its plans were not available for sale. *Popular Home Magazine*, Small Homes Review issue, 1949.

39 *Everyday Art Quarterly: A Guide to Well Designed Products*," 1952, Walker Art Center Archives.

40 Andrew Blauvelt, with Jill Vetter and Martha Ruddy, "The Idea House Project," in *Ideas for Modern Living: The Idea House Project/Everyday Art Gallery*, exhibition catalog (Minneapolis: Walker Art Center, 2000), 5.

41 The Walker exhibition was the first in the United States to feature a full-scale demonstration house on museum premises. Both Idea Houses I and II predated the Museum of Modern Art's famous Exhibition House, designed by Gregory Ain and built in the museum's garden in 1950.

42 Blauvelt, *Ideas for Modern Living*, 7.

43 Blauvelt, 14. Other participating architects and firms included Gerhardt Brandhorst, Humphrey and Hardenbergh, Long and Thorshov, and Harlan E. McClure. Although Ellerbe & Company was also on the original list of designers, the firm did not ultimately participate. Instead, a group of students from the School of Architecture at the University of Minnesota contributed a juried design.

44 Cover notes for *Everyday Art Quarterly*, Fall 1947, Walker Art Center Archives.

45 Reiss, who was three years older than Lisl, was a member of the Communist Party and a vocal opponent of Hitler. She came to New York in 1933. Tanja Poppelretuer, "German-Speaking Refugee Women Architects before the Second World War" (unpublished essay, University of Salford, Manchester, 2018). Lisl and Reiss are two of six women architects "who fled to the United States between 1933 and 1945" whom Poppelreuter profiles in her essay. In fact, Lisl arrived in the United States in 1932.

46 Alexandra Griffith Winton, " 'A Man's House Is His Art': The Walker Art Center's *Idea House* Project and the Marketing of Domestic Design 1941–1947," *Journal of Design History* 17, no. 4 (2004): 397. Walker Art Center Archives.

47 All quotations in this paragraph from D. S. Defenbacher to Miss Mary Davis Gillies, April 23, 1947, Walker Art Center Archives. Gillies was the interior and architectural editor of *McCall's*. No drawings of any of the projects could be found in the Walker Art Center Archives.

48 "Idea House Oral History Project, 1999–2000," Walker Art Center Archives.

49 "Idea House Oral History Project." Idea House I was demolished in 1961 to make way for the construction of the Ralph Rapson–designed Tyrone Guthrie Theater, and House II was bulldozed in 1969 for a Guthrie expansion. The Guthrie Theater was demolished in 2006 to make way for a green space at the Walker.

50 Blauvelt, *Ideas for Modern Living*, 14.

51 Donald R. Torbert, "The Architect and the City," *Everyday Art Quarterly*, Spring 1952.

52 Torbert, "The Architect and the City."

53 Aileen Reynolds, "On Old Home Problems: Husband–Wife Architect Team in Remodeling Clinic," *Minneapolis Star*, April 10, 1952.

54 "57 Houses for a Better '57," *House & Home*, October 1956.

55 "Today and Tomorrow at Garden City: 2,000 New Homes Planned in Future for Garden City," undated clipping, Roy M. Close Family Papers. Garden City was built on land donated by Earle Brown to the University of Minnesota in 1949. As the university's advisory architect, Winston Close developed land studies and site plans for the community eventually known as Garden City. In 1954 the university sold the land to two developers: the Winston Brothers of Minneapolis and Hal B. Hayes of California. They hired Lisl to design model homes; Hayes, a colorful entrepreneur based in Hollywood, planned to make Garden City America's first "A-Bomb-Proof City." His elaborate scheme was not realized.

56 Unless otherwise noted, quotations in this paragraph are from "Two ideas make this two-story house a Minnesota pioneer," *House & Home*, October 1956. The trusses were fabricated by the G. M. Stewart Lumber Company of Minneapolis.

57 "Lumber Giant Widens Aid to Dealers and Builders," *House & Home*, August 1964, 11.
58 "Lumber Giant Widens Aid to Dealers and Builders."
59 "New Boost for Lumber Dealers: This Wood-Promotion House," *House & Home*, September 1965, 82–83.
60 Contractually, architects were responsible for providing floor, foundation, and site plans, interior and exterior elevations, millwork details, electrical layouts, and room finish schedules. Weyerhaeuser supplied component and shop drawings, joist layouts, sheathing plans, and material lists. "Weyerhaeuser Registered Homes Outline of Plan Requirements for Regional Architects; Program," n.d., Close Associate Papers.
61 Elizabeth S. Close to Fred C. Knipher, January 3, 1964, Close Associates Papers.
62 Elizabeth S. Close to James Fenelon, September 20, 1965, Close Associates Papers.
63 "New Boost for Lumber Dealers."
64 "New Boost for Lumber Dealers."
65 The retractable cover did appear in a study model of the house constructed by the firm. Close Associates Papers.
66 "New Boost for Lumber Dealers."
67 "House with a Natural Point of View," *Good Housekeeping*, October 1965, 128.
68 Hargens interview.
69 Untitled article, *St. Paul Pioneer Press*, August 7, 1949.
70 Rood House problem statement, n.d. Close Associates Papers.
71 Roy Close email to author, July 2, 2018.
72 According to Hargens, Lisl's design included "innovative ceiling radiant heating and cooling." Gar Hargens email to author, October 7, 2018.
73 Joel Hoekstra, "Art House," *Architecture MN*, November/December 2014.
74 "Edina Home Has European Flavor," *Minneapolis Tribune*, October 4, 1964.
75 Marri Oskam interview with author, August 28, 2014, Edina, Minnesota.
76 "Edina Home Has European Flavor."
77 The northern white cedar posts were purchased from the Page & Hill Company, for whom Lisl had previously designed prefabricated houses. Page & Hill Inc. invoice, November 4, 1963, Close Associates Papers.
78 "Walkout Windows" advertisement, *Newsweek*, July 1970.
79 Quotations in this paragraph from Oskam interview. The well-preserved, original furniture remains in the house today.
80 As of this writing, Marri still lives in the Oskam House. Edina Heritage Landmark, Hendrick [*sic*] and Marri Oskam House, August 5, 2015, https://edinamn.gov.
81 Marri Oskam interview.
82 Quotations in this paragraph and the previous one from Hargens interview. Crab Orchard stone is a sandstone quarried from Crab Orchard Mountain in Tennessee. https:// tennesseeencyclopedia.net.
83 Hargens interview.
84 "25-Year Award," *Architecture Minnesota*, January/February 1989, 46.
85 "House for Mr. & Mrs. P. S. Duff," problem and significance statement, November 1988, Close Associates Papers.
86 Hargens interview.
87 Mack, "Women Architects Make Their Way in an Old Boys' Profession."
88 "About Us," Iseman Homes, https://isemanhomes.com.
89 Lloyd L. Reaves to Mrs. Close, August 13, 1968, Close Associates Papers.
90 Lloyd L. Reaves to Mrs. Close, September 12, 1968, Close Associates Papers.
91 All quotations in this paragraph and the next are from Elizabeth Close to Lloyd L. Reaves, August 30, 1968, Close Associates Papers.
92 "14 Award-Winning Apartments and Townhouses," *House & Home*, July 1965.
93 Lora Lee Watson, "Housing Study Lauds, Blames Cities Designs," *Minneapolis Tribune*, May 28, 1967.
94 Quotations and general information in this paragraph from James I. Brown, "Cleveland Terrace—Twin Cities First Architecturally-Designed Condominium," *Northwest Architect*, January/February 1972, 24–25, 38, and "First Condominium Built," *St. Paul Sunday Pioneer Press*, July 5, 1970.
95 The consortium included the Eberhardt Management Company, McGough Construction, and landscape architect Herb Baldwin.
96 Jim Fuller, "Builders Start on Windslope Housing," *Minneapolis Tribune*, December 8, 1976.
97 "Statement on the Colors of Windslope," undated document, Close Associates Papers.
98 Fuller, "Builders Start on Windslope Housing."
99 "Statement on the Colors of Windslope" and "Legal Action Possible to Change Color of Windslope Siding," *Eden Prairie News*, March 31, 1977.
100 Close Oral History, May 15, 2000.

CHAPTER 6 BUILDINGS FOR WORK AND PLAY

1 Gar Hargens email to author, October 7, 2018.

2 The Closes designed and added a wing to the building in 1970.

3 *A History of Elliot Park's Healthcare and Social Services*, report by Lindberg Consulting, February 2012, 25–26, www.minneapolismn.gov.

4 According to Hargens, such a venture was "not all that common but very appropriate here." Hargens email to author, October 7, 2018.

5 Close Oral History, February 5, 2001.

6 Gar Hargens interview with author, July 24, 2018, Minneapolis, Minnesota.

7 General information from "Gordon A. Friesen, 1909–1992," Bellwetherleague.org, and Adam Moore, "Satellite Recovery," February 24, 2012, www.interiorsandsources.com.

8 The Co/Struc system was invented and patented by Robert Propst, president of the Herman Miller Research Corporation, who in the 1960s "initiated research into the troubled state of patient care delivery in hospitals." www.hermanmiller.com.

9 Hargens interview, July 24, 2018. Prior to installation, the system was tested by the nursing staff.

10 Hargens interview, July 24, 2018.

11 Lyman E. Wakefield obituary, *StarTribune*, December 13, 2001. The obituary also notes that Wakefield was a member of the "North American Championship Fours," a now discontinued precision skating competition for teams of two women and two men.

12 Quotations and general information in this paragraph from Elizabeth S. Close to Greta Lockhart (Trane Co.), October 1, 1958, Close Associates Papers.

13 "Lyman and Louise Wakefield, 'Something for the Whole Family,' " *Sports Illustrated*, February 16, 1959.

14 "Brother, It's Cold INSIDE . . ." *Minneapolis Star*, August 1959.

15 Close Oral History, February 5, 2001.

16 Emerson Goble, "Behind the Record: A Memorial Is a Memorial," *Architectural Record*, February 1961, 9.

17 "Franklin Delano Roosevelt Memorial Competition," project statement, Close Associates Papers.

18 All quotations in this paragraph from "Franklin Delano Roosevelt Memorial Competition," project statement.

19 Close Oral History, February 5, 2001.

20 Close Oral History, February 5, 2001.

21 "Pedersen and Tilney Win FDR Memorial Competition," *Architectural Record*, February 1961, 13.

22 Benjamin Forgey, "Like the Man, the Memorial Breaks with Tradition," *Washington Post*, April 27, 1997. Interestingly (and graciously) enough, the Closes submitted a letter in support of the winning design: "The ageless, simple dignity of the tablets is subtly anchored to our time by contemporary structural techniques and by the sensitive arrangement of forms and spaces. It is this combination which places the design at the level of the great monument of earlier ages." Elizabeth and Winston Close to Francis Biddle (chairman of the Franklin Delano Roosevelt Memorial Competition), March 10, 1961, Close Associates Papers.

23 Founded as F. H. Peavey & Company, in Sioux City, Iowa, the organization changed its name to the Peavey Company in 1962. The company, which initially developed "the Peavey system" of grain elevators, had interests in flour milling and later diversified into food processing and specialty retail. Generally, "Peavey Company Records, 1870–1984," Manuscripts Collection, Minnesota Historical Society, www.mnhs.org.

24 *Peavey Technical Center*, unpublished booklet prepared by Close Associates, circa 1974, Close Associates Papers.

25 Hargens interview with author, November 18, 2015.

26 General information and quotation in this paragraph, *Peavey Technical Center.*

27 Peavey Technical Center problem statement, undated document, Close Associates Papers.

28 Three years after the completion of the building, Close Associates conducted a review of the facility "to assess the validity of the initial concepts, and the effectiveness of the solutions." Except for a few minor issues, the audit found the building to be "very satisfactory and flexible in use," according to company director Dr. John Nelson. *Peavey Technical Center.*

29 *FWBI Freshwater Biological Institute*, Close Associates project brochure, Roy M. Close Family Papers.

30 "May 6, 1965 Tornadoes," Minnesota Department of Natural Resources, www.dnr.stat.mn.us.

31 Unless otherwise noted, quotations in this paragraph from Dick Gray, "Looking Back: Tornadoes, Ugly Algae Spurred Community Campaign That Built a Lab and Freshwater Society," January 20, 2010, https://freshwater.org.

32 "Personality: Elizabeth Scheu Close," *Facets of Freshwater*, Fall 1972, Winter–Spring 1972 to 1973.

33 Close Oral History, May 15, 2000. According to Lisl, Wilcox, a graduate of the School of Architecture at the University of Minnesota, was "one of Bucky's Boys" referring to his association with visionary inventor R. Buckminster Fuller, who was a frequent visiting lecturer at the school. Fuller, known for his creation of the geodesic dome, worked with students, Wilcox among them, on several dome proj-

ects during his visits. When Lisl and Win became Fellows in the American Institute of Architects in 1969, Wilcox presented them with a hand-crafted "geodesic bauble," inspired by Fuller's invention. The bauble hung in the office, and later the Closes' home, for many years. It remains in the family today.

34 Hargens interview, November 18, 2015.

35 *FWBI.*

36 Close Oral History, May 15, 2000.

37 Close Oral History, May 15, 2000.

38 *FWBI.*

39 Gar Hargens email to author, October 7, 2018. He credits Lisl with conceiving this key and innovative use of space, one he believes is "still being copied and 'discovered' around the country."

40 Gar Hargens email to author, October 7, 2018.

41 Gar Hargens email to author, October 7, 2018.

42 Steve Woods, executive director of Freshwater, email to author, August 15, 2018.

43 Close Oral History, May 15, 2000.

44 "Facets of Freshwater," *Freshwater Biological Research Foundation*, Summer–Fall–Winter 1975–1976, Roy M. Close Family Papers.

45 Unless otherwise noted, quotations and general information in this section from *Donald N. Ferguson Hall 1985*, dedication book, University of Minnesota, Roy M. Close Family Papers. A year later additional funds were appropriated, including $1.3 million for a music library and $1.6 million toward a performance laboratory and education concert hall.

46 Bruce N. Wright, "An Architectural Coda," *Architecture Minnesota*, September–October 1986, 48–51.

47 *Donald N. Ferguson Hall 1985.*

48 Gar Hargens email to author, October 7, 2018.

49 *Donald N. Ferguson Hall 1985.*

50 Gar Hargens email to author, August 14, 2018.

51 Gar Hargens email to author, August 14, 2018.

52 Hargens interview, November 18, 2015.

53 *The International School of Choueifat: Centenary 1886–1986*, brochure, Close Associates Papers.

54 Memo to the Eden Prairie Planning Commission from Tracy S. Whitehead, director of operations and community affairs, International School, February 19, 1987, Close Associates Papers.

55 *The International School of Choueifat.*

56 Memo to the Eden Prairie Planning Commission.

57 Memo to the Eden Prairie Planning Commission.

58 James Steilen to the Members of the Planning Commission, February 23, 1987, Close Associates Papers. Steilen was an attorney with the Minneapolis firm of Popham, Haik, Schnobrich, Kaufman & Doty, Ltd.

59 All quotations in this paragraph, unless otherwise noted, are from "International School: Design Implications, Eden Prairie Site," Close Associates Inc. memo, n.d., Close Associates Papers.

EPILOGUE

1 "Fellowship," www.aia.org.

2 *The American Institute of Architects College of Fellows History and Directory, 2017 Edition* (Washington, D.C.: American Institute of Architects College of Fellows, 2017).

3 "Pioneers" quotation from press release from Edwin Neuger & Associates for the Minnesota Society of Architects, AIA, May 17, 1969. "Contributory force" quotation from "Sponsor" letter to the American Institute of Architects College of Fellows, 1969. Roy M. Close Family Papers.

4 Press release from Edwin Neuger & Associates.

5 Victor Gruen to Jury of Fellows, American Institute of Architects, January 15, 1969. Roy M. Close Family Papers.

6 Victor Gruen to Jury of Fellows.

7 Elmer L. Andersen to Jury of Fellows, American Institute of Architects, January 20, 1969, Roy M. Close Family Papers.

8 Hargens interview, November 18, 2015.

9 Georgia Bizios interview with author, June 3, 2012, Minneapolis.

10 Hargens interview, November 18, 2015.

11 Linda Mack, "Winston Close Dies at 91: Was Pioneer of Architecture," *Minneapolis Star Tribune*, June 17, 1997.

12 "Sponsor" letter to the American Institute of Architects College of Fellows, 1969. Roy M. Close Family Papers.

13 "Elizabeth Close, FAIA, Gold Medal Winner," *Sparks*, September 2002.

14 Linda Mack, "Gold-Medal Graciousness," *Minneapolis Star Tribune*, December 13, 2002.

15 "Elizabeth Close Receives Honorary Degree," CALA press release, May 7, 2003.
16 "Honorary Degree Recipients," University Awards and Honors, uawards.dl.umn.edu.
17 Julia Robinson telephone interview with author, September 28, 2018.
18 Bizios interview.
19 Mary Abbe, "A Modern Woman Who Made Modern Public Buildings," *Minneapolis Star Tribune*, December 2, 2011.
20 Bizios interview.

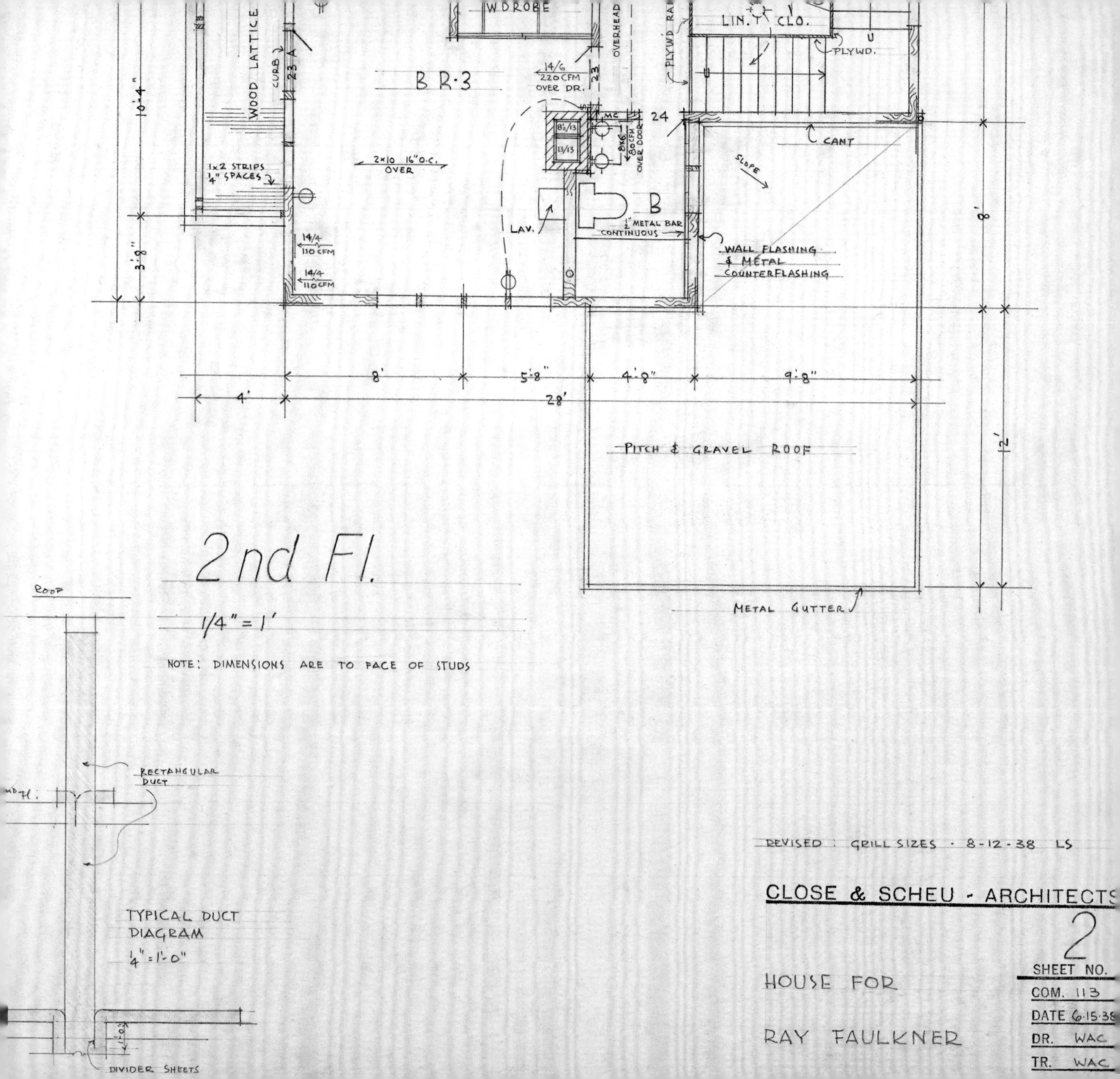
WDROBE
LIN. CLO.
PLYWD.
OVERHEAD
PLYWD RA
WOOD LATTICE
CURB
23 A
BR·3
14/6
220 CFM
OVER DR.
23
24
10'-4"
1x2 STRIPS
1/4" SPACES
2x10 16" O.C.
OVER
MC
8 1/2/13
13/13
8x6
180 CFM
OVER DOOR
CANT
SLOPE
LAV.
B
1/2" METAL BAR
CONTINUOUS
WALL FLASHING
& METAL
COUNTERFLASHING
14/4
110 CFM
14/4
110 CFM
3'-8"
8'
8'
5'-8"
4'-8"
9'-8"
4'
28'
PITCH & GRAVEL ROOF
12'
2nd Fl.
1/4" = 1'
NOTE: DIMENSIONS ARE TO FACE OF STUDS
METAL GUTTER
ROOF
RECTANGULAR
DUCT
TYPICAL DUCT
DIAGRAM
1/4" = 1'-0"
1'-0"
DIVIDER SHEETS
REVISED : GRILL SIZES · 8-12-38 LS
CLOSE & SCHEU - ARCHITECTS
2
SHEET NO.
HOUSE FOR
RAY FAULKNER
COM. 113
DATE 6·15·38
DR. WAC
TR. WAC

Index

Page numbers in italics refer to figures.

Jane King Hession, an architectural historian specializing in modernism, is a founding partner of Modern House Productions. She is coauthor of *John Howe, Architect: From Taliesin Apprentice to Master of Organic Design* (Minnesota, 2015), *Frank Lloyd Wright in New York: The Plaza Years, 1954–1959*, and *Ralph Rapson: Sixty Years of Modern Design*, and the author of *The Frank Lloyd Wright House in Ebsworth Park: The Kraus House*.

Joan Soranno is design principal with HGA in Minneapolis. Her award-winning projects of cultural and religious architecture include Lakewood Cemetery Garden Mausoleum, the entry pavilion for the Walker Art Center, and Bigelow Chapel at United Theological Seminary of the Twin Cities.